BOXING
GREATS

AN ILLUSTRATED HISTORY OF THE LEGENDS OF THE RING

5067 Boxing Greats

First published in the United States in 1998 by Courage Books

9 8 7 6 5 4 3 2 1

Digit on the right indicates the number of this printing

Library of Congress Cataloging-in-Publication Number 98-72148
ISBN 0-7624-0402-7

CREDITS

Project Editor: Chris Stone
Designer: Peter Laws
Copy-editor: Jillian Stewart
Production: Neil Randles, Ruth Arthur, Karen Staff
Director of Production: Graeme Procter
Color reproduction: Global Colour, Malaysia
Printed and bound: Graficromo, S.A.

Published by Courage Books, an imprint of
Running Press Book Publishers
125 South Twenty-second Street
Philadelphia, Pennsylvania 19103-4399

BOXING GREATS

AN ILLUSTRATED HISTORY OF THE LEGENDS OF THE RING

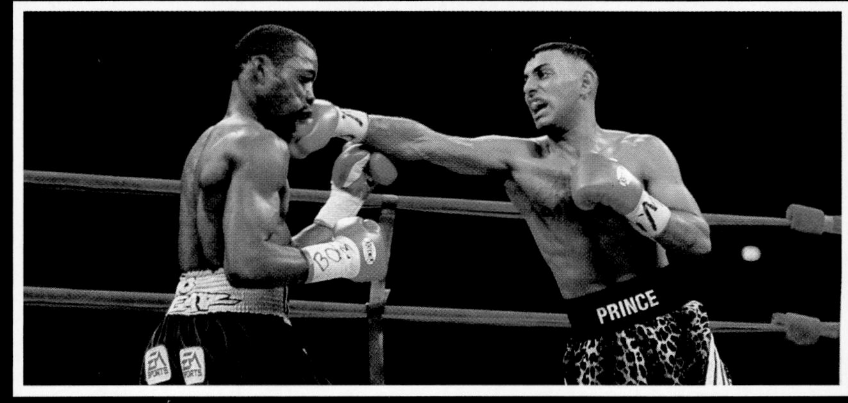

Steve Bunce

WITH BOB MEE

Contents

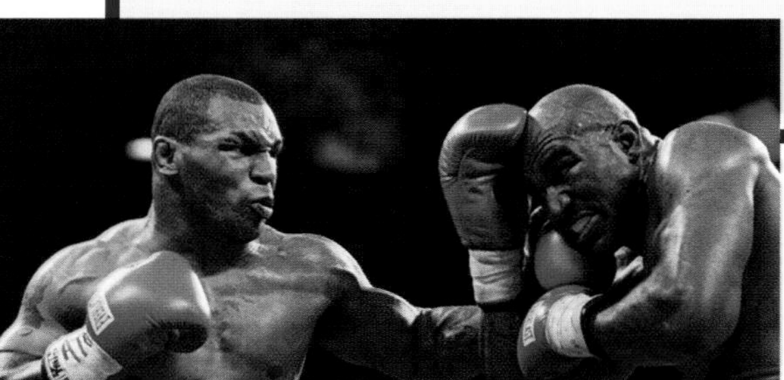

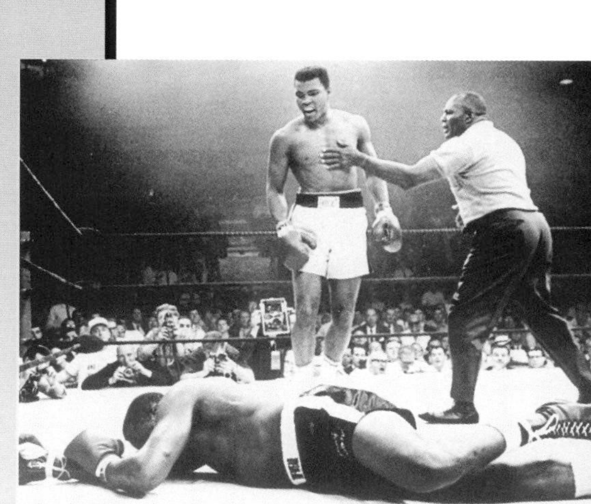

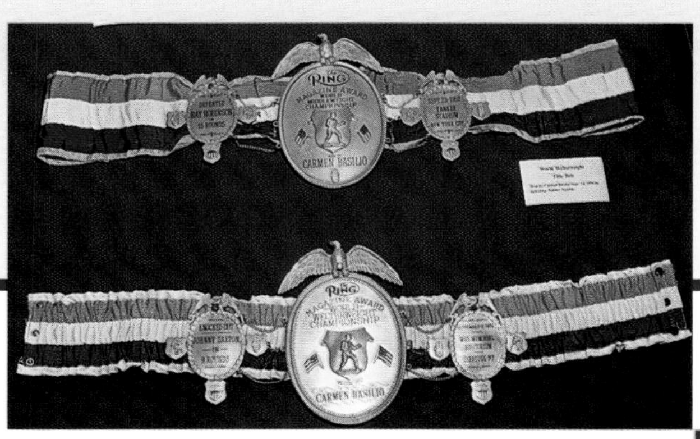

Foreword

"Boxing a sport of kings that is as old as the human race itself. That from the time of an archaic past the love to win, the struggle to conquer, has been the predominating thought in all men."

There is something compelling about men who do battle with other men. The lives of many of boxing's best practitioners, both in and out of the ring, have often rivalled any movie script, from the great John L. Sullivan who boasted he could "lick any son of a bitch in the house" to Muhammad Ali, who swore he was "the Greatest of All Time".

Personalities aside, boxing often mirrored political and social events of the time. Joe Louis vs. Max Schmeling transcended the sport of boxing; to some it was good vs evil, black vs. white, Democracy vs. Nazism. Not that Louis or Schmeling personally embodied any of these – Schmeling was not a Nazi – but their nations and fans rallied around them as symbols of what was right in their mind. Before he became the most beloved athlete of all time, Muhammad Ali was as reviled a sports figure as ever for his refusal – on religious grounds – to serve his country and fight in Vietnam. Kept out of the game at his peak for three years, Ali earned respect for his steadfast religious convictions and, as it turned out, Vietnam became one of the most controversial wars in history.

These are just some of the intriguing stories that *Boxing Greats* will walk you through. Each of its 10 chapters outlines an important period in boxing's illustrious history, from the Queensberry Rules to present day stars like Oscar De La Hoya, Naseem Hamed and Evander Holyfield.

Die hard fans of the sweet science will enjoy this recap of boxing's past and new fans will surely marvel at the history of the sport. *Boxing Greats* is for anyone who appreciates the international sport of boxing. Enjoy!

Ed Brophy

EDWARD BROPHY,
EXECUTIVE DIRECTOR INTERNATIONAL BOXING HALL OF FAME

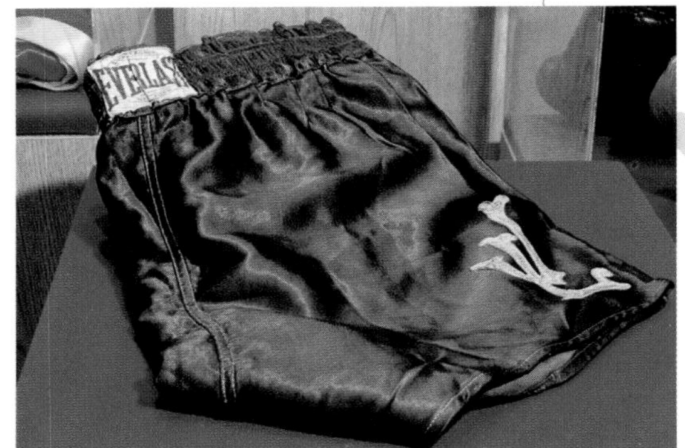

▲ **THE CHAMPION'S SHORTS**
A pair of Joe Louis's purple shorts which can been seen on display at the International Boxing Hall of Fame, Canastota, New York. Before the introduction of television coverage, all world champions were required to wear purple shorts in order to assist their identification by the huge crowds.

▶ **BOXING MEMORABILIA**
Big fight promotional posters and an array of old-fashioned boxing equipment: just two of the many exhibits on display at the International Boxing Hall of Fame.

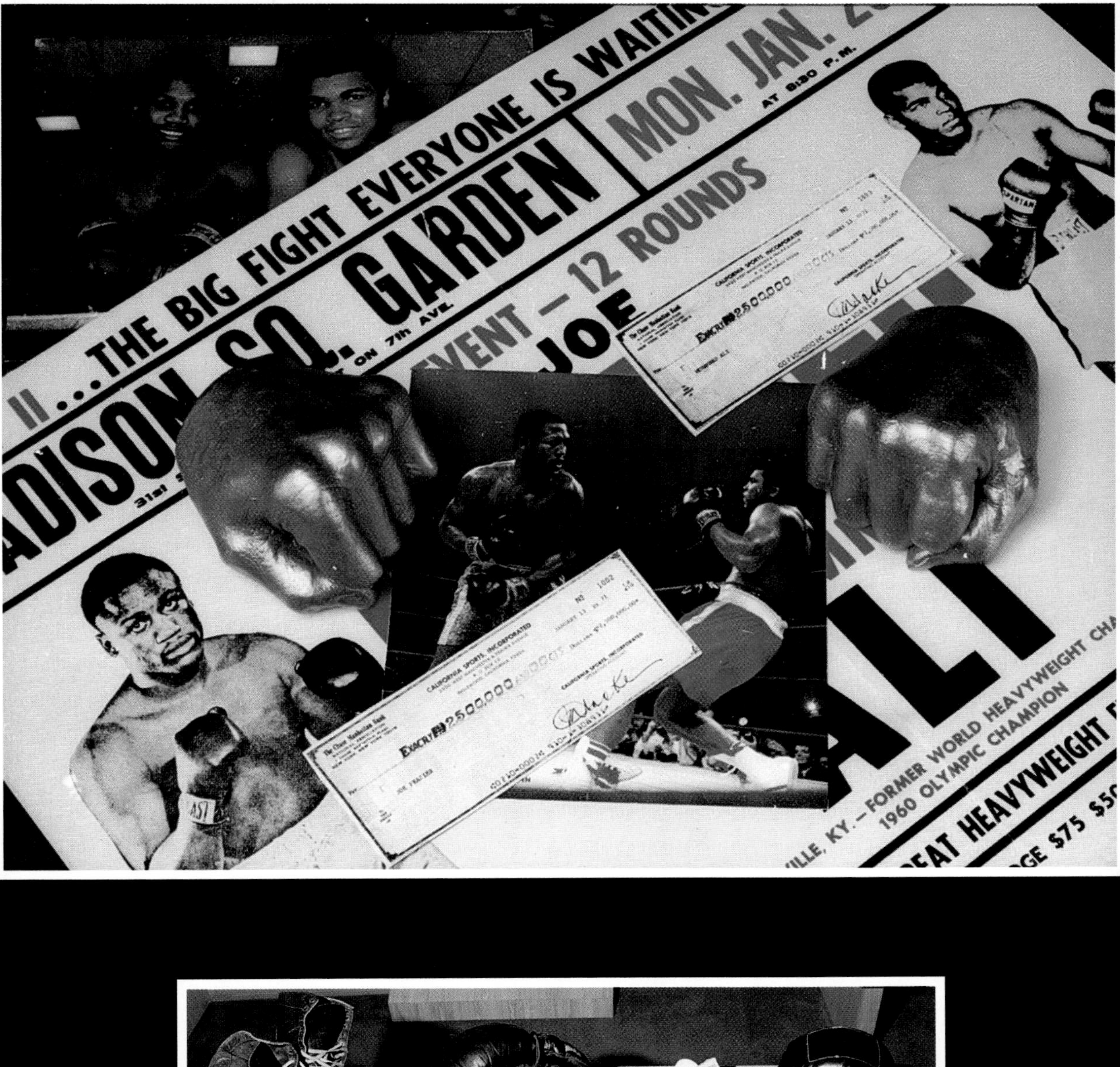
...THE BIG FIGHT EVERYONE IS
SQ. GARDEN
ON 7th AVE.
MON. JAN.
AT 8:30 P.M.
EVENT — 12 ROUNDS
JOE
CALIFORNIA SPORTS, INCORPORATED
JOE FRAZIER
ALI
FORMER WORLD HEAVYWEIGHT
1960 OLYMPIC CHAMPION
HEAVYWEIGHT
$75

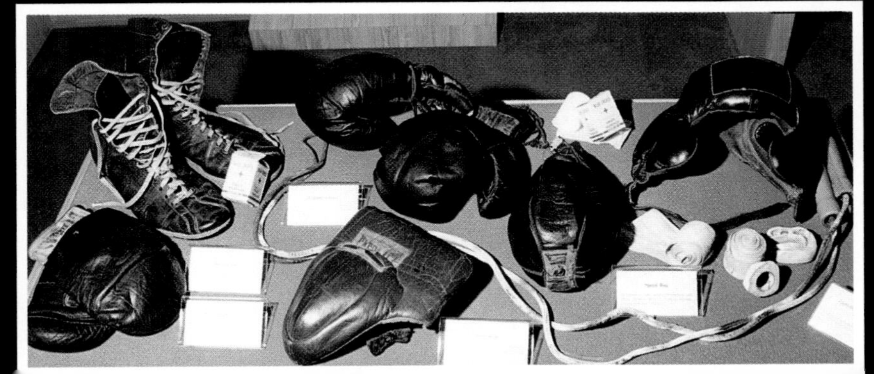

Ancient PUGS *and* TORIAN GENTLEN

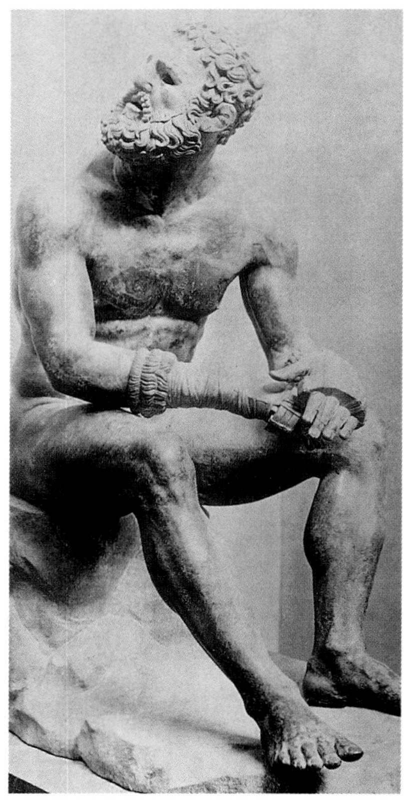

▲ **FAMILIAR FACE OF BOXING**
Ancient statues and works of art clearly demonstrate that boxing was a bloody and gruesome sport. The heavily-bound fists of this Roman boxer would certainly have inflicted serious injury.

The fist-fight boxers are the fathers of the sport and although their fights have long disappeared from the public consciousness, their presence is still felt. Boxing is an ancient recreation which has always resisted change, yet despite its inevitable evolution its essential spirit remains intact.

THE FIST-FIGHT ERA

When Mike Tyson's gold teeth bit off part of Evander Holyfield's right ear in 1997, the bloody and brutal business of boxing returned to its dark past. Tyson broke the rules, but his was a senseless act of inhumanity while so much of the violence in boxing's long history has been necessary or demanded. "A boxer's victory is gained in blood," reads one inscription from an ancient Greek vase. In Tyson's case, his shame was gained in blood.

The antiquity of the sport is reflected by the fact that Homer wrote vivid descriptions of fighting contests as early as 688 BC – when the first boxing bouts were held at the 23rd Olympiad. The description of the fight between Amycus and Polydeuces is strangely reminiscent of a modern event. First, the fans arrived and formed a ring for the action, then the two boxers bound leather thongs to their hands and arms for protection before the fighting began. In the ring the pair sparred for position, careful to avoid the sun in their eyes. The fight ended with a straight right to the temple – Amycus was down and out.

Following the Greeks, the Romans increased the level of violence in boxing matches by preparing the fighters in camps. Prisoners, criminals and guilty slaves were instructed in the horrible arts of slaughter by *lanistae* – the Roman coaches and cornermen – who were freed slaves. The thongs worn by the Greeks were adapted by the Roman *lanistae* and altered to look like a lethal weapon, called a *cestus*, a cross between a knuckle-duster and an iron bar. Roman methods of sporting amusement were extreme. Mutilations and death were common, but violence has always characterized the sport.

From James Figg – the notorious prizefighter, swordsman, and bear-baiter – to Oscar De La Hoya, the blood has flowed. In fact, when Figg beat Ned Sutton in 1720 there was probably less blood on the stage than there was spread over the canvas when De La Hoya beat Julio Cesar Chavez in 1996.

Boxers in the 20th century are faster and better prepared than ever, but they nevertheless bleed and

◀ **BRAWLING WARRIORS**
Previous page: A sketch by Rowlandson depicting Ward versus Quirk from June, 1812.

suffer in much the same way. Heads and thumbs, it seems, always have and always will be used. Ancient Greek vases clearly illustrate boxers throwing punches with their thumbs extended to gouge at their opponent's eyes. This is just one of the dirty tactics still used, in spite of thumbless gloves, as demonstrated by the foul-ridden contests between Sandy Saddler and Willie Pep in the 1950s.

A fervent debate still rages over the safety of gloves and there is good reason to believe that a return to bare-knuckles would actually lead to a reduction in deaths, although mutilations would be increased. The prizefighters who boxed before the introduction of gloves, in 1867, hit each other far less than any of today's boxers, because each round was normally over after one or two punches.

The people involved at the center of the sport of boxing have always resisted inevitable change. There was resistance when the first rules, written by Jack Broughton in 1743, outlawed grabbing a man below the waist, and the outrage at change continued when world championship fights were reduced from 15 to 12 rounds 250 years later.

When the bare-knuckle breed started to move their feet, the flat-nosed, proud brawlers from the past were dismayed at the development. When some fighters started to use gloves, even the "fair-sized gloves" which could mean skin-tight leather wraps, there was a feeling that pugilism was at an end.

During this century people complained when Jack Johnson, boxing's first black heavyweight champion, struck from the ropes, when Muhammad Ali connected with punches nobody saw and when Naseem Hamed slowly beat opponents like an animal gently playing with his kill. Traditional fighters, losers, and men with more heart than sense, will always be the favorites in the hearts of the people.

Each generation of fighters, fans and experts have mourned a bygone era. In the early 18th century in James Figg's pleasure palace of combat, situated in a field in north London, it was common practice to watch cats and rats fight in a burning barrel, as entertainment between the animal baiting, the sword play and the boxing. However, when Jack Broughton took over the house, in 1743, social constraints were such that this attraction was banned – much to the consternation of Broughton's punters!

Similarly, when the formidable lightweight Benny Leonard was landing punches from odd angles and avoiding punches with style in the early part of this century, his technique was criticized by many of the sport's relics. He is now accepted as a modern master.

Most of the old heroes are no longer our heroes, but out of respect the last breed of bare-knuckle fighters and their gloved companions, who never quite mastered the differences in the sport, are still held in high esteem. Men like John L. Sullivan and James J. Jeffries belong with Figg and Broughton, not Ali and Joe Louis. Figg and Broughton could so easily have been gladiators at games in ancient Rome or a Greek festival of sport.

Boxing's development over the centuries has limited the extremes of the early contests, but fights can still end in death. Each year new victims are added to the list of the men who have lost their lives in the boxing ring. No amount of change will ever completely eliminate the risk.

▼ THE FIRST OLYMPIC SPORT *Boxing, wrestling and other combat sports formed part of the early Olympics. The two fighters in the center of this vase are probably competing in a* pankration *fight, a mix of boxing and wrestling. Deaths were common in* pankration, *which was part of the 33rd Olympiad.*

The top pugilists were in demand as the sport began to expand

▲ **A FIGHT AT THE RACES**

A bout between Spring and Langan at Worcester racecourse in 1824. Most of the main fights in the 19th century took place at race tracks because all the key "players" were there: bookmakers, people with and without money, rogues and prostitutes!

The art of boxing was born at the Bear Gardens, by the River Thames in London, in the mid-17th century. The vulgar idols of the day, however, were not the pugilists, but fighting bears with names like Goldilocks, Rose of Bedlam and Mad Besse. The fist-fights took place on the same bill as the bear-baiting, in the sheds and scaffolds of London, but were considered a lesser attraction at the time.

In 1684, a so-called Boarded House, in fields near what is now Oxford Circus in central London, was used to bait bears, bulls and dogs. In 1719 the owner formed a partnership with James Figg and the Boarded House soon took on a new guise as an "entertainment" center which boasted a wide variety of combat games. Figg was a touring swordsman who took advantage of his new base to explore the building's gore-stained past. He combined fist and sword with women, freaks and wild animals during a six-year reign of original spectator events. On Figg's stage women fought dwarfs and men crossed sabres, after which Figg, following displays with sword, dagger, buckler and quarter staff, would box. The grotesque shows flourished as his sporting retreat attracted the full spectrum of London life. Figg's gruesome exhibitions are part of boxing's bloody and savage heritage.

In the 1720s Figg fought Ned Sutton from Kent. It was a challenge, a duel in three stages. First there was the backsword, followed by a break for port; second was the pugilism section and finally, after another break for port, the cudgels were used. Figg broke Sutton's knee to win. Contemporary accounts create a vivid image of the fighting. Figg was bleeding heavily before winning and several people fainted!

▲ **ACTION WAS RARE!**
Top: A good deal of moving and posing was common in 18th-century fights. Many of the contests lasted for hours, but the action was usually limited to quick flurries, throws and pulls.

▲ **DEDICATED TO THE FANCY**
Showrooms for gentlemen to punch each other opened up all over London in the early part of the 19th century. Poets and dandies were instructed in the manly art of self-defense by retired prizefighters.

MILESTONES OF BOXING

JACK BROUGHTON'S RULES

1743

THE RING

RULES

TO BE OBSERVED IN ALL BATTLES ON THE STAGE

I. THAT a ſquare of a Yard be chalked in the middle of the Stage; and on every freſh ſet-to after a fall, or being parted from the rails, each Second is to bring his Man to the ſide of the ſquare, and place him oppoſite to the other, and till they are fairly ſet-to at the Lines, it ſhall not be lawful for one to ſtrike at the other.

II. That, in order to prevent any Diſputes, the time a Man lies after a fall, if the Second does not bring his Man to the ſide of the ſquare, within the ſpace of half a minute, he ſhall be deemed a beaten Man.

III. That in every main Battle, no perſon whatever ſhall be upon the Stage, except the Principals and their Seconds; the ſame rule to be obſerved in bye-battles, except that in the latter, Mr. Broughton is allowed to be upon the Stage to keep decorum, and to aſſiſt Gentlemen in getting to their places, provided always he does not interfere in the Battle; and whoever pretends to infringe theſe Rules to be turned immediately out of the houſe. Every body is to quit the Stage as ſoon as the Champions are ſtripped, before the ſet-to.

IV. That no Champion be deemed beaten, unleſs he fails coming up to the line in the limited time, or that his own Second declares him beaten. No Second is to be allowed to aſk his man's Adverſary any queſtions, or adviſe him to give out.

V. That in bye-battles, the winning man to have two-thirds of the Money given, which ſhall be publicly divided upon the Stage, notwithſtanding any private agreements to the contrary.

VI. That to prevent Diſputes, in every main Battle the Principals ſhall, on coming on the Stage, chooſe from among the gentlemen preſent two Umpires, who ſhall abſolutely decide all Diſputes that may ariſe about the Battle; and if the two Umpires cannot agree, the ſaid Umpires to chooſe a third, who is to determine it.

VII. That no perſon is to hit his Adverſary when he is down, or ſeize him by the ham, the breeches, or any part below the waiſt: a man on his knees to be reckoned down.

Boxing's first rules were read to a gathering of pugilists by Jack Broughton in August 1743. The seven rules were written by Broughton and Captain John Godfrey.

The rules were not designed to help the sport of boxing, but to promote interest from the gambling fraternity, which was crucial to the sport's development.

Following the implementation of the rules, fighters were permitted just 30 seconds to recover and get back to the line for the next round. Broughton was given the right to enter the ring to restore "decorum" in rule three, while rule six dealt with the selection of two officials "to decide all disputes." Boxing bouts needed clean finishes, the gamblers needed a clear winner and the rules provided this. Only rule seven dealt with the fighting itself, by excluding grabbing a man below the waist and hitting an adversary "when he is down." There was no mention, even in those days, of more creative infringements such as biting an opponent's ear!

FATHERS OF THE FIST
Jack Broughton (left) and James Figg (right) never fought. Instead both men ran their theatres of the physically grotesque from the safety of the stage.

Boxing was one of the more civilized attractions at the Boarded House

Jack Broughton was known as the father of modern pugilism. His rules, which were essentially gambling concessions, were written by himself and Captain Godfrey and published in August 1743. Godfrey also wrote boxing's first book.

Broughton had first fought in the many sporting booths in central London, but took over the Boarded House in 1743. Two years earlier he had been involved in a fight at the booths with George Stevenson, which ended with modern boxing's first death, when Stevenson died some weeks later in Broughton's arms.

Many have sought to link the birth of the rules with a desire to safeguard the sport after Stevenson's death, but in truth Broughton was an entrepreneur and without rules and guidelines the sport would have continued to be dogged by unsatisfactory conclusions to fights and was therefore in danger of losing its gamblers. The rules helped persuade gentlemen gamblers, wealthy merchants and royal patrons to continue their support of pugilism.

Broughton enticed his fans with theatrical sideshows at the Boarded House and in 1748 he opened a boxing academy in the Haymarket, London, where gloves, or "mufflers", as they were known, were first used. Broughton started a tradition for performers in the "manly art" to earn money away from the ring as trainers to the rich and famous. His newspaper advertisements claimed: "Persons of quality and distinction will be given the utmost tenderness, for which reasons mufflers are provided, that will effectually secure them from the inconveniency of black eyes, broken jaws and bloody noses."

▲ MEN OF DISTINCTION

The sparring sessions at Fives Court in London took place in the middle of the Real Tennis court, in this case involving Randall and Turpin in 1805. Boxing was an important part of the sporting revolution at the end of the 18th century and later during the first half of the 19th century.

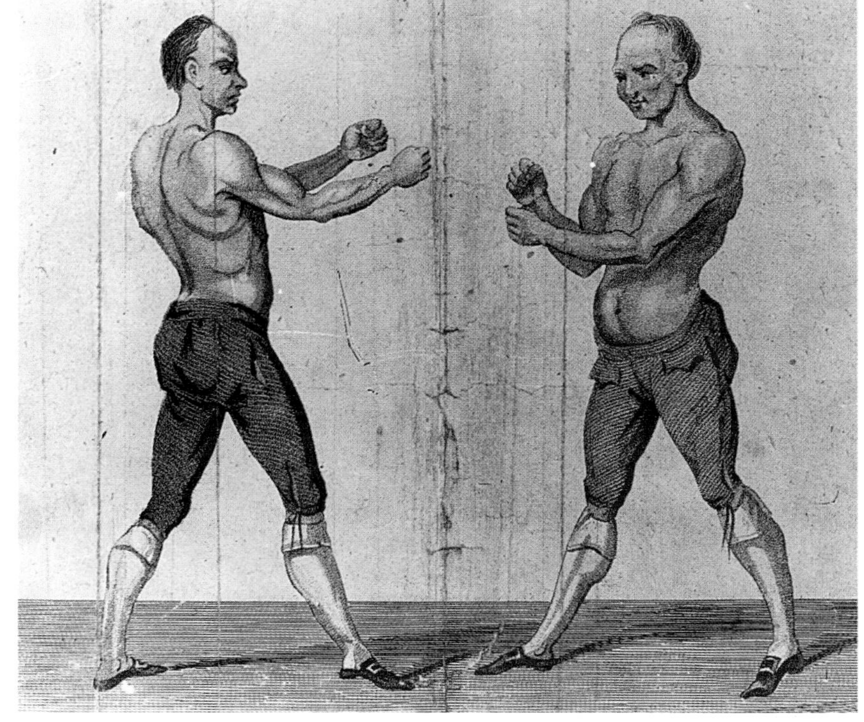

◄ HEROES OF THE FIST

Jack Broughton and Jack Slack fighting on April 10, 1750. The fight only lasted 14 minutes with Broughton defeated when his eyes were closed by Slack's punches. Broughton's patron, the Duke of Cumberland, was most upset – the odds on a Slack win were high.

The Queensberry Rules saved the sport from the Victorian bruisers

▶ **CRIBB V MOLINEAUX**

There was more than a title at stake when Tom Molineaux arrived in Britain from America, in 1809. Upon arrival he sought and found another freed slave, Bill Richmond. After the rematch with Cribb, it was alleged that Richmond (pictured standing behind Molineaux) had dissuaded his man from training hard.

From Broughton's retirement, in 1754, until the Queensberry Rules in 1867, prizefighting went through varying stages of popularity, but the steady arrival of black fighters from America and the West Indies created much interest.

One such immigrant was Tom Molineaux. In 1810, Molineaux, a former slave, was cheated out of victory when he met champion Tom Cribb. Cribb was knocked senseless in round 28, prompting his cornerman, Jem Ward, to walk across to Molineaux's corner during the 30 second break and strike up a debate. He was possibly trying to increase the bet. At any rate, the ruse worked and Cribb was given extra time to recover – he went on to win in round 34.

Angelo Dundee did the same thing when he helped tear Cassius Clay's glove after a brutal knockdown against Britain's Henry Cooper in 1963. Clay was also given extra time to recover.

The rematch between Cribb and Molineaux in 1811 was watched by over 20,000 spectators. However, Molineaux was weary from a publicity tour and was easily beaten in 11 rounds.

By the 1860s a new sport was needed. "These fellows are, indeed, amongst the curiosities of civilization", wrote one spectator. In 1860, the great international fight between America's John Heenan and Britain's Tom Sayers ended in confusion when Sayers quit the ring. It was bare-knuckle prize fighting's first grand goodbye. A newspaper of the time called it "a blot upon the social history of the year." That history soon underwent a drastic change with the introduction of the Queensberry Rules.

◀ **MOLINEAUX V BARCLAY**
The black immigrant, Tom Molineaux, is pictured breaking Capt. Robert Barclay's ribs during a sparring session. Capt. Barclay was the most prolific trainer from the period and trained a number of athletes. Tom Cribb hired Barclay to train him for his return fight with Molineaux.

MILESTONES OF BOXING

•••••••••••••••••

BOXING'S FIRST BOOK

In 1747 Captain John Godfrey's *A Treatise upon the Useful Science of Defence* was published. Such was its appeal that fakes appeared the very same year.

Godfrey was a friend of Broughton, but had first trained under James Figg, and was also an accomplished swordsman and renowned man about town. He introduced Broughton to the Duke of Cumberland, who was later to become the prizefighter's backer!

The descriptions in the book of a boxer's balance are still valid today. Godfrey was obsessed as a boxer and swordsman with gravity, the proper distance between the legs. "A less degree of Art will tell far more than a considerably greater strength. Strength is certainly what the boxer ought to set out with, but without Art he will succeed but poorly."

The MODERN *business*

1867-1919

ETCHEL
PAPK

The end of traditional boxing was in sight before the introduction of the Queensberry Rules in 1867. The new men on the horizon may have taken their essential tactics from the bare-knuckle bruisers, but they refined their punches and within 50 years developed a style that was radically different.

THE BIRTH OF THE NOBLE ART

▲ **SULLIVAN V MITCHELL**
John L. Sullivan beat British-born Charlie Mitchell in a gloved bout at Madison Square Garden in 1883. The return fight (above) was staged in Chantilly, France, without gloves, in 1888. After an exhaustive three hours and 10 minutes of combat the contest was declared a draw.

◀ **KETCHEL V PAPKE**
Previous page: Stanley Ketchel (left) and Billy Papke engage in a spell of holding during their fight in 1908.

The Queensberry Rules were responsible for initiating a drastic and civilizing change on the world of boxing and Jack Johnson, who emerged in the heavyweight division as the last boxer from the ancient days and the first of a new breed of gifted technicians, finally kissed the "gory" days goodbye when he won the world heavyweight title in 1908. After Johnson, many fighters continued to be referred to as "throw-backs" – men who fought both with and without gloves – but as the years passed the ways of the turf fighters slowly faded and a sweeter science was perfected.

The new sport of boxing was part of a larger movement of athleticism that was taking place toward the end of the 19th century. For this was a period of transition when many increasingly popular sports were developing and refining their rules. In 1880, the Amateur Boxing Association (ABA) in London followed suit, releasing their own stringent rules to further distance the descendants of James Figg's "house of pain" from the Victorian sportsmen. A period of professionalism followed and the possibilities opened up by boxing's new, more commercially viable image quickly established it as the glorious frontier for willing sports entrepreneurs.

The bare-knuckle warriors were rapidly running out of time. A new breed of nimble, mobile fighters with cult followings were taking control of the sport. The critics, not surprisingly, were divided. Boxing journalists have never liked change and have always mourned a previous golden era. So it was in the 1890s, a period of comic nostalgia among the boxing fraternity. But between the Queensberry Rules and Johnson winning the world title in 1908, boxing had to change. To survive it needed to evolve from the dark days of the muddy pits and secret fights.

The new rules were not enough at first to make the new sport of "glove-fighting", as many critics called it, a legitimate business. Money slowly changed everything. By 1889 the fighting business, which many considered a travesty of the original, was established on both sides of the Atlantic. In 1890 the world championship was in transition. There were bare-knuckle claimants to some titles, while men in gloves claimed status as world champions at other weights. As the sport started to develop, men on the outside of the ropes disagreed about who the "true" champions were.

The last bare-knuckle champion was John L. Sullivan. In 1889 he beat Jake Kilrain in 75 rounds without gloves, won a side bet of $10,000 and retired to gloat. During his absent reign Sullivan ignored Peter Jackson, a black fighter who was born in the West Indies, but based in Australia. "I will not fight a negro", insisted Sullivan. Jackson, however, went on to meet Gentleman James J. Corbett, who boxed as an amateur, in a fight that was considered the real battle for the real heavyweight championship. The fight between Corbett and Jackson was declared a no-contest after 61 rounds. It was arguably the first big heavyweight fight to be a dreadful letdown. A few weeks later Corbett sparred with Sullivan and the following year he beat Sullivan, leaving the old man in a dreadful bloody mess after 21 rounds.

Sullivan made over one million dollars during his lifetime – the first fighter to do so. The epitome of the old-style prizefighter, he was, not surprisingly, a folk hero. In boxing's time-dishonored tradition he drank as much of his fortune as possible. While Sullivan was establishing his reputation – both as a fighter and as a womanizing hard man – in far away Galveston, Texas, Jack Johnson was just starting, meeting men who were good enough to be worth beating.

In 1897 British-born Bob Fitzsimmons, who grew up in New Zealand, but would later become an American citizen, knocked Corbett out with a body shot. It was, he said, "a bloomin' good belly clout". Fitzsimmons was 33 at the time and weighed less than today's super-middleweight limit of 168 pounds.

In 1899 Fitzsimmons, who would fight for a total of 31 years and become the first man to win three world titles at different weights, was beaten by James J. Jeffries. Between 1899 and 1904 Jeffries defended the title seven times but hid behind a "color bar" of his own making. In 1905 he nominated Marvin Hart, who somehow outpointed Johnson in a non-title fight, to fight for the heavyweight championship. After beating Jack Root, Hart lost the title to the diminutive Canadian Tommy Burns in 1906.

During this time Johnson had to wait, biding his time with wins over black fighters such as Joe Jeannette, Sam McVey and Sam Langford. In those days, waiting for a title fight was itself a hazardous business. It was all too easy to succumb to injury or ill health before you had your shot at the title, a fact typified by the death of Peter Jackson, in 1901, from consumption. The alternative for Johnson was to stick to fighting black opponents; a strategy that Langford adopted, fighting the same seven black fighters a total of 96 times between 1905 and 1921. Half a century later Archie Moore, Charlie Burley and Holman Williams experienced similar problems during a different climate of ignorance.

The wait finally came to an end for Johnson in 1908 when, after two years of pursuing Burns around the globe, he forced him to fight in Sydney. The result was never in doubt, the massacre was total and Johnson was the world champion, instead of merely the "black" champion. However, the search for the Great White Hope to beat him now began in earnest and the campaign of hatred that had been waged against Johnson intensified. The "Get Dead Quick" cards had arrived from the Ku Klux Klan before Johnson had even arrived back in America.

▼ JACKSON V CORBETT
Peter Jackson and James J. Corbett fought 61 rounds in California, in 1891. At the time John L. Sullivan was the world champion, but he was becoming far more interested in his theatrical career. Corbett had to wait until 1892 for his chance at the title, while Jackson was ignored by Sullivan because he was black.

Johnson's infamy outside the ring often overshadowed his boxing

▲ THE LAST RUN
James J. Jeffries looks like an old man, while Jack Johnson resembles a young athlete in this publicity photograph for their heavyweight title fight in 1910. Former champions, Sullivan and Corbett were drafted in to help support Jeffries in one of the most hyped campaigns in boxing history.

Having beaten Burns for the title, Johnson then defeated middleweight champion Stanley Ketchel. His next defense was against the former champion James J. Jeffries. The fight generated unprecedented interest and attracted 36 bids from willing promoters, but it was newcomer, Tex Rickard, who won the tussle to promote the fight by guaranteeing each fighter over $100,000 and a substantial share of the film rights.

The fight took place in Reno, Nevada – transforming the pioneer town. Thousands arrived by train – and 15,760 paid – to witness what they thought would be the end of Johnson's reign. The blatant hatred of the crowd for Johnson was left intact, however, when he destroyed Jeffries in 15 rounds. A young Jack Dempsey was in the angry audience.

After one more defense Johnson was forced to flee America, having been found guilty by an all-white jury of crossing a state line with a white woman. He avoided a prison sentence by fleeing to Paris via Canada later that year.

Johnson's absence created hope for those desperate for a white champion. Gunboat Smith, Art Pelkey and Luther McCarty were acclaimed as "white" heavyweight champions of the world after Johnson beat Burns. It was a spurious accolade. In 1914 Frenchman Georges Carpentier beat Gunboat Smith in London to win the title.

Attention now switched to Jess Willard, who had fought two unexceptional no decision bouts with Pelkey and McCarty, and lost to Smith. However, Willard was tall and heavy and was, many believed, the man, the white man, to beat Johnson.

▶ JAMES J. JEFFRIES
Jeffries quit the ring in 1904 and selected Canada's Tommy Burns and Jack Root to fight for the vacant heavyweight championship. Jeffries was the referee and counted Root out in round 12.

▼ THE OLD CHAMP
The heavy tape used to bind fighters' hands is clearly visible on Jeffries as he is introduced to the crowd before his fight with Johnson. From the outset Jeffries never stood a chance and was eventually stopped in round 15 of the one-sided savaging.

MILESTONES OF BOXING

THE QUEENSBERRY RULES

The Queensberry Rules saved boxing from extinction. Before the 12 rules were published in 1867, the sport of prizefighting was stuck in the fields, sheds and bars. Boxing needed a more civilized look and a set of rules that altered its arbitrary nature.

The rules were compiled by John Graham Chambers, a graduate of Cambridge University, and keen sportsman John Sholto Graham, the eighth Marquess of Queensberry (above). They introduced gloves to competition, a time limit of three minutes a round (although seldom in the history of the prize ring had rounds lasted that long, anyway), a rest period of one minute between each round and a maximum recovery period of 10 seconds. They also banned wrestling. However, there was no limit to the number of rounds. Regulation was the key factor.

The introduction of gloves disgusted old-timers and the introduction of the 10 second recovery period ruined forever the bare-knuckle methods. The ancient breed of pugilists were in immediate trouble. Their sport, and their wild catch-hold-hit-and-maul style, was all but finished.

JACK JOHNSON

Boxing's First Controversial Figure

▼ **JACK AND HIS WOMEN**
Johnson's career was ruined because of women – white women. He chased them, he married them, he was forced out of America with one, and served time in prison due to another. As Muhammad Ali once said of Johnson, "Back in 1919 when you got lynched for looking at a white woman, he married a white woman."

The public drama of Jack Johnson's life, reign and death undoubtedly secured his place as a prominent figure in sporting history. Johnson courted controversy from the beginning. From his smiles of total scorn during fights to his hedonistic pursuit of chaos outside the ropes, he was news. Often bad news. His contemporary, Ed Gunboat Smith, the main "white" heavyweight champion of the time, was ready to brawl with him after watching Johnson abuse his first wife. His second wife, who Smith thought was a "bum," later killed herself. It all added to Johnson's wild image. Johnson also enjoyed chasing white women, a trait that seemed to further infuriate the masses.

It seemed likely that Johnson's career would end in turmoil and his life, most probably, in a nasty death. It is amazing then that he survived until he was 68, when he crashed his car en route to the Joe Louis-Billy Conn rematch, in 1946.

Born in Galveston, Texas, Johnson began fighting at the age of 13 and took part in his first professional fight in 1897. His trouble with white America started before he won the world title. By 1912, police in several states had questioned him in connection with the Mann Act, which prohibited men taking women across state boundaries for immoral purposes. Johnson liked fast cars and equally fast women, and he broke the law in style. He was sentenced to one year and one day in prison in 1913 and ordered to pay $1,000 after a former mistress confessed, but he fled to Europe while on bail. His place in history secure, Johnson continued to win fights in defense of his portion of the world title. He got into the business of running bars and became a celebrity in Europe. His fitness began to deteriorate and his eventual defeat at the hands of Jess Willard was inevitable, if unexpected.

"There had been some miserable times in my life before the Willard fight," claimed Johnson. When it was over and Johnson was back in his dressing room the inquest started and the legitimacy of Willard's win was under scrutiny. "I sure know it was hot in there and 26 rounds is a long time to go before you throw a fight," was Willard's response to the suggestion that Johnson had taken a dive.

After Willard beat him in Havana in 1915, Johnson continued his roaming, but eventually returned to America to serve his sentence in 1920. After his release he sought a fight with Jack Dempsey, but it never took place and Johnson was all but finished, fighting only eight more times in different places. His last professional fight was in 1928, although he returned for exhibitions until 1945.

In 1956, Nat Fleischer, editor and founder of *The Ring*, published a letter claiming he had paid Johnson $250 for the letter of guilt, over the Willard fight, in 1916. Fleischer never believed Johnson's account of the fight's conclusion. In the missive of confession Johnson said he had taken a dive "A dive after 26 rounds in the heat?" experts asked. Opinion is still divided and it remains an enigmatic moment in the mad history of heavyweight boxing; just one of Johnson's bizarre contributions.

▲ **THE OTHER LOVE** *Johnson, pictured here in June 1911, loved cars. According to frightened passengers, however, he was a terrible driver.*

Willard's surprise victory put an end to the panic on the streets

▲ MAYHEM IN THE RING
A beleaguered Jack Johnson starts to lift himself from the canvas in Havana after the challenger, Jess Willard, connected with a light combination in round 26 of their fight in April, 1915.

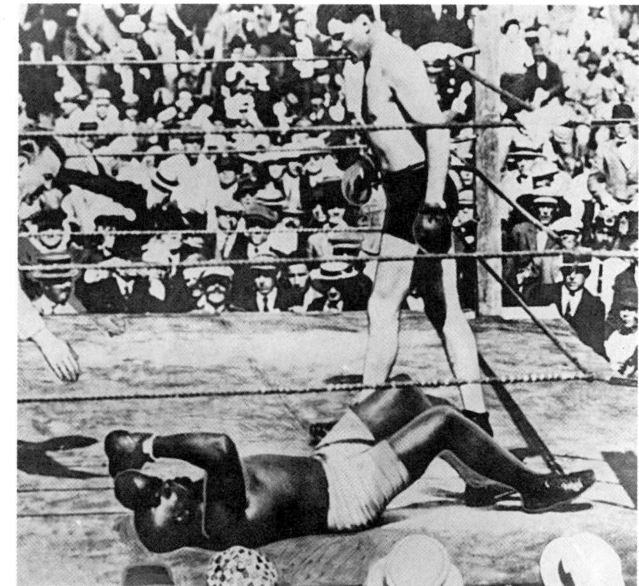

▶ WAS HE REALLY OUT?
Johnson appears to be shielding his eyes from the sun – surely not the actions of a man out of his senses. The debate surrounding the fight still rages.

When Jack Johnson and Jess Willard met in Cuba in 1915, Johnson was 37 and was keen to return to America after nearly three years in exile. The fight ended in round 26 with Johnson sprawled on the canvas, shielding his eyes from the burning sun. He had been floored by a seemingly innocuous punch, a light right to his exposed jaw. "I threw the fight," he offered as explanation the following year. Johnson had won 20 of the 25 completed rounds. Willard was simply too slow and too easy to hit, but Johnson was in bad shape.

Controversy still surrounds the fight today, but nobody cared at the time. The man perceived as the black menace was beaten. Willard kept the title for over four years, but he was an unexceptional fighter at a time of tremendous transition. A distant reminder of the slow fighters of boxing's past, Willard won his title two decades too late.

Far removed from the style of Willard was the New Yorker, Benny Leonard, the lightweight champion of the time. Leonard was the first wizard of the modern business of boxing, while Willard was one of the last exponents of the ancient art of milling. A few years later, the infamous Primo Carnera would take over the role played by Willard.

◀ WILLARD UNDER FIRE
Willard was bloody and bruised at the end of the contest, having been forced to endure a lot of punishment before Johnson's eventual collapse. Willard's resolve was formidable throughout. "He caught me but I just kept going. I had to win, I had to keep going," he said.

MILESTONES OF BOXING

FIRST HEAVYWEIGHT CHAMPIONSHIP FIGHT TO BE FILMED

Not only was Bob Fitzsimmons of a very similar stature to the movie hero, Rocky, played by Sylvester Stallone in the film of the same name, but the pair also share a cinematic allegiance. When Fitzsimmons knocked out James J. Corbett in round 14 to win the world heavyweight title in March 1897, it was the first heavyweight championship fight to be filmed. The film was later discovered by Jim Jacobs, Mike Tyson's first manager, in 1958 and restored.

Enoch J. Rector's film of the fight was such an immediate international success that fakes, with actors playing the two boxers, were made. However, it was not the first fight to be filmed as Thomas Edison had printed an exhibition involving Mike Leonard and Jack Cushing in 1894.

An earlier attempt to make a commercial film of a Fitzsimmons's fight had ended in disaster when Fitzsimmons demanded his share of the film's expected profits. The promoter, Dan Stuart, told him: "You are paid to fight, not act." "OK, no money, no moving picture," Fitzsimmons replied. The fight lasted 95 seconds, with Fitzsimmons displaying supreme arrogance by refusing to move before knocking out Peter Maher with his first punch.

BENNY LEONARD

Boxing's First Folk Hero

▼ LEONARD V TENDLER
The stylish Benny Leonard (left) engages in a gentlemanly handshake with Lew Tendler before their non-title fight in 1922. The fight was declared a no decision contest, but in the rematch the following year Leonard outpointed Tendler over 15 rounds.

Benjamin Leiner became Benny Leonard when the ring lights illuminated his genius and he became the first folk hero of boxing. He was a poor kid from a bad neighbourhood on New York's East Side, and his career started with a knockout defeat in 1911.

By 1916 he was arguably the best lightweight in the world. He had fought Johnny Dundee and Freddie Welsh in so-called no decision fights when local pressmen voted against him on both occasions. In 1917, however, he took his revenge by beating Welsh for the lightweight title. He was a man with both perfectly placed feet in the 20th century.

Leonard was an intelligent fighter, not a vicious man. "I would rather not hurt them," he said. He was also quick to identify the difficulties that young champions experienced once they won titles: "Friends want to throw a party. The bad part is if you don't take them in, your friends start complaining that you are now a swell head and don't want to have anything to do with them any more. More guys have lost their titles because they were partied to death than for any other reason."

In the ring Leonard was too cute for his day. After three losses in the first three years of his caree,r he went undefeated – with the exception of one dubious disqualification – from January 1914 until his last ring appearance in 1932, against future welterweight champion Jimmy McLarnin. During his 209-fight career, he lost just five, won 88 and had 115 no decision fights.

In May 1917 Leonard won the lightweight title by knocking Freddie Welsh to the floor three times, forcing a ninth-round stoppage. The two men had met twice before in 10-round no decision fights. It was during this time that Leonard met Ad Wolgast, Willie Ritchie, Rocky Kansas and Ritchie Mitchell, all members of an elite club of exceptional lightweights of which Leonard slowly took control.

Leonard was a great fighter. It's true that Johnson delivered his punches from a defensive stance with accuracy, but Leonard was even more precise. He could also move and, as a lightweight, boxed faster. His fights were watched in New York by crowds in excess of 50,000 and often generated nearly half a million dollars in gate receipts. When he fought Lew Tendler in 1922 he taunted his opponent "Is that the best you can do," he asked. "I expected more." The ringside *cognoscenti* were thrilled by the latest weapon in Leonard's endless repertoire. The fans loved him too and after each fight he delighted them by slicking back his black hair – it was his trademark, his shuffle, his back flip.

There remains, however, an odd cloud of controversy over Leonard's career. In 1922 he was just seconds away from winning the world welterweight title from Jack Britton when he walked across the ring and hit Britton, who at the time was on one knee recovering from a legitimate knockdown. Leonard, the favorite with the bookies, was disqualified.

His last fight, which was part of a sad comeback necessitated by the loss of his fortune in the Wall Street crash of 1929, was a knockout loss to Jimmy McLarnin. Leonard was 36 at the time, his famous sleek black hair thin and receding. He quit boxing for the last time in 1932 and in April 1947, after serving in the Second World War, died of a heart attack in the ring while refereeing a fight at the St. Nicholas Arena in New York.

▲ **LEONARD IN HIS PRIME** *During a time of great prejudice Leonard courted controversy by refusing to discriminate against black opponents.*

The demise of Willard at the hands of Dempsey was a turning point

▲ **THE WILDE EFFECT**
Pal Moore attempts to block Jimmy Wilde's punches during a brutal 20-round contest at Olympia, in London, which Wilde won. Gene Tunney, a heavyweight champion of the period and the recipient of boxing's first million-dollar purse, considered Wilde to be "the greatest fighter I ever saw." There were many others who agreed.

In the lighter weight divisions, fighters like Benny Leonard were adapting to the changing times with more ease than the heavyweights. They were moving faster and were more inventive with their punches.

Leonard was the best, but Welshman Jimmy Wilde was also exceptional. Wilde won universal acceptance as flyweight champion in 1916. He weighed less than 100 pounds for many of his fights and was a curious specimen, with power in both hands and an ability to knock people out from many angles. He started boxing in the coal mines, continued in touring booths, and fought for the last time in 1923, when he lost his title to Pancho Villa at the Polo Grounds, New York, in front of 23,000 people. It is possible that during his celebrated career, Wilde took part in over 800 fights.

In 1914, Kid Blackie started boxing. He would later become known as Jack Dempsey, the hobo warrior, the Manassa Mauler, a man with a past that satisfied the critics and a style that pleased the crowds. His progress was interrupted when Jim Flynn, a veteran, knocked him out in 1917, but two years later he was ready for Willard having knocked out Flynn in a rematch. He had also knocked Arthur Pelkey out in one round and Gunboat Smith in two.

The Willard-Dempsey fight, which took place in July, 1919, was to change boxing forever. The program for the fight called it a boxing exhibition. It was not. It was a sickening and brutal spectacle that exposed Jess Willard's towering limitations. In many ways Johnson had been a champion with a lenient streak, but Dempsey was cruel in the ring, a ferocious fighter who showed no mercy.

◀ **A GIANT IN THE RING**

Although slightly built, Wilde was incredibly strong in the ring and was able to use his outward appearance to his advantage in fights. "My opponents could not believe I would still be standing after two rounds. They thought I looked too fragile to survive."

▶ **KID BLACKIE STARTS TO BOX**

Jack Dempsey was first known as Kid Blackie. He was a young hobo warrior and a ruthless puncher. In 1919 he finally got his chance when he was matched with Jess Willard.

MILESTONES OF BOXING

FIRST BLACK HEAVYWEIGHT CHAMPION

Jack Johnson was the first black world heavyweight champion. Always a controversial figure, Johnson's idea of fun was risking a lynching by taunting opponents and he succeeded in angering most of white America in the process. He beat Canadian Tommy Burns in 1908 to win the title, but the contest was a clear mismatch. Burns was short, brave and ideal fodder for Johnson's calculated style. As the rounds passed it was clear Johnson would leave Sydney with the championship. "It was a massacre," many of the journalists reported. The local police intervened in round 14 to bring the slaughter to an end. Johnson was unmarked; Burns unrecognizable.

For Johnson it was the end of a long journey in pursuit of Burns and the start of his decline as a fighter. He made five successful defenses before agreeing to fight Jess Willard in 1915. He lost and it was 22 years before another black fighter, Joe Louis, fought for the title.

Louis won the championship in 1937 and from the start everything possible was done to ensure he was not perceived as another Johnson.

BEYOND
the ring

1919-1937

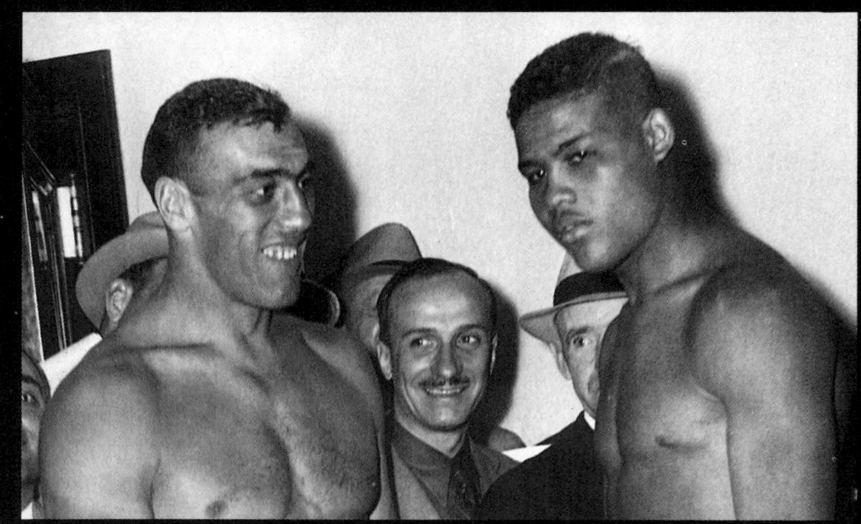

After Jack Johnson fell victim to the Havana sun it was just a matter of time before someone else emerged to take control of the sport. That man was Jack Dempsey, a fighter from the asphalt jungle, a hobo off the tracks with a dark past. He was boxing's new savage idol.

DEMPSEY'S RING TERROR

▲ TWO OF A KIND
Jack Dempsey and George "Tex" Rickard both left school when they were young. Similarly, both were drifters until they discovered boxing. Rickard promoted Dempsey's world title victory over Jess Willard in 1919, which was not a great financial success. However, both men went on to be involved in the sport's first million-dollar gate fights.

◀ THE SHELBY FIASCO!
Previous page: Jack Dempsey and Tom Gibbons in the 1923 fight that bankrupted the small town of Shelby, Montana.

Jack Dempsey, his manager Doc Kearns and his promoter Tex Rickard changed the sport. The change started with Dempsey's first left hook in front of 70,000 people in Toledo, Ohio. Willard was on the floor seven times in the first round. He was helpless from the first seconds. It finally ended at the close of round three when Willard decided to remain on his seat, the blood forming on the floor at his feet. Dempsey was accused of having his fists taped with insulation tape, so-called loaded bandages. Kearns's son said his father admitted using a mixture to harden the bandages, but either way it would have made little difference as Willard was out of condition and easy to hit. Dempsey reigned as the first sentinel at the gates of boxing's future.

From the start men pursued Dempsey. Johnson wanted a fight, as did another black fighter, Harry Wills. Wills came closer but he too was held at bay. "There was a color bar. We could have made money but there was nowhere to put the fight on", claimed Dempsey. At one point tickets for the fight with Wills were printed, a ruse on the part of Rickard.

Rickard did, however, set up crowd-pulling events for Dempsey. In 1921 Dempsey took part in the first fight to take one million dollars at the gate. In fact, Dempsey would go on to draw a million dollars at each of his next five fights. In one small town venue, betting on a Dempsey fight virtually broke the bank. Dempsey's status as an icon may have been gradual but his appeal was immediate. He was a hungry man, a poor guy with a hobo past whose rise to the top made him the classic all-American hero. After his career was finished, there was a 10-year gap before another fighter was held in the same esteem.

Between Willard's bloody end and the predictable victory of Louis in 1937, the sport of boxing evolved more drastically than in practically any other period in its history. Boxers from other divisions started to emerge, there were rivalries that attracted crowds and increased publicity and coverage meant boxing appealed to more and more people. By the time Louis was in control, the sport had changed drastically from the business which Jack Johnson had plundered.

In 1926 Dempsey lost to Gene Tunney. It was a shock, but Dempsey, like so many champions before and after him, had taken too much time out – too many nights away from the ring and days away from the gym. In defeat, Dempsey's legend was secured when he embraced Tunney.

Before a rematch Dempsey knocked out Jack Sharkey who, at the time, was the leading contender for Tunney's title. Sharkey won the heavyweight title in 1932 at the second attempt. Just before the fight with Dempsey, the unpredictable and outspoken Sharkey beat Harry Wills – the black fighter who had earlier been denied a fight with Dempsey – on a 13th-round foul. Wills, however, was 37 when he fouled Sharkey and over 30 when he should have met Dempsey. The unfortunate Wills remains one of boxing's lost fighters, a casualty of the politics of the sport at the time.

Tunney agreed to a rematch with Dempsey. In their second fight both were on the floor – Tunney for 14 seconds in the notorious "long count" – before he eventually won again. Dempsey enhanced his reputation when he stated that Tunney could have got up before the count reached 10. It was, Dempsey admitted, his own fault as he always stood over opponents instead of moving back to allow the referee to count. "I don't know if I could have licked Gene at my best," he said.

Dempsey retired shortly after the Tunney fight, but still took part in over 50 exhibitions until the early 1940s, and in 1940 – nearly 15 years after his last official fight – he fought twice in licenced contests.

When Tunney retired in 1929 boxing was in need of somebody to take control. The leading pack of heavyweights consisted of Max Schmeling, Jack Sharkey, Johnny Risko, Young Stribling, King Levinsky, Ernie Schaaf and Paolino Uzcudun, but the eventual champion came from another source. The lull in talent encouraged the creation of Italy's Primo Carnera, a lump of flesh that eventually wrested the world title from Sharkey in 1933.

Carnera's life was a pantomime of exploitation and he fell hardest of all the heavyweight champions until the lunatics from boxing's lost generation of heavyweights like Tony Tucker, Michael Dokes and Tony Tubbs ruined what could have been brilliant careers with a sad descent into drugs.

However, even without a clear leader, the heavyweights were still the main men at the box-office. In 1929, a non-title fight between two Europeans – Max Schmeling, from Germany, and Paolino Uzcudun, from Spain, drew over 40,000 to Yankee Stadium. It was a time of tremendous matches. In 1935, as a regal and baby-faced Joe Louis moved closer to the title, 88,000 people filled Yankee Stadium to watch him beat former champion Max Baer.

Middleweights, however, like Mickey Walker, who took over the mantle from Harry Greb and Tiger Flowers, were establishing the lower orders with potential for big gates and repeat fights. Greb was the only man to beat Tunney, and in 1931 Walker drew with Sharkey.

▲ **WILLARD AWAITS HIS FATE**
Jack Dempsey and Jess Willard in the ring in Toledo, Ohio, July 4, 1919. Dempsey dropped Willard seven times in the first three minutes of a bloody and brutal contest that lasted just three rounds. Willard had made only one defense of his title in four years and was unprepared for the onslaught. "He hit me quick and it hurt. I never recovered, but I kept getting up," said Willard.

Greb, Flowers and Walker: the battle between the middleweights

▶ **GREB V WILSON**
Harry Greb moves away from Johnny Wilson's teasing jab before their world middleweight title fight in New York, on August 31, 1923. Greb won over 15 rounds and made seven defenses before losing to Tiger Flowers in 1926.

▲ **THE GEORGIA DEACON**
Tiger Flowers died before he had a chance to consolidate his position in the middleweight division. "He was an inspiration not only to the youth of his race, but to all boys and all young men – to live cleanly, speak softly, trust in God, and fight hard and fair," said Gene Tunney at Flowers's funeral in 1927.

Tiger Flowers became the first black middleweight champion in 1926 when he beat Harry Greb. The two were completely different characters: Flowers was a gentle man, a church deacon from Georgia, while Greb was a hellraiser and a dirty fighter.

Their two title fights were awful brawls, where filthy tactics dominated and Greb repeatedly used his thumb to bloody Flowers's eye sockets. In their second world title fight of 1926 Flowers said to Greb, whose mouth was as foul as his tactics: "Mister Greb, put my eye out if you like, but please don't take the name of the Lord in vain."

Harry Greb died just two months after the middleweight title rematch against Tiger Flowers. Greb's punishing fight program had included 299 bouts in 13 years. In October 1926 he underwent an operation to have scar tissue removed from above his eyes and have his nose straightened following an automobile accident, but died after surgery.

Tiger Flowers lost a close decision, and his title, to Mickey Walker the same year. Walker had lost a fight to Greb in 1925, when he had outpointed him with the assistance of his thumb.

Flowers died in November 1927, just four days after winning his last fight. Amazingly, in the week before his death he fought a 10-round draw with future light-heavyweight champion Maxie Rosenbloom. At the time of his death Flowers had a contract with Jack Doc Kearns for a rematch against Walker. Both Greb and Flowers were 32 when they died. A tremendous series of fights died with them.

Walker beat some of the best heavyweights at the time, in addition to engaging in an infamous late-night altercation with Harry Greb several hours after their fight! Only Archie Moore, fighting 20 years later, would compile a record to compare with the magnificent achievements of Walker in a division where he often conceded 50 pounds.

▶ GREB LIVED BY NIGHT
Harry Greb was a notorious hellraiser who loved a good time, whether it was in the ring, at the gym or out on the town.

▼ THE TOY BULLDOG
Mickey Walker was an extraordinary boxer. He won the middleweight title with a dubious decision over Tiger Flowers in 1926, but he was willing to meet anybody, at any weight, anytime!

MILESTONES OF BOXING

FIRST MILLION-DOLLAR GATE

Jack Dempsey was ruthless. The bad guy. Frenchman Georges Carpentier – who was given the subtle sobriquet "Orchid Man" by promoter Tex Rickard's publicist, Ike Dorgan – was handsome and a war veteran. He may have been a foreign boxer but he was seen as the good guy in the first fight to take over $1,000,000 at the gate.

The fight took place at Boyle's 30 Acres, in New Jersey, on July 2, 1921. It was Dempsey's third defense, his only fight in 1921 and he was paid $300,000 from the gross of $1,789,074. A crowd of over 80,000 watched Dempsey knock Carpentier out in the fourth round. The fight, however, helped make boxing respectable.

DEMPSEY V FIRPO

Boxing's Most Ferocious Round

▶ THE FINAL KNOCKDOWN
Dempsey walks away from the stricken Luis Angel Firpo after the ninth and final knockdown. "I knew it was the last time," said Dempsey after the fight, "He had taken too many and would not take any more."

▼ A SAVAGE NIGHT FOR FIRPO
Dempsey and Firpo met to dispute Dempsey's world heavyweight championship in 1923. Firpo found there was no way out and, after the notorious first round, proceedings came to a sudden halt in round two.

The press at the time claimed the "last shred of civilization had snapped," during round one of the Jack Dempsey-Luis Angel Firpo heavyweight title fight at the Polo Grounds, New York, in September 1923. It was boxing's second million-dollar fight and arguably the sport's most ferocious round.

"Blood thirsty savages watching a struggle to the death between two fight-crazy maniacs," was how one journalist described the action. By the end of the first minute of round two, Firpo had been dropped nine times, the final time for the full count, while Dempsey had been knocked through the ropes and saved by the outstretched hands of dumbstruck sportswriters.

"The bell rang right away and that saved me," recalled Dempsey nearly 50 years later. When he was thrown back in the ring he was too dazed to move from the ropes and Firpo lost his chance when the bell was somehow heard above the howls of the 82,000 crowd.

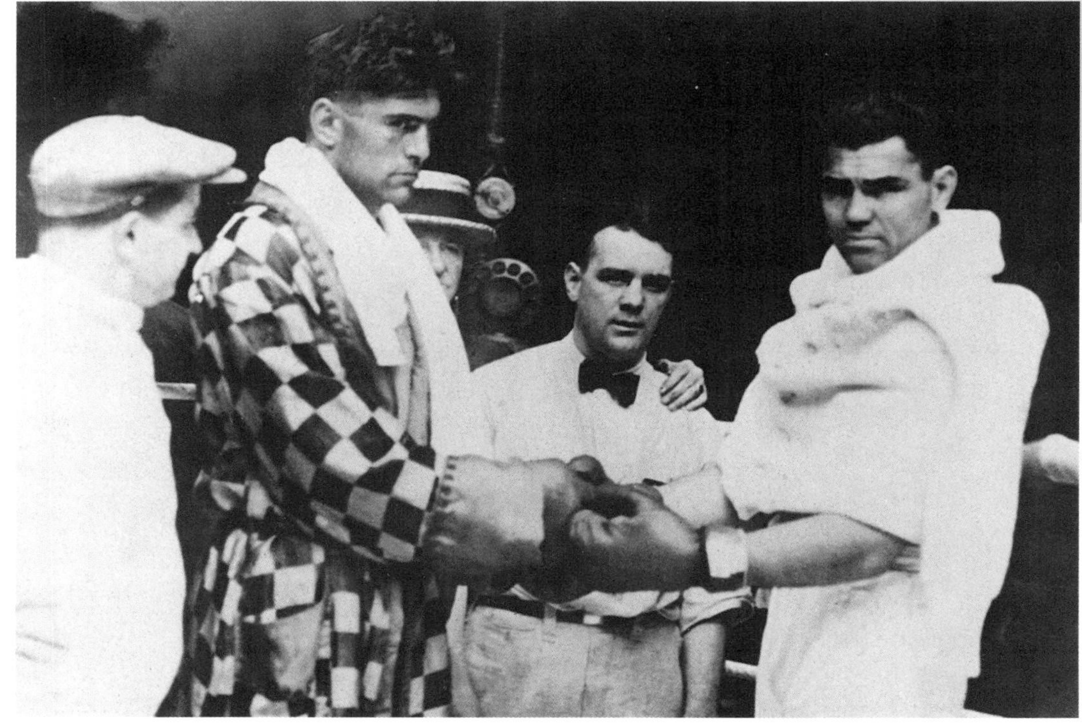

Tex Rickard needed the Dempsey-Firpo fight to be a success. Two months earlier Dempsey and his manager, Doc Kearns, had fled from the town of Shelby, Montana in the hour after Dempsey outpointed Tommy Gibbons, when the town – which had put up the finance – was bankrupted by the flop. Before leaving, Kearns had cleared the final $56,000 from the gate receipts. The Firpo fight restored Rickard's reputation as sport's top promoter, with Dempsey, sport's richest prize, at his side.

Rickard matched Firpo with Jess Willard in Jersey City, just a few days after the Dempsey-Gibbons fiasco in Montana. Firpo won in eight rounds and the dream fight with Dempsey picked up momentum. Earlier attempts to foist Firpo, whom Rickard claimed he discovered in Argentina, on the boxing writers had failed. Beating Willard somehow convinced the cynics.

When it came to fighting Dempsey, however, Firpo was simply too tough for his own limited skills and went down on one knee at the start of the first round. Firpo was then caught with a left hook and went down again. From that moment, until the final 30 seconds of the fight, Firpo was down six more times. Some were clean knockdowns and some the result of Dempsey's fury and his knack of standing directly above a stricken boxer.

After seven knockdowns Firpo landed a desperate lunge to Dempsey's chest and then a right. The world champion tipped from the ring, his feet flipping up as his body sank onto the ringside press tables. He was hurt but he scrambled back, with the help of the writers. Firpo's last effort to end the fight in the few seconds remaining of the first round failed. In the second Firpo was over twice more, the final time from a right, for the full count. The fight was over.

In New York, Jack "Kid" Berg was seen as a new lord from an old land

▲ THE BOY FROM THE EAST
Jack "Kid" Berg was born in London's East End. He was called the Whitechapel Whirlwind, and had an immediate impact in New York, winning 14 of his 15 fights between May 1929 and January 1930. Berg's showmanship raised his profile to cult status.

When Benny Leonard retired from the lightweight division in 1925, Tony Canzoneri was just starting. Between Leonard and Henry Armstrong a succession of brilliant lightweights won and lost titles and fights.

Tony Canzoneri was one of the best, becoming only the sixth fighter to win world titles at three weights – feather, lightweight and junior-welterweight – during a time when good fighters fought the best opposition at regular intervals, and often at short

▲ BERG SHOWS NO FEAR
In one fight, against Billy Pertrolle in 1930, Berg returned to his corner after round one having been subjected to a thunderous body shot. Asked by his concerned trainer, Ray Arcel, how he felt, the fearless Berg replied, "Lovely thank you. And you?"

MILESTONES OF BOXING

THE FIRST MILLION-DOLLAR PURSE

Gene Tunney was once described as "a book-reading dude" by a contemporary journalist. He is seldom described as a great fighter yet when he retired in 1929 he had lost just once in 87 fights. He was clearly a calculated boxer.

In 1926, when he beat Dempsey, he was paid $200,000. His payment for the rematch was a much more complicated affair. Tunney was initially given $999,445 for the fight. He then wrote Rickard a check for $9,555 and was in return paid with a check for one million dollars. The rematch – a controversial match which Tunney won – was watched by 104,943 eager spectators and took $2,658,660 in gate receipts.

Tunney left the ring for good after beating Tom Heeney in 1928. He never wandered back, never had the urge to fight again that so many former champions had had before and after him. Tunney was content with his money and his glory.

notice. It was an active scene. Not necessarily a fair time, but a time of terrific matches. Few fighters won world titles with unbeaten records before the 1960s.

In early 1930 Canzoneri lost a decision to Britain's Jack "Kid" Berg. The same year Berg, who at the time was only 21, put an end to Kid Chocolate's unbeaten run of 160 fights. Berg was a cult fighter, a brilliant showman whose career was effectively over by the time he was 23.

In 1928 Berg arrived in America. By 1930 he was the champion of the junior-welterweight division, which was not at that time universally recognized. Nevertheless, Berg and his non-stop style had a large following. In New York's Madison Square Garden, the fighter from London's East End proved a huge attraction with nearly 20,000 paying to see his first performance in 1929.

Berg entered the ring wearing a sacred Jewish shawl, a *tallith*, and strips of leather, *tvillan*, strapped to his arms (*tvillan* are a reminder of god's presence). It took Berg several minutes to remove the religious items and after he had kissed each *tvillan*, his trainer, Ray Arcel, would place them in an embroidered, velvet bag. The crowd loved it.

◀ **SWEET SMELL OF SUCCESS**
Tony Canzoneri was a remarkable fighter. During his career he held three world titles, fought 22 championship fights at four different weights and lost only 24 times in 141 fights between 1925 and 1929. He fought the full list of greats from a period of excellence: Johnny Dundee, Lou Ambers, Sammy Mandell, Billy Petrolle, Kid Chocolate, Jack "Kid" Berg, Barney Ross and Jimmy McLarnin.

SHORT-TERM HEAVYWEIGHT CHAMPIONS

Boxing's Time-dishonored Tradition

BRADDOCK'S FAIRYTALE
James J. Braddock was an unlikely heavyweight champion. His career appeared to be over in the early 1930s, but wins in late 1934 and early 1935 resurrected his fading hopes. In June 1935 his dream came true when he beat Max Baer to win the championship.

From the moment Gene Tunney's left fist started to tame Jack Dempsey, until a night 10 years later when James J.Braddock collapsed against Joe Louis, the heavyweight scene was awash with controversial figures and events. The first fighter to emerge after Tunney was Jack Sharkey who, having beaten top black fighters Harry Wills and George Godfrey in 1926, was knocked out by Dempsey in 1927 as he turned to the referee. Until that moment Sharkey was winning the fight. "What the hell was he doing looking away," asked Dempsey. It was the question on everyone's lips.

In 1930 Sharkey lost a vacant heavyweight title fight when he landed a low blow, a short left hook, and Max Schmeling, a German with a Jewish-American manager, fell in agony to the floor. It was the first time the heavyweight title was won on a foul. It was an accident, but many fights at the time were decided on intentional fouls.

In boxing's time-dishonored tradition, the title split after Sharkey's fist plunged deep into Schmeling's groin. Schmeling was the linear champion, but in 1931 Primo Carnera was matched with Sharkey for a version of the championship. The Italian lost – a surprise considering the men who controlled his career.

In 1932 Sharkey beat Schmeling in a rematch. There was an outcry from Schmeling's manager, Joe Jacobs, and one of boxing's most often quoted expressions entered the sporting lexicon. As Schmeling ducked his head in defeat Jacobs screamed in disgust: "We wuz robbed – we shoulda stood in bed."

The Sharkey-Carnera rematch was made for June 1933. It was a strange fight from the start and in round six it ended with Sharkey on the canvas. It was another setback. Nobody had faith in Carnera's abilities, but he was now the champion. Mickey Walker, who fought at a lighter weight altogether, beat better heavyweights, but in the 1930s anything went.

Light-heavyweight champion Tommy Loughran is a perfect example of the confusing state of the sport at this time. Loughran fought a no decision bout with Tunney in 1922 and beat Georges Carpentier, Harry Greb, Mickey Walker, Johnny Risko, Ernie Schaaf, King Levinsky, Young Stribling and future heavyweight champions, James J. Braddock and Max Baer. He fought Greb six times (with one win, two losses, one draw and two no decision affairs) and claimed that Tunney refused him a rematch on five occasions.

Loughran was knocked out by Sharkey in 1929 but beat him in a rematch after the Boston Gob, as Sharkey was known, lost his title to Carnera. In 1934 Loughran lost on points to the Italian, whose ring sobriquet, the Ambling Alp, was often referred to as an exaggeration of his speed!

After Carnera came Max Baer, who beat Carnera in the same way Dempsey beat Willard. In 1935 Baer lost to Braddock. The carnival had turned bizarre. Braddock, understandably dubbed the Cinderella Man, had lost 11 of his previous 20 fights before he toyed with Baer. He could fight though; he was an old-fashioned grafter. Braddock should have fought Schmeling but 1937 was a difficult time and the pair never met. Braddock's manager Joe Gould claimed he spoke personally to Joseph Goebbels about the proposed fight. Joe Louis, however, had other plans for Schmeling, in the shape of a revenge bid for his painful first defeat in 1936 when Schmeling knocked him out.

It was only a matter of time before Louis was matched with Braddock. After a gap of 24 months the fight was made and Louis won in 8 rounds in June 1937. Tunney, Schmeling, Sharkey, Carnera, Baer and Braddock had managed just five successful defenses between them in 11 years.

▲ **ON DANGEROUS GROUND**
Max Schmeling shaking hands with New York governor Franklin D. Roosevelt before his rematch with Jack Sharkey in 1932.

▲ **BAER AND TUNNEY**
Max Baer (top) had his day in the sun as champion while ignoring most of pugilism's sacred rules. His clowning antics may have endeared him to the fans, but it ultimately ruined his career. By contrast, Gene Tunney (above) was a consummate artist. "I've seen Dempsey fight and I was impressed with his lack of knowledge," he said before outpointing him in 1926.

When Louis and Armstrong entered the ring quality fighters suffered

▲ **LOUIS IS NOT AMUSED**

Joe Louis was not one to smile easily. He was certainly not amused by the grinning Primo Carnera at the scales before their 1935 fight. Carnera was ruined in six rounds. The ruthless Louis also disposed of Max Baer in four rounds and Jack Sharkey in three, but in 1936 he was unexpectedly beaten by Max Schmeling.

In 1931 Tony Canzoneri knocked out "Kid" Berg and later in the year outpointed him, although Berg was still considered world super-lightweight champion by *The Ring* until 1932. Berg started to box at the age of 14 at Premierland, not far from where he was born in London's Whitechapel.

He was in decline after the last Canzoneri fight and although he continued to win, he was never the same. "Berg could tear the hearts out of the toughest pugs," claimed Arcel. Sadly, his timing faded and Berg, like so many others, lost his edge at an early age.

It was a time of transition. There were still relics from the past but increasingly fighters were starting to look more and more modern. Television was just a few years away and stars were needed to fulfil a new role on the small screen. It was possibly the last period of innocence for boxing. At the end of the decade, revenue from television and the manipulative powers of businessmen and influential organizations started to form the bloody business of boxing that we have today.

By 1937 two new fighters, Henry Armstrong and Joe Louis, had become established and during the next few years they would dominate the sport. At the same time, a young kid called Walker Smith was dazzling the experts in New York's gyms. In the competitive ring, Smith used the name Ray Robinson, Sugar Ray. In the late 1930s boxing's future was secure in the fists of this trio of great fighters. In the 1940s, Rocky Graziano, Tony Zale, Jake La Motta and Marcel Cerdan – whose battles are still used to measure levels of heart, sacrifice and brutality in the boxing ring – would take over their mantle. The middleweights would have their glorious time but in 1937, The Brown Bomber, Joe Louis, was the only fighter who really mattered.

◄ **CANZONERI BOWS OUT**
Tony Canzoneri decided to quit the ring when he was knocked out in 1939. It was his first stoppage in an incredible career. "There is no point in another fight," he said.

▼ **HANK THE HOBO WARRIOR**
This publicity shot of Henry Armstrong was taken at Joe Louis's training camp in Pompton Lakes, New Jersey, just before he won the second of his three world titles in 1938. Armstrong's career was a genuine rags to riches story.

THE OTHER SIDE OF BOXING

PRIMO CARNERA

Carnera was never meant to be a fighter. He was discovered in Italy by French sports entrepreneur, Leon See, and guided like a hopeless child from obscurity to the championship by men with the right connections. He beat opponents who were told to lose during a shameful time in boxing's history. Carnera's great love was food and he often met the press in restaurants, hence the many pictures of him eating.

Carnera is famous as the mob's fighter and sadly his legacy has done more to shape the perception of boxing than that of most fighters. Many people are familiar with the story of Primo Carnera, but few know about James J. Braddock, whose journey from the docks and poverty to the world heavyweight title during the same period was a much happier affair.

Following a succession of fixed fights, Carnera won the heavyweight title by beating Jack Sharkey in unconvincing fashion in 1933. Following two successful defenses, he was soundly beaten by Max Baer the next year. The end of Carnera was easy to predict and his free fall, once it was obvious the game was up, remains one of boxing's most disgraceful incidents. He eventually turned to wrestling, all 6ft 7in and 260 pounds of fragile Italian granite.

LOUIS *and Hank*

1937-1945

"The idol of his people, the one and only Joe Louis", announced the MC Joe Humphreys from the ring before a 1935 fight. It was not an exaggeration. The expectations placed on the young Joe Louis were enormous.

THE CHAMP CALLED JOE

▲ **A BURDENED CHAMPION**
Joe Louis won the world heavyweight title in 1937, but he was an isolated champion who was constantly dictated to by those around him. Louis's management even drew up a list of rules, in an effort to ensure that their man did not repeat the mistakes of the notorious Jack Johnson.

◀ **LOUIS LOOKS GOOD**
Previous page: Joe Louis prepares for his first title defense, against Tommy Farr, in 1937.

Not only was Joe Louis expected to win the world heavyweight title, but he was expected to raise the stature of black fighters from the negative image that that had persisted from the days of Jack Johnson. This he did in time, but in 1936 his early promise counted for nothing when he suffered an unexpected and ignominious defeat at the hands of Max Schmeling. His spell as a fallen idol, however, was brief.

Louis, known as the Brown Bomber, was just 22 years old when he met former champion Max Schmeling for the first time. Louis was unbeaten in 27 fights, including 4 exhibitions, with 23 knockouts. He had beaten Max Baer, once described as a lethal playboy, Primo Carnera and six other heavyweights from the top 10. Schmeling was meant to be an easy fight, but it turned hellish for Louis as the rounds passed and the German's experience started to show. "I saw a fault and I studied him," Schmeling said. In round 12 Louis went down. "I had taken such a terrible beating that I just couldn't get up," he commented later. The result put in doubt his proposed championship fight with James J.Braddock. However, Louis returned to the ring, seemingly unaffected, with a stoppage win over Jack Sharkey. He was duly matched with Braddock in June 1937 at Comiskey Park, Chicago, in front of 45,000 expectant fight fans.

Louis arrived at the fight in style in a pink Cadillac, and eventually won in eight rounds, having been on the floor in round one. With this victory he became the first black heavyweight champion for 22 years. Louis kept the title for 11 years and eight months and during that time made a total 25 defenses. Both these records still stand.

On two occasions he donated his purses from title defenses to the Army and Navy Relief Funds. There were some unimpressive performances against mediocre fighters, watched by small crowds. These defenses became known as the "Bum of the Month" campaign. There were also great wins against the best opponents of the era. Louis just kept winning and obeying the rules set down by his manager John Roxborough, which included: no fixed fights, no soft fights, no gloating and no photographs with white women. The "Louis Rules" had been born out of the aftermath left by Carnera and the legacy of Jack Johnson.

There was still one important engagement for Louis. After three defenses, including a dour struggle with Welshman Tommy Farr, Louis was matched with Schmeling once again. The plight of Jews in Nazi Germany was starting to cause international outrage and the fight became something other than a mere world heavyweight championship contest. "I'm not champion yet," said Louis, "Wait till I beat Schmeling, then I'll be champion." The fight was ferocious, and the outcome never in doubt from the opening seconds. Louis had reached perfection.

During this period, in the lower weight divisions, Henry Armstrong had to compete with Louis's fame. It wasn't easy, despite the fact that Armstrong held world titles at three weights simultaneously. He remains the only fighter to do so. Armstrong had started fighting under the name Mellody Jackson, before changing it to Henry Armstrong, and was known, at different points in his career, as Mammy Boy (Al Jolson had bought a part of his contract), Homicide Hank and Hurricane Hank.

Between October 1937 and August 1938 Armstrong won the featherweight, then beat Barney Ross for the welterweight, before dropping down to win the lightweight championship. It was a stunning achievement. His decline began in 1940, when he drew with previous victim Ceferino Garcia for the middleweight title and lost the welterweight to Fritzie Zivic. He was, and remains, a boxing enigma.

By 1942, several fighters who would forever shape the history of boxing had begun their careers. Sugar Ray Robinson met Jake La Motta; and Archie Moore, having turned pro in 1936, finally won his first title – the Californian middleweight championship in 1943. Moore's fight tally is still virtually impossible to sort out due to inconsistencies in boxing records, but he was prolific to say the least. By the time he was 29 he had fought over 60 times and was still fighting in 1962 when he was dropped, danced over and soundly beaten by Cassius Clay.

Most of the championships were interrupted by the onset of war in the 1930s, when many of the contenders and champions went off to fight in a very different kind of battle. Nearly 50 former, contemporary or future world champions served in the war, including Schmeling and Louis. Some, like Barney Ross, were decorated for their bravery. Careers were effectively put on hold – the case of Tony Zale being a perfect example. Zale won the middleweight title in 1941 but due to war commitments his first defense was not until 1946, when he won the first of his three fights with Rocky Graziano.

▲ **PANIC IN THE RING**

Henry "Homicide" Armstrong never let his opponents settle. He outpointed Britain's Ernie Roderick (above) at Haringay Arena, London, in May 1939, to retain his world welterweight title. He made 11 successful defenses of this crown in 1939, but lost his lightweight title to Lou Ambers the same year.

"He can run but he can't hide" – Louis before the Conn rematch

▲ **NO WAY BACK FOR CONN**
Louis never lost control of the fight and slowly ruined Conn's hopes of winning the world heavyweight title, when they met in a rematch in June 1946. Their first fight, in 1941, had ended dramatically when Conn, who was leading, was stopped in round 13.

Before the Schmeling rematch Louis made three quick defenses, although only the first – a surprisingly hard 15-round decision over Welshman Tommy Farr – is generally considered of much relevance. Farr was an accomplished boxer who had beaten former champion Max Baer four months earlier.

The decision by Louis's promoter, Mike Jacobs, to match Louis against Farr postponed the Schmeling rematch. It also put an end to Schmeling's planned fight with Farr; a contest that would have been an ideal warm-up for his fight with Louis. Farr had no option: the money was good and he accepted.

In August 1937, the two met at New York's Yankee Stadium. Farr left his changing room 20 minutes early and chose to sit through a four-round preliminary bout. In the ring before the first bell, Jack Johnson, who had gone to watch the contest, sensationally ignored Louis and shook Farr's hand instead. During the fight itself, Farr survived punches that had left many other fighters on the canvas, but in the end Louis was a clear winner.

After Farr came two easy defenses and then Schmeling in the rematch. The German crumpled in one savage round and Louis started his "Bum of the Month" tour. Most of his opponents were average and some were bad, but not all. Certainly not Billy Conn, who had held the world light-heavyweight title and was considered a master boxer. The pair met at

▶ **THE FIGHT IS LOST**

The suffering of Billy Conn is complete as he fails to beat the count during round eight of his second fight with Louis at Yankee Stadium. Conn's blood-soaked face is evidence of the success of Louis's punches, although his facial lacerations failed to temper his critics, who accused him of quitting.

▼ **THE BOY FROM THE VALLEYS**

Welshman Tommy Farr beat Max Baer in London, in 1937, and lost on points to Louis the same year. Farr (right) returned to New York to face Baer (left) in a rematch the following year, but was beaten on points. "He is the kinda guy who has no respect for another guy's face," said Baer, a prolific playboy and prankster.

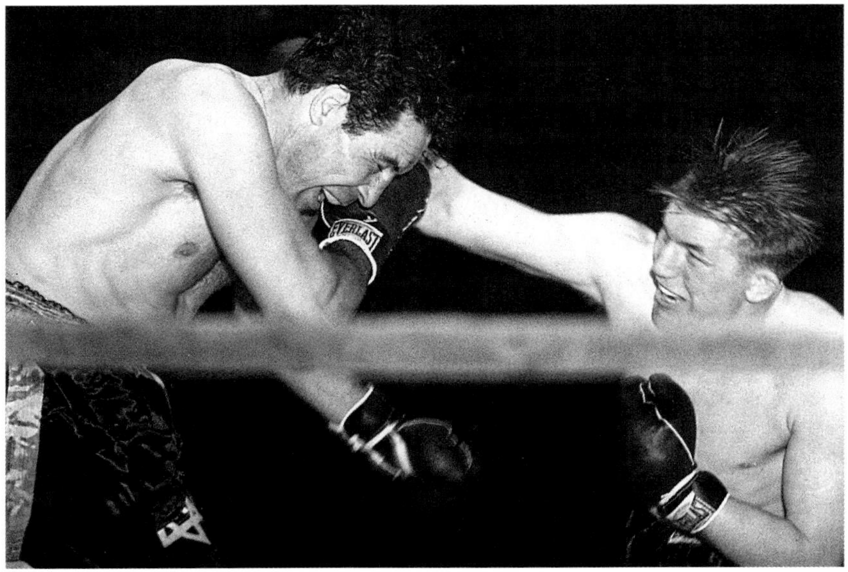

the Polo Grounds, in New York, in front of 55,000 fans. Conn boxed skillfully and by the end of the 12th he was clearly winning the fight and ahead on all three judges' cards. The title was his if he simply stuck to what he was doing. He listened, instead, to a mad tune in his head, abandoned his tactics, and rashly decided to try to knock out Louis. In the 12th a left hook hurt Louis and there was a moment at the start of the 13th when Louis looked in deep trouble. However, with the last punch of the contest, Conn was floored and counted out with two seconds left.

Louis's comeback in the fight against Conn was exceptional, but his title defense in 1938 against Schmeling was without doubt his best.

LOUIS v SCHMELING

A Dark Night in the Ring

▼ REVENGE IS SWEET

A relaxed Louis greets Schmeling prior to their second fight. Before the first fight Louis had been too relaxed and was duly defeated. In the build up to their 1938 rematch the hype surrounding the contest was an unnecessary reminder that nothing exceeds like excess!

On the day of Joe Louis's rematch with Max Schmeling, a syndicated newspaper column published an article in which Louis wrote: "I fight for America." In reality, Louis was not beating the drum for his country's cause, but specifically fighting for black America. In the run-up to both fights Louis and Schmeling became helpless pawns in the political games of their respective leaders.

Schmeling became an unwilling propaganda tool of Nazi Germany long before the rematch. "Your victory is a German victory. Heil Hitler," Joseph Goebbels told Schmeling after his first fight with Louis in June, 1936. Before the second fight, Louis met with American president Franklin Roosevelt, who pinched the boxer's muscles and told him: "That is the type of muscle we need in America." Meanwhile, as Hitler entertained Schmeling, German troops moved east. The second Louis-Schmeling fight is possibly the most politically relevant bout in history. Prior to the contest, Schmeling had watched a film of the first fight as a guest of Hitler, who apparently slapped the fighter's leg every time Louis was hit. "Hitler invited me for lunch. I went, I had to go," he explained in later life

The rematch with Schmeling was a much delayed affair which fell through four times. The German, who received parity in the first fight, was negotiating for 30 per cent of the rematch. Eventually, he settled for 20 per cent and a slice of the radio and movie rights. The radio rights were sold for $50,000; double the film rights for the fight.

In 1936, Schmeling, who was at ringside when Louis beat Paulino Uzcudun in 1935, watched films of the American as part of his preparation. For the rematch, Louis studied Schmeling. As the fight approached, the event took on symbolic importance. Schmeling was disturbed by the hatred directed at him. "I'm a fighter, not a politician," he pleaded, but the press claimed bouquets of flowers bedecked with swastika ribbons in his house were sent by Hitler. As a result, Louis became a symbol of good and Schmeling a figure of hate. The plot was simple and Louis appeared at the time to be a willing participant. "Joe, the Negro, found himself unwittingly in the role of a national hero, of all Americans," wrote Schmeling in his autobiography. In truth, Louis was not the hero of all Americans. A number of sportswriters from the southern states, for instance, predicted, and hoped for, a German victory.

Schmeling was too old and slow by the time the rematch was finally made, whereas Louis was fast and focused. From the first bell the German never stood a chance. The moment before the first knockdown when Louis pulls Schmeling off the ropes is one of boxing's defining moments – hard to defend and impossible to ignore. Louis dropped Schmeling three times in the fight. Before the fight, he had spoken of his fear of killing Schmeling and both corners invaded the ring after the third knockdown. It was a win that shaped the patriotic conscience of the nation. The film of the fight can still silence an audience and it is said that years later the young Mike Tyson watched the fight repeatedly when he was a teenager at Cus D'Amato's retreat in upstate New York.

In 1951 an old and bloated Louis was defeated by Rocky Marciano. In Louis's changing room after the fight, Sugar Ray Robinson and Marciano cried, while on television the second fight with Schmeling was shown as consolation to the former champion's fans.

▲ **THE CALM AFTER THE STORM** *The fight is over and Schmeling is down on all fours in pain, while Louis calmly glares at him from his corner.*

▶ **COMING TO THE END**
A mature-looking Joe Louis pictured just six days before losing to Ezzard Charles in 1950. "It was missing that night and I could see the openings but my punches never filled them," said Louis, who was outpointed over 15 rounds.

▼ **MEN AT THE TOP**
Louis, his left eye still damaged, gives his promoter Mike Jacobs the gloves from his win over Jersey Joe Walcott, in 1948. Jacobs gives Louis his check! Jacobs had control of the sport during this period because he had Louis – and that meant power.

Louis's "Bum of the Month" circus

Billy Conn had to wait five years for a rematch with Louis, when the war denied him a chance to make amends for his rash mistake in the previous contest. When they met again, Louis ruined him in eight rounds.

As well as fighting some of the best men around, Louis fought many opponents who qualified for the "Bum of the Month" tag. Jack Roper, for instance, went over in one round, Johnny Paychek in two and Abe Simon, in perhaps the most one-sided bout of all, in six.

The spirit of the time and the allure of Louis's fights were perfectly captured by his encounter with one of boxing's genuine characters, Tony Galento, in a memorable defense in 1939. Galento was known as Two-Ton Tony. He trained in bars, the publicity said, and had the gut to prove it. Nearly 40,000 spectators showed up at Yankee Stadium for Galento's fistic wake. Galento continued to bad-mouth Louis even when they reached the ring. Incredibly, Louis went over briefly in round three, but the contest came to a bloody end in round four with Galento in a terrible state, barely able to walk and smeared in his own blood.

After the first of two defenses against Chile's Arturo Godoy, a fight that was roundly booed for being such a poor display, some sportswriters believed Louis was losing his edge. "He is nearing the end of his reign," said one. The low-key search for a white hope, however, was proving fruitless.

In the early 1940s Jersey Joe Walcott, once a sparring partner of Louis, and Ezzard Charles were waiting in line and in 1947 Rocky Marciano turned pro. But despite the wealth of talent queueing up to take his crown, Louis remained champion until 1949.

▶ CONN'S TORMENT

When Billy Conn won the world light-heavyweight title in 1939 he was the kid with the matinee-idol looks and the golden fists. He relinquished the title, however, in order to fight Louis in 1941 – a fight which was in his grasp but he let slip. "I used to have nightmares about that fight," said Conn. "I play back the last round each time and it is always the same ending."

▼ GALENTO BEYOND FEAR

Joe Louis was covered in Tony Galento's blood following their 1939 title fight. As he was led away in round four Galento may have had the usual loser's scarlet veil over his face, but he still appeared to want more.

GIANTS OF THE RING

HENRY ARMSTRONG

1912–1988

When Henry Armstrong simultaneously held the feather, lightweight and welterweight titles he set a record in boxing history that will never be broken. It was a freak achievement by today's standards, but at the time many fighters dipped in and out of different weights just to stay busy or stay in contention.

Armstrong was born on a plantation in Mississippi, but grew up in St. Louis. He decided to box after reading tales about Kid Chocolate, a Cuban world champion with a fondness for spending his money lavishly. His passage from poverty-stricken dreamer to triple champion is a story that beggars belief, considering that it was achieved at a time when many boxers were struggling simply to survive.

Armstrong bought some gloves and toured the streets of the North Side of St. Louis – where he was known as Little Samson – looking for money. He found fights, eventually found a gym and, through hard work and perseverance, in time became one of the greatest ever fighters at the lower weights.

Armstrong's triple success will never be repeated

▶ **ARMSTRONG V GARCIA**
Ceferino Garcia (left) and Henry Armstrong met for the first time in 1938. Armstrong retained his welterweight title on that occasion, but in 1940 they drew in a fight for the middleweight title. "It was never easy with Henry," said Garcia, "he was punching and moving all the time."

In the late 1930s the lightweight division had a number of quality champions – among them Tony Canzoneri, Lou Ambers and Henry Armstrong – and surprisingly few weak links. "Them were the good old days", claimed Lou Ambers years later.

Ambers began as a bootleg fighter for $5. In 1938, he lost his lightweight championship to Henry Armstrong but won it back the following year. Both fights were hard and the second dirty – Armstrong's illegal punches costing him five rounds and the title. A mooted third fight never happened. When Ambers was stopped by Lew Jenkins in 1940 for the New York version of the championship, he was only 26. Nearly 100 fights had taken their toll and he was old in ring years before his time. "When a fellow gets old in this game, you're going to weaken," he acknowledged.

Beau Jack – another promising lightweight of the period – was 21 when he won the New York version of the title. Jack was the main attraction at Madison Square Garden 21 times, beating Tippy Larkin for the title and then winning just one of three title fights with Bob Montgomery between 1943 and 1944. In 1944 Jack beat Montgomery, who at the time was still champion, in a non-title fight as part of a war bonds drive. Jack, who started and ended his working life shining shoes, first boxed in Battle Royals, a form of boxing that owed more to the entertainment values of the ancient Romans than war-time boxing. In a Battle Royal, four or five black fighters would be blindfolded and would slug away until just two were left. Then they would box. Armstrong had refused to take part in Battle Royals, but Jack had little alternative.

▲ **"MAIN EVENT" JACK**
Armstrong was in the twilight days of his fighting life when he met Beau Jack (right) at Madison Square Garden in April 1943. Jack held the New York version of the world lightweight title at the time and had just beaten Fritzie Zivic. During his career, Jack fought in 21 main events at Madison Square Garden in front of a total of 335,000 fight fans.

◄ **THE HERKIMER HURRICANE**
Lou Ambers found the bright lights after years in boxing's wilderness – winning and losing the world lightweight title on two occasions between 1936 and 1940. He had started fighting in boxing booths, where he fought more than 150 times. His record in the ring was 86 wins, eight losses and six draws.

HENRY ARMSTRONG

A Unique Entry in Boxing Folklore

When Henry Armstrong was left penniless and stranded in Mexico after losing a disputed decision to Baby Arizmendi in 1934, his reaction was to fight his way out. It was not the first or the last setback in an eventful career.

Armstrong was born Henry Jackson in Mississippi in 1912. Like so many other boxers before and after him, he was born into poverty and as a teenager took up boxing as a means of earning money. Having fought his first professional fight in 1931, he bummed his way on the railroad to Los Angeles, where he fought his first two fights – a win and a loss – under the name Mellody Jackson. Returning to the amateur ranks as Henry Armstrong, he fought his way across California taking part in a huge number of contests and gathering a strong following.

▲ **FROM HOBO TO CHAMP**
Despite losing his first ever professional fight, Henry Armstrong went on to dominate the lower weight orders throughout the 1930s and early 1940s.

His success spurred him to relaunch his pro career and, in 1937, he won the featherweight title from Petey Sarron. Gaining weight he then went for the welterweight title, beating Barney Ross on points. His next goal was the lightweight crown, which he took from Lou Ambers in a fierce battle. In less than a year Armstrong had won three titles and defied all of boxing's rules by moving up and down in weight classes without gaining, or having to lose, much weight.

When Armstrong met Barney Ross for the welterweight title at Long Island in 1938, it would be Ross's last fight and possibly Armstrong's finest. To bulk up for the contest, Armstrong drank beer while at Pompton Lakes, in New Jersey, with Joe Louis, who was preparing for his rematch with Schmeling.

Ross was a quality champion but one at the end of his career. Reports of what happened during the fight seem strangely out of character for Armstrong, given that some of his fights were foul-filled affairs. At the start of the 12th round, with featherweight champion Armstrong so far in front that there were calls of mercy from the crowd, the boxers spoke to each other during a clinch. "How, you feel Barney?" "I'm dead," Ross replied. "Jab and run, and I'll make it look good," said Armstrong. The pair went through the motions for the remainder of the fight and fought the last two rounds in loving slow motion!

It was Armstrong who kept the public interested in the other divisions during the late 1930s and early 1940s when Louis fever dominated. The crowds loved him. He may not have been a slayer of ogres like Jack Dempsey, but he was exceptional at overwhelming his opponents with his perpetual motion style.

Armstrong lost his last title, the welterweight championship, to Fritzie Zivic in 1940, when he was just 18 pounds heavier than he had been when he won the featherweight version in 1937. In this 48 month period Armstrong had fought 40 times, a total of 26 world championship fights and lost just twice, to Lou Ambers in a lightweight rematch, and to Zivic.

Despite losing his last title, Armstrong kept up a relentless schedule against the best boxers of the time. He beat many former champions during this time, but was easily outpointed by a young Sugar Ray Robinson at Madison Square Garden in 1943. The crowd booed Robinson's caution.

Armstrong starred in a film of his life called *Keep Punching*, but lost money on the project. When he gave up boxing in 1945 he turned to drink. After many years he managed to conquer his addiction and entered the ministry. He died at the age of 76 in Los Angeles.

▲ **THE MERCIFUL CHAMPION** *Armstrong (left) consoles an exhausted Barney Ross at the end of their fight in May 1938. It was Ross's last fight.*

Middleweight brutality was fearsome

▲ **THE END OF ZALE**

Tony Zale (left) is near the end of his reign as middleweight champion as Frenchman, Marcel Cerdan connects with another right in September 1948. "I will put Cerdan to sleep within five rounds," Zale had claimed before the fight. It all came to an end when Zale failed to come out for round 12 – he never fought again.

The middleweight division was also experiencing a busy period during the 1940s. Tony Zale won the unified world middleweight title in 1941, although his first defense was not until 1946, against Rocky Graziano. The pair fought three times in all, with Zale winning twice. All three fights remain as eloquent examples of the struggles from the 1940s and 1950s, fights that would later come to be recognized as some of boxing's epic encounters. The Sandy Saddler and Willie Pep fights at featherweight are equally famous – just as brutal, but far dirtier. All four fights set a standard for illegality that remains to this day.

In the first Zale-Graziano fight – watched by 39,827 at Yankee Stadium – Graziano, the challenger and younger man by nine years, was over in the first round. He got up to put Zale down in the following round and by the end of the fifth, Zale was cut and shaken. Zale turned the tables in round six, however, by knocking Graziano clean out. It was a truly incredible fight that typified the era. Years later Graziano commented: "The Zale fights were almost identical. It was just who got the better punch in first." Zale did in both the first and the final fight.

Meanwhile, Sugar Ray Robinson was learning his trade, getting ready for his first title in 1946 by fighting future middleweight champion, Jake La Motta, a total of five times between 1942 and 1945. All were non-title fights, but in 1951 Robinson stopped La Motta in round 13 of a middleweight championship fight.

La Motta is one of the few champions and contenders from the period to give Holman Williams, a black fighter who was avoided by other boxers, a chance. La Motta beat Williams on points. Charley Burley, another overlooked black boxer of the period, was snubbed by Robinson and is one of the rare fighters in the International Boxing Hall of Fame to have never won a world title.

▲ **ROCKY GRAZIANO**

Having come through the chaos of his early life, Rocky Graziano fought like a man on a detour from the abyss. His trio of fights against Zale are a testimony to boxing's pain, suffering and raw excitement.

▶ **ZALE – A MAN OF STEEL**

Despite turning pro in 1934 and winning the NBA middleweight title in 1940, Tony Zale is best remembered for his trio of brawls with Rocky Graziano, the first of which was not until 1946.

GIANTS OF THE RING

JOE LOUIS

1914–1981

Joe Louis, his handlers insisted, had no vices. He read the Bible before fights, loved his mother and never dated white women. It looked good, it sounded good and, following the career of Johnson, it was a necessary part of creating an acceptable black fighter who could dominate the sport of boxing.

Where Jack Johnson had laughed or glared at his opponents, Louis rarely looked at them, even when they were sprawled on the canvas. Louis was not allowed at any cost to repeat Johnson's sins. Certainly not in public. He had to be respectful and was forced to ignore all references to "jungle beasts" with which the sportswriters baited him.

In later life, after his financial situation had left him at the mercy of people he had earlier inspired – such as Frank Sinatra, who paid for his care – an angrier and far less subservient Louis often emerged. In one particular incident, when he was working as a greeter at Caesars Palace in Las Vegas, he lost his cool with a customer. Perhaps Louis finally realized, at that late stage, that he had been performing for far too long.

A climate of ignorance ruled the day

▲ A SWEET MOVER
Ezzard Charles moves smoothly away from Jersey Joe Walcott's right in the opening round of the first of their four heavyweight title fights. Charles won this 1949 contest, and their 1951 fight, but was knocked out later the same year and outpointed in 1952. Their rivalry is, sadly, one of the least celebrated in heavyweight history.

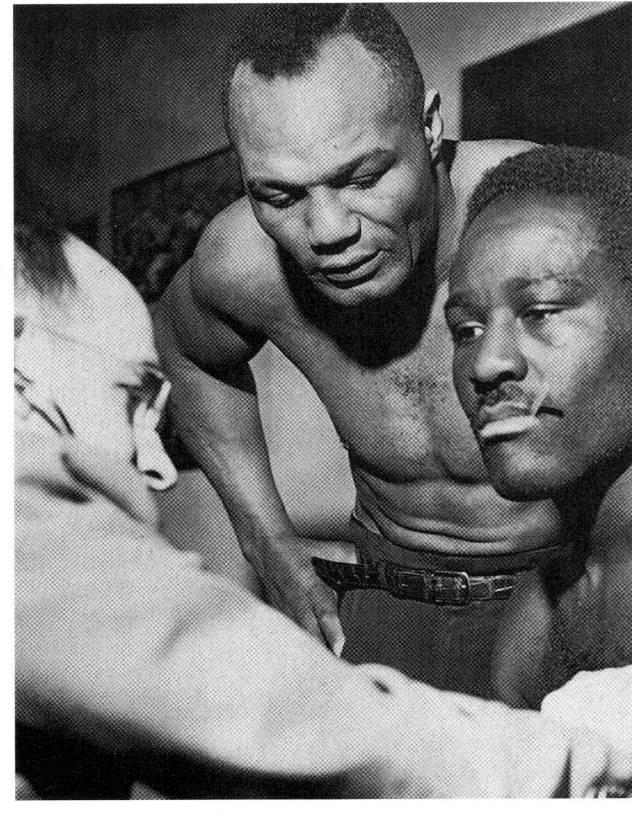

▶ A PRE-FIGHT CHECK-UP
Walcott looks on as the fight doctor checks Ezzard Charles before their second meeting in 1951.

In 1944 Charley Burley beat Jack Chase to win the Californian middleweight title. Chase had beaten Archie Moore for it and in 1944 Burley beat Moore, but his form would leave him forever on the sidelines in a sport that has perfected all methods of ostracism. During this period there were several notable examples of fighters left on the fringe of stardom; forced to wait undue lengths of time for shots at titles.

Another top middleweight at the time, Ezzard Charles, beat Burley twice on points in 1942 and despite beating other top fighters was denied a chance at the middleweight title. His response was to make a permanent move to the heavyweight division, where he beat Jersey Joe Walcott for the heavyweight championship in 1949. Walcott had also had a few problems, and was almost denied the chance to challenge Louis for the title in 1947 because of what was thought to be an unimpressive record.

During their careers both Walcott and Charles met Joey Maxim, who is widely regarded as having served one of boxing's hardest apprenticeships. Maxim, a good-looking Italian fighter who was christened Giuseppe Antonio Berardinelli, was a pro for nine years before he eventually won the world light-heavyweight title in 1950. In addition to Walcott and Charles, Maxim met another fighter from the period – another black heavyweight who was often overlooked – Jimmy Bivins.

However, it was not just the black fighters who were ignored. It is hard to imagine a good-looking kid like Maxim having to endure so many hard fights to get to the top, even then. The case of Joey Giardello – real name Carmine Orlando Tilelli – is similar. It took Giardello 16 years to win a title, something that would never happen today.

Joey Maxim eventually gained fame and is remembered for several reasons but primarily for his championship defence against Robinson, who collapsed at the end of round 13 from heat exhaustion. Maxim also showed his class when, after 13 years as a pro, he outpointed Floyd Patterson in 1954. It was Patterson's first defeat and, sadly, one of Maxim's last wins.

◀ **MOORE V MAXIM**

In 1952, after 16 years as a pro, Archie Moore beat Joey Maxim (left) to win the world light-heavyweight title. Moore was 39 at the time and had fought almost 170 times. Moore received just $800, not including expenses. Moore may have won the world title but it cost him money.

THE OTHER SIDE OF BOXING

WAR CHAMPIONS LOSE THE BATTLE IN THE RING

The war effort ruined Billy Conn. He lost his chance for a quick rematch with Joe Louis and when he did fight him again it was too late. Similarly, Tony Zale lost four years at his prime and other champions were in decline when World War II ended.

Louis (pictured) was the army's favorite boxing recruit and toured during the war, often performing a double act with another leading contender at the time, Sugar Ray Robinson. In one particular incident, Robinson flatly refused to spar an exhibition at an army training camp unless black soldiers were allowed to watch. The general of the camp duly got special permission from the war department and the exhibition went ahead.

Barney Ross was the champion who did the most fighting. Ross lost his world welterweight title to Henry Armstrong in 1938 and then enlisted in the marines, winning medals for bravery at Guadalcanal. By the time the war ended, Ross was hooked on the morphine that had been administered to relieve the pain caused by his war injuries.

DAYS OF *Sugar*

1945-1952

G & S

▲ **A BAD END**
Freddie Mills could take a beating. He was on the wrong end of several savage attacks before winning the world light-heavyweight title in 1948, when he outpointed American veteran Gus Lesnevich. In 1965 Mills was found shot dead in an alley behind his club in London's Soho.

◀ **ROBINSON SPARKLES**
Previous page: Sugar Ray pictured in training at Blooms Gymnasium in London's West End.

Sugar Ray Robinson was one of the greats and was involved in many fights that will forever be remembered as among boxing's finest. He held history in his fists for nearly 20 years and shaped generations, to whom he was a role model, hero and genius in the ring.

ROBINSON: THE NEW BABE

Sugar Ray Robinson was the sweetest thing to enter a boxing ring. His long career and fights against former, present and past world champions amount to possibly the finest record ever accomplished by a fighter. He won his first world title fight in 1946 and lost his last in 1961. Boxing changed to such an extent during Robinson's career that when he finally retired in 1965 he was a living icon to a sport that many believed would never be as good again.

His first few years as champion – when he won the welterweight, the middleweight and failed in the most dramatic way to win Joey Maxim's light-heavyweight championship in 1952 – were his best.

Robinson was not alone, however, he fought alongside a number of other legends. Just as Robinson was in the ascendant, Joe Louis was winding down. At the end of World War II, Louis had aged, his face losing its youthful appearance after the four-year break. In 1946, Louis met and soundly beat Billy Conn in a rematch, but his timing was not what it had been.

One fight each in 1947 and 1948, both against Jersey Joe Walcott, kept Louis in the public eye but he was starting to look and fight like an old man. In 1949 Louis quit but his absence was temporary and in 1950 he lost for only the second time when Ezzard Charles, the new heavyweight champion, outpointed him over 15 gruelling rounds.

At the same time Rocky Marciano was just starting to fight men with reputations. A dubious win over Roland La Starza seemed to suggest, however, that Marciano was not quite ready to move from the safety of easy workouts to the dangers of exposure in harder fights. In 1951 an ideal compromise was found and

Joe Louis, who had won eight in a row since his Charles defeat, was given to Marciano. It was a harder fight than is generally recognized but it ended in round eight. Louis was trapped on the ropes and helpless. It was his last fight. Marciano won the title the next year.

It is Robinson, sometimes known as the Black Angel, who has inspired fighters since the moment he first won a title. He had the style in and away from the ring to alter the way people thought about fighters. However, he was as ruthless as any boxer before or after him. In 1947 Robinson defended his welterweight title for the first time when he met Jimmy Doyle. A left hook to the head dropped Doyle in round eight. He later died in hospital from injuries sustained during the fight. When Robinson was asked by the coroner: "Couldn't you see that Doyle had been hurt and was groggy?", he replied "Mister, that's what my business is – to hurt people." There was criticism for the honest reply and Robinson set up a $10,000 trust fund for Doyle's mother. His critics were numerous, and as Muhammad Ali would discover 15 years later, any seemingly callous comment could be taken out of context and used as proof of insensitivity or arrogance.

While Robinson and Louis were at different stages in their careers, the business of boxing was under the control of the gangsters. Fixed fights were nothing new to boxing, but in the late 1940s and throughout the 1950s, the entire business operated under a dark cloud of corrupt officials.

In January 1947 Rocky Graziano, less than four months after losing a world middleweight title fight to Tony Zale, was questioned at the DA's office in New York about an attempt to bribe him to lose a fight. Graziano denied the bribe offer was serious. "It was just some punk talking to me on the phone. It never meant nothing", Graziano claimed. The DA disagreed, informed the New York State Athletic Commission and in February 1947 Graziano's license to fight in his native city was revoked.

In April Graziano's attempt to regain his status in New York failed but in July of the same year, fighting under an Illinois license, he knocked Tony Zale out to win the world title. It was a genuine win but Graziano's refusal to take a dive, or "tank a fight," as they called it, only served to heighten the involvement of the mobsters.

After Graziano beat Zale there was a celebration party in his Chicago hotel room. One of the guests was the notorious gangster Paul John Carbo, alias Frankie Carbo, alias Paul Carbo, alias Frank Carbo, alias Frank Russo, alias John Paul Carbo!

It was Carbo, a man convicted of manslaughter, who came to be recognized, alongside Frank "Blinky" Palermo, as one of the criminal leaders in the boxing business. Some despaired of their influence. Others saw them as pioneers.

In reality, they were just doing business according to one of boxing's oldest maxims: you get what you negotiate, not what you deserve. Both Carbo and Palermo knew a thing or two about negotiating.

▲ **ARMSTRONG V ROBINSON**

"Fight man. I ain't never been booed in the Garden," said Henry Armstrong (right) to Sugar Ray Robinson when they met at Madison Square Garden on August 27, 1943. Robinson won on points after 10 rounds of calculated boxing, beating his hero while never once risking defeat.

The middleweight division was devastated in 1949 when former champion, Marcel Cerdan, died in a plane crash as he returned to America for an eagerly awaited rematch with Jake La Motta.

In 1948 Cerdan had battered Tony Zale to become the champion. The following year, he injured his shoulder against La Motta in a title fight, but continued until the end of the ninth. He fought like an American and the crowds liked that. La Motta lost the title to his old nemesis Robinson in 1951.

Throughout this time Graziano continued to fight. After losing the third fight to Zale in 1948 he won 20 in a row, all by stoppage or knockout. He was popular, but his opponents were often undemanding. His popularity was still evident in 1952 but the opposition had improved and he was stopped in three brutal rounds by Robinson.

Graziano fought just once more, losing a decision to TV-dinner fighter Chuck Davey – a nice white kid with a college education, whose personality sparkled and whose skills were easily enhanced by the men in power; men like Carbo and Palermo who had a controlling interest in the new industry of TV-boxing. Davey was a boxing matinee idol and the house-fighter of the International Boxing Club (IBC) and its president Jim Norris, who was linked with Carbo and Palermo. Business was good for them all at this time, and it was particularly good for Davey.

In 1960, however, when boxing's bad guys were on trial, La Motta admitted that he had taken a dive in a 1947 fight with Billy Fox. Carbo ended up on Alcatraz. A proposed bout between La Motta and Graziano failed to take place after a series of mysterious events. It was this series of events that moved Norris and the IBC closer to the underworld.

The boxing world was stunned by the sudden death of Marcel Cerdan

▲ **BATTERED AND BRUISED**
Tony Zale walks away from the collapsed form of Rocky Graziano in round three of their middleweight title fight in June 1948. Graziano's distorted face is one of boxing's most vivid images.

▲ **RAGING BULL IN AGONY**
Sugar Ray Robinson won the middleweight title when Jake La Motta was saved from further punishment in round 13 of their fight in 1951. La Motta fought 10 more times before quitting in 1954.

▶ **DEATH OF A FRENCH IDOL**
Marcel Cerdan (right) shakes Jake La Motta's hand before their proposed rematch in October 1949. Cerdan later died in a plane crash en route to the fight.

GIANTS OF THE RING

ROCKY GRAZIANO

1922–1990

Despite the fact that he was not the best middleweight ever, not even the best middleweight of his generation, Rocky Graziano became one of boxing's best-known characters. A reform-school boy whose past would never leave him, Graziano was often in trouble and served time at Riker's Island. He went AWOL from the army after assaulting an officer and was eventually given a dishonorable discharge.

After winning and losing the world middleweight title in a three-fight series against Tony Zale, the Rock's career slowed down. He was a celebrity because of his excessive lifestyle, rather than his boxing. He competed with another celebrity middleweight champion, Jake La Motta, for the headlines out of the ring. The pair never met because the people in charge could not find an ideal way to split the spoils. Graziano's book, *Somebody Up There Likes Me*, was made into a movie starring Paul Newman.

PEP v SADDLER

Unkind History Neglects Saddler

▼ **TRUE CHAMPION, NICE GUY**
Sandy Saddler may look just like an innocent kid in this photograph, but during his four wild fights with Willie Pep between 1948 and 1951 the pair perfected all the established boxing infringements, while also inventing a repertoire of new ones!

The featherweight division in the 1940s and 1950s was dominated by a series of fights between Willie Pep and Sandy Saddler. They met in four of boxing's dirtiest and most memorable fights, with Saddler emerging victorious on three occasions. During their fourth brawl, in 1951, which ended in the ninth, both boxers had their licenses suspended by the New York State Athletic Commission – Saddler's for 60 days and Pep's for life, although Pep was later reinstated after 20 months.

Saddler had won 43 of his 46 fights in 22 months and was the younger man, but he was seen as the underdog in their first fight. Pep had been champion for six years, had beaten men who had beaten Saddler, and had lost just once in 136 fights. The fight ended in round four with Pep out cold. "He made me forget I was clever," said Pep.

The rematch was arguably Pep's finest performance. Madison Square Garden was packed with 19,097 people who set a record for a featherweight bout by paying $87,563. The sensible money was on Saddler to repeat his first shock win. The sentimental money was on Pep, however, and from the first bell he was smart – his reputation was at stake."I had to keep moving because his confidence was high. He had knocked me out once and he believed he could do it again. I kept moving, outboxed him and won back the title," said Pep. He was champion again after 15 rounds. "It was the greatest fight of his life and the greatest fight of my life," Pep insisted. But it was still a brutal affair. After the fight both boxers required stitches to their faces: Pep 11 and Saddler seven.

The victory secured Pep's status, but Saddler was remorseless in pursuit. "I just had to get him back in the ring – that was all I wanted." By the time they met again, the level and quality of their dirty fighting had improved, but there is still a debate about which of their last two fights was the dirtiest. Some say it was the third and others the fourth.

For the third fight the crowd of 38,781 at Yankee Stadium had paid a new featherweight record of $262,150 to watch the contest. By the end of round seven, Pep was clearly winning the fight but he remained on his stool in the ring at the beginning of round eight. Saddler was unconvinced when Pep claimed an injured shoulder.

Their final encounter ended with Pep on his stool again. This time his eyes were injured – the left one was shut and the right one was cut – and he sensibly decided that enough was enough. Saddler had done the damage with his thumbs. Both fighters had perfected a way to jab with knuckle and thumb.

"He made me lose my head and that was my mistake. I played for him when I lost my head," Pep later claimed. Saddler was more understanding of Pep's decision to stop fighting in the fourth fight. "I guess he couldn't see and that is not good," he said.

In 1973 they were back in the ring at Madison Square Garden for an exhibition bout. Saddler was 46 and Pep 50. It only lasted just one round. The two men were friends but it upset Saddler that whenever they were introduced before big fights his name always came second. It was always the great Willie Pep and another featherweight champion, Sandy Saddler. "It was me that retired as the undefeated featherweight champion of the world," Saddler correctly points out.

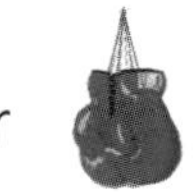

▲ **DODGING AND WEAVING** *Willie Pep once famously won the third round of a fight against Jackie Graves, in 1946, without throwing a single punch!*

Robinson made contenders bid farewell to their hopes and dreams

▲ **SUGAR RAY IN PARIS**

Sugar Ray Robinson completes his training in Paris before his first world middleweight title fight with Britain's Randolph Turpin in July 1951. Turpin, unlike other fall guys, refused to be fazed by the legend's reputation and won on points.

Sugar Ray Robinson was a busy champion but he was largely untested after he won the welterweight title in 1946. He had beaten top fighters at the start of his career but there was a distinct lack of quality opponents in the welterweight division. In 1947 and 1948 Robinson made only three defenses despite fighting 15 times. He stopped nine opponents and, after a non-title fight in 1948, defended his title in 1949 against Cuba's Kid Gavilan, the only welterweight star in waiting during Robinson's time as champion. Gavilan, or The Hawk as he was known, would win the welterweight title in 1951 but was linked to several fixed fights. Before meeting Robinson one of Gavilan's opponents refused an offer of $100,000 to take a dive.

Gavilan outscored Johnny Bratton for the vacant undisputed title in 1951. In the same year, in his first defense of the title, Gavilan was extremely fortunate

to get the decision over Billy Graham, but in 1954 he was on the receiving end of a terrible injustice when he lost his world title to Johnny Saxton. The fight was a dreadful fix and Saxton was the chosen winner. Gavilan only started to fight in the last round of the great hitless mazurka. Gavilan denied knowledge of all the fixed fights but the defeat against Saxton remains one of the fights that will forever inextricably link gangsterism with boxing.

By 1950 Robinson was contemplating the spoils in the middleweight division. In June he won the Philadelphia version of the title, in August he retained his welterweight version for the last time and in January 1951 he stopped old foe Jake La Motta for the undisputed middleweight championship of the world. It was the start of his amazing years as middleweight champion and boxing troubadour.

◀ ROBINSON V FUSARI
Robinson throws a right at Charlie Fusari on his way to retaining the world welterweight title for the fifth and final time over 15 rounds in August 1950.

▲ THE CUBAN HAWK
The career of Kid Gavilan was never easy. His name was unjustly linked with the gangsters following his infamous fight with Johnny Saxton in 1954. Things failed to improve for Gavilan after the end of his ring days in 1958. He lost his farm, just outside Havana, in his native Cuba, and eventually ended up as part of Muhammad Ali's touring entourage.

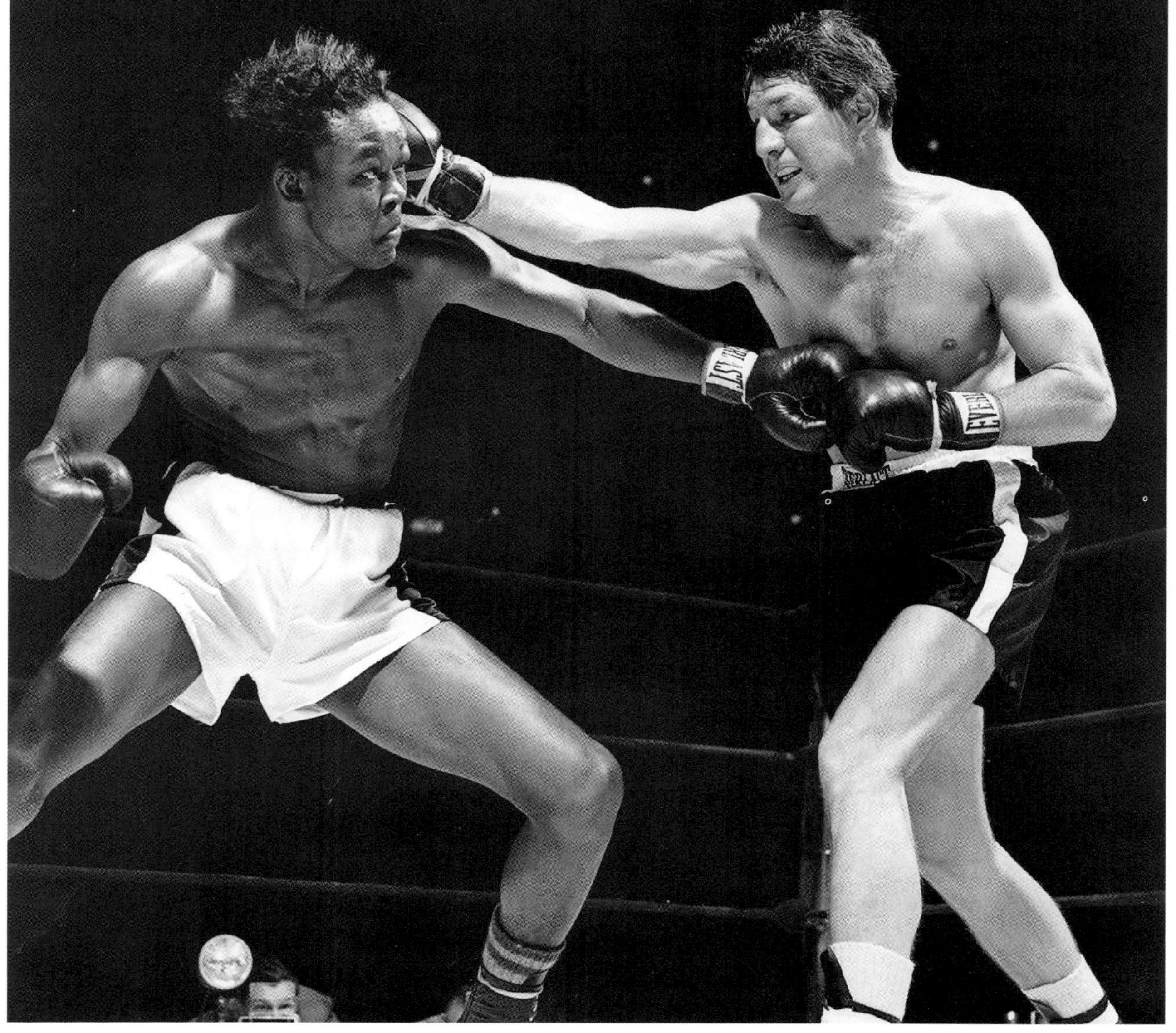

◀ GAVILAN WINDS UP A RIGHT
Gavilan easily outpoints Billy Graham (right) in their second fight in November 1950. They fought four times in total – twice for Gavilan's welterweight crown.

Money problems force Louis's return

▲ **SO CLOSE TO THE END**

Joe Louis almost lost his fight with Jersey Joe Walcott in 1947. He felt like an old man, but in their rematch in June 1948, Louis (right) stopped Walcott in round 11. It was to be Louis's 25th and last defense of the world heavyweight championship. He retired the following year, but soon returned.

Too many fighters neglect the signs of disintegration and continue fighting. Joe Louis, sadly, was one of them.

When Louis defended his title against Jersey Joe Walcott in 1947, he won a close and disputed decision. Walcott had been a sparring partner in the Louis camp in 1938 but, despite the outcome of the fight, it was obvious time had been kinder to the understudy.

Louis was over twice, in rounds one and four, and tried to leave the ring before the decision was announced."I made it tough. I saw openings I didn't use. I beat him, but next time I will knock him out," promised Louis. The rematch was in 1948 and Louis fulfilled his promise, knocking Walcott out in round 11. It was the 25th and last title defense of Louis's 11 years as champion.

When Louis retired the following year, he was undefeated champion. Unfortunately tax problems forced him to make a comeback when he should have been enjoying his retirement. In 1950 he was back. He challenged Ezzard Charles, who held a version of the championship, for the vacant world title. Louis was paid $9,000 less for this fight than he had received for winning the title from James J. Braddock in 1937. His tax problems remained.

Charles won easily and hurt Louis on several occasions. When it was over, Charles said: "I never wanted to hurt the old fellow who did so much for the Negro in boxing." But he still left Louis stumbling. However, it was not the end. That awful night would come 13 months later against Rocky Marciano.

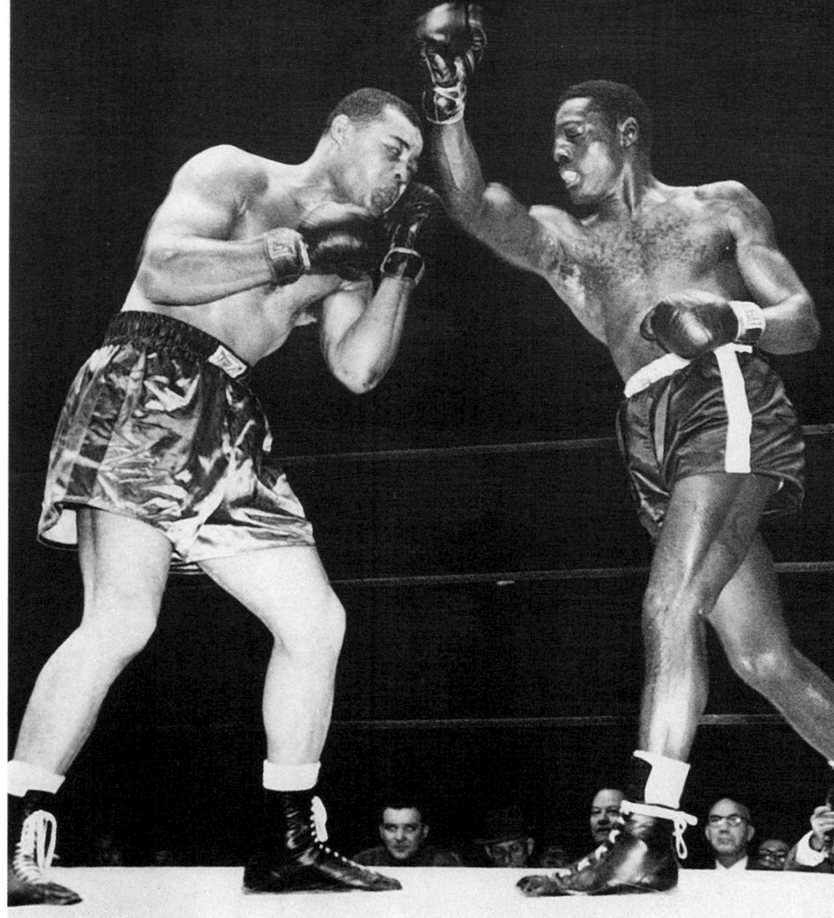

▲ **A FADED FORMER CHAMP**
Louis came out of retirement to be beaten up by Ezzard Charles in a world title fight in September 1950 (top). Charles won the contest easily, but Louis refused to fade away and came back to face Lee Savold the following year.

▲ **LOUIS DESTROYS SAVOLD**
A battered Lee Savold (above left) tumbles down the ropes after Louis's final onslaught of punches in June 1951. Savold had won a version of the world title after Louis retired in 1949, but Charles was considered the true champion.

GIANTS OF THE RING

SANDY SADDLER

1926–

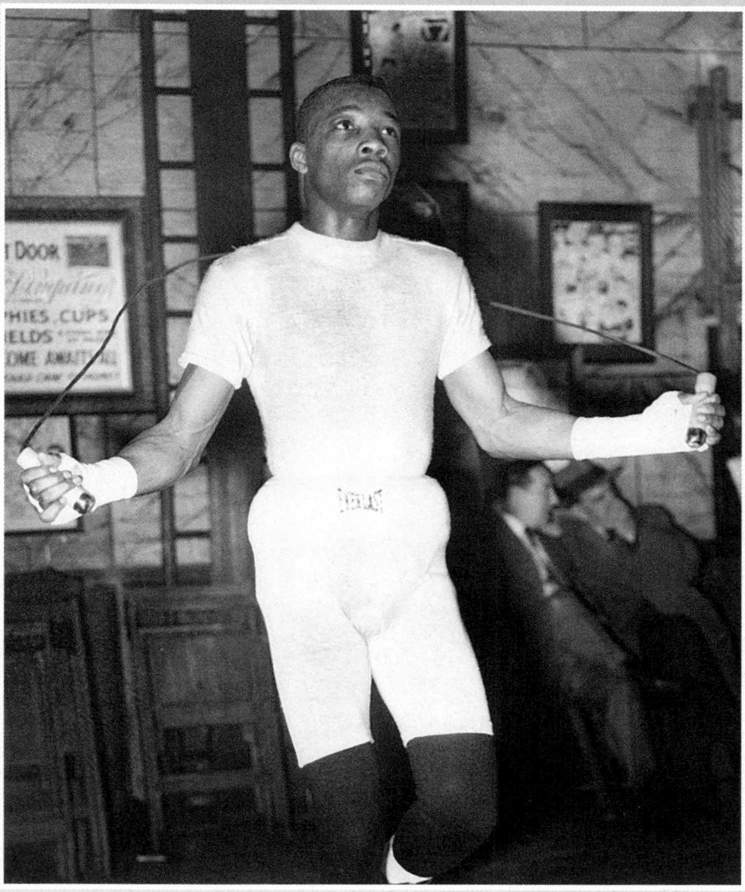

It is hard to imagine just what goes through Sandy Saddler's head each time he is introduced as a "former featherweight champion of the world." The comment hardly does him justice. He also held the junior-lightweight title but he was much more than a champion. He was quite simply brilliant.

His four fights with Willie Pep are proof. When he had to adjust against Pep he was clever. His timing was perfect and his arms were long enough to surprise many opponents from the edge of the ring. His last featherweight defense in 1956 – eight years after first winning the title – against Gabriel "Flash" Elorde, from the Philippines, is an indication of just how great he was. Saddler stopped Elorde in round 13. It was revenge for a non-title fight points defeat the year before.

LOUIS v MARCIANO

Tears Flow as Louis Bows Out

▶ LOUIS'S SAD SWANSONG

"There ain't no sentimental money in boxing," Joe Louis once observed. He was an old man long before his last fight against Marciano and although he could still mix it with the best of them, his baby face had grown weary during his years of military service.

Joe Louis beat some good men after losing to Ezzard Charles. The wins discredit the popular notion that he was wheeled out of retirement and offered as a sacrifice to Rocky Marciano. He was clearly past his best but he was still a quality fighter.

The way Louis destroyed Lee Savold in 1951 was reminiscent of an earlier and far more lethal Brown Bomber. Despite the fact that he had lost his speed, his skill and punching power still existed. Few people, however, believed that Louis could beat Marciano. Louis was 37, Marciano 28 and unbeaten. It was a fight made to judge just how far Marciano's career could go.

Madison Square Garden was buzzing as Joe Louis led the final chorus of approval at his own fighting wake. It was not a massacre, just a fight that had only one possible ending. In round eight Louis was over. At ringside Sugar Ray Robinson left his seat and moved to the fallen champion's corner. On the canvas was his idol. Louis regained his feet, but was knocked senseless seconds later and finally dumped on the other side of the ropes. It was an ignoble resting place for one of boxing's greatest fighters. Robinson was one of the first in the ring to help him.

Marciano never forgot the final punch, even though it was the previous left hooks that had left Louis upright but unconscious. "The right hand I threw shoved him through the ropes out of the ring and on to the apron, and that's where he got counted out," Marciano later recalled in a magazine article. It was a matter-of-fact description, typical of Marciano.

The fight was shown on television. When it was over, and it was clear that Louis had left the ring, a recording of the night in 1938 when Louis secured a place in the hearts and minds of the nation, by knocking out Max Schmeling, was shown. It was just one way to show respect for a fighting great. As it was being shown there was misery in the changing room of the nation's first black sporting hero and both Robinson and Marciano were in tears.

Marciano had firmly established himself as the main contender and appeared to have silenced the critics who insisted he should actually have lost the fight against Roland La Starza at the Garden in 1950. With Louis ruined and in retirement, there was just Jersey Joe Walcott and Ezzard Charles between Marciano and the world heavyweight title. His chance came against Walcott in 1952.

▲ **THE OLD MAN SUFFERS** *Marciano connects with a vicious right uppercut during their fight and Louis's face is frozen with pain.*

Turpin reigns for just 64 days

▲ **ROBINSON CAUGHT COLD**
Sugar Ray Robinson prepared in halls in various European cities for his 1951 middleweight title defense against Randolph Turpin. Turpin won on the night, but his reign lasted just 64 days. Robinson, the clear favorite, had lost for only the second time in 133 fights.

Sugar Ray Robinson's first defense of his middleweight title was in London in July 1951, against the British champion Randolph Turpin. A few days prior to the event, Robinson – with his personal entourage of extroverts in attendance – discussed the fight with a group of British reporters. "I'd like it (the fight) to be just one round. But they tell me that Turpin won't co-operate. So – I guess – it won't go more than 15 rounds," Robinson stated.

In the previous four months he had fought eight times – six times in Europe – and defeating Turpin, who was good enough to be worth beating, looked like the ideal way to end a wonderful summer.

It all went wrong, however, in front of 18,000 people at Earls Court. Turpin was relentless, while Robinson looked old. When it was over, Robinson's first reign as middleweight champion was at an end and Turpin's 64 days as champion had started. It is still one of the best wins in British boxing history.

The rematch was made for September at the Polo Grounds in New York. Interest in the fight was such that it set a record, with 61,370 people watching and paying $767,626 – the biggest non-heavyweight gate at that point in boxing's financial history.

At the end of nine oddly muted rounds the fight was close. The referee, Ruby Goldstein, had it four

▶ TURPIN IN TROUBLE
Robinson connects with a left hook in his first fight with Turpin. "In Britain they treat me like a real champion and I will fight like a real champion," promised Robinson before the fight. But Turpin was relentless and within hours of that statement Robinson had lost his title.

rounds each with one even. In round 10 Robinson was cut, a deep ugly wound above his left eye that oozed blood. The injury, however, seemed to motivate the former champion and he charged Turpin.

It was the beginning of the end of Turpin's short reign. Robinson landed with two rights and Turpin was down. He climbed up, groggy and near collapse and for nearly one minute the brave British fighter remarkably withstood Robinson's onslaught until with just eight seconds left in round 10, the referee moved forward to end the fight. Robinson's second reign as middleweight champion had begun.

▶ ROBINSON'S REVENGE
Turpin is dropped in the 10th and final round of his rematch with Robinson at the Polo Grounds, New York. The fight was even after nine rounds but Robinson responded viciously when cut in round 10 to regain his crown.

CHARLEY BURLEY

Burley's Sorrow, Boxing's Shame

▼ ZIVIC'S DUBIOUS TACTICS
Fritzie Zivic (below) lost twice to Charley Burley, and after winning the world welterweight title from Henry Armstrong in 1940, he bought out Burley's contract. "I don't blame Fritzie," said Burley after the event, "he was just doing what any champion would do if he had the chance to avoid me."

Few names cause as much wonder and confusion in the history of boxing as Charley Burley. He was without doubt one of the sport's greats, possibly the best fighter never to win a world title. In 1992 partial justice was served when Burley was made a member of Boxing's Hall of Fame, but a position next to the champions from the 1930s, 1940s and 1950s is scant reward for a fighter who was never given a chance because he was black, honest and simply too good for his peers.

Burley's class is obvious from his record and there are many, including veteran trainers Ray Arcel and Eddie Futch, who make bold claims on Burley's behalf. They certainly agree he was the best fighter never to win a title and they should know, as their association with boxing started in the 1920s.

Sugar Ray Robinson was the most famous fighter to avoid Burley. According to Burley, he was offered a fight with Robinson if he took a dive in the first round. Futch has also claimed that Robinson would not fight Burley. Their careers overlap and they could have fought in 1943 or 1944 but by the time Robinson was champion at welterweight, Burley was possibly too big, and when Robinson was middleweight champion it was too late for him.

In 1938 Burley won and lost in fights with Fritzie Zivic and beat him again in 1939. The same year, Zivic won the world welterweight title from Henry Armstrong. To add insult to the injustice Zivic, while champion, actually bought Burley's contract which meant he managed the man he should have been fighting! Sense got the better of Zivic's conscience, however, and Burley was soon back to fighting bigger men. In 1938 he beat Billy Soose and in 1940 Soose beat world middleweight champion Tony Zale in a non-title fight. He claimed the title the following year.

Burley fought Holman Williams – another black fighter who never quite got his break – a total of seven times. They each won three with one no-contest. Burley also lost twice to Ezzard Charles on points in 1942. In 1944, however, Burley beat Archie Moore. Veteran trainer Eddie Futch remembers the night: "Burley left work, went home, got his gear, hopped on a bus, came up the 125 miles to Hollywood, went into the ring, and gave Archie a good 10-round licking." Moore has never disputed the beating, and once described Burley's style as "slick as lard and twice as greasy." "I wasn't that big but I could beat the heavyweights. I knew when their punches was coming, let it miss, slip a little and then start punching," Burley later added.

Charley Burley could have and should have won a world title. It was a time of ferocious competition and even more savage discrimination, but despite this he held a world ranking from 1939 until 1946, first in the welterweight top five and then in the middleweight top three. In 1947 Burley, who was 30, had to go to work as a garbage collector because he had trouble finding opponents. As Burley himself commented, "It was never easy for me. I could see what was happening but what could I do if people never wanted to fight me. I could get close to a title, have people tell me it was gonna happen, but it just never fell the right way for me in the end."

Before Burley died in 1992 he was asked what would have happened if Robinson had agreed to fight him. "He woulda been in trouble. I guess I woulda been, too. Ray ducked me. I wanted him. But it wasn't for me."

◀ **THE TALENTED OUTCAST** *Charley Burley was highly rated, and avoided for that very reason. In 1942, future world heavyweight champion, Ezzard Charles outpointed him twice but never stopped him. Archie Moore said he was the hardest man he had ever fought. He gained respect despite being sidelined and died in 1992, shortly after being inducted into the Boxing Hall of Fame in Canastota, New York.*

Sugar Ray finds Joey Maxim too hot to handle in New York

▲ **GLORY FOR MOORE**

Archie Moore survived for 16 long years as boxing's most notorious outsider, before finally winning the world light-heavyweight from Joey Maxim (right) in 1952.

The city was sweltering when Sugar Ray Robinson met Joey Maxim for the world light-heavyweight title in New York. The fight was delayed for two days because of rain but when it finally took place on June 25, 1952 the temperature was 104 degrees and it was the hottest 25th of June in the city's history.

When the pair weighed in for the first time the difference in size was obvious. Robinson was three pounds inside the middleweight limit of 160 pounds, whereas Maxim was just 4 ounces under the light-heavyweight limit of 175 pounds. When they visited the scales 48 hours later Maxim had dropped to 173 and Robinson was 157 $^1/_2$.

In round seven Robinson's sweet left hook and then a right sent Maxim back to the ropes. There was an attempt at holding but Robinson moved back slightly, out of Maxim's grip, and landed a perfect bolo punch. Both were breathing heavily when the round ended. Robinson was winning before the heat started to ruin him. The referee, Ruby Goldstein, was also suffering from heat exhaustion and had to be replaced in round 11 by Ray Miller. Robinson was fading fast. In round 13 he fell over from exhaustion when he missed with a punch and at the start of round 14 he remained on his stool, unable to continue in the overwhelming heat. It was over, he was finished and the old warrior Maxim was still champion.

"The heat talk is an alibi," claimed veteran manager Doc Kearns, but Maxim knew better. "That heat sure affects you strangely. When Robinson was down I wanted to step on his face – anything so he'd just stay down. I never felt like that before," he said.

The fight took a heavy toll on both fighters. Robinson lost a staggering 11 pounds during the fight and Maxim nine pounds. Six months later Robinson retired. The night before his retirement, on December 17, 1952, Archie Moore finally won a world title when he beat Joey Maxim. The Old Mongoose, as Moore was known, had been a professional boxer since 1936.

▲ THE HEAT OF THE NIGHT

Joey Maxim stands menacingly over the exhausted form of Sugar Ray after Robinson missed with a wild punch in the 13th round. Robinson was leading on the judges' cards after this round, but the intense heat had taken its toll on both fighters. When Robinson stayed on his stool at the start of round 14, his challenge was over.

GIANTS OF THE RING

SUGAR RAY ROBINSON

1921–1989

So much of the debate surrounding Sugar Ray Robinson's place in boxing history focuses exclusively on his better known, and often more entertaining, middleweight fights. His days as welterweight champion – arguably the best welterweight who ever fought – are often overlooked.

Having turned pro in 1940 he won an astonishing number of fights before taking the welterweight title from Tommy Bell in 1946. He never lost the title, holding it until 1950. As a welterweight Robinson had grace and speed and could avoid the wars he so often had to endure as a middleweight. If Robinson had won a welterweight title earlier, and had more challengers, his first spell as world champion would have been considered as close to perfect as any fighter has ever managed.

The YEARS *of Rock*

1952-1964

After Joe Louis, Ezzard Charles and Jersey Joe Walcott came Rocky Marciano. The heavyweight title was often in a lull in the few years between the demise of Louis and the emergence of Marciano and his relentless pursuit of blood. Archie Moore proved to be the sentinel at the edge of changing history.

ROCKY TIMES

▲ **THE OLD WARRIOR MOORE**
Some people say that Archie Moore had two birthdays each year – one his real age, the other his fighting age (which was allegedly three years younger). He was certainly old in boxing years when he fought for the heavyweight championship.

◀ **THE ROCK AND MOORE**
Previous page: Marciano misses with a wild uppercut during the third round of his fight with Moore.

Rocky Marciano once said: "In a fight you just go in there and go crazy if necessary." The strategy obviously worked given that he never let himself down in any of his 49 fights and was able to retire as undefeated world heavyweight champion in 1956.

After his famous victory over Louis, Marciano's next fight was with Jersey Joe Walcott for the title. Walcott had become the oldest man to win the championship when, at the fifth attempt, he beat Ezzard Charles in 1951. The fight with Marciano should have been in New York but it was switched to Philadelphia because Felix Bocchicchio, Walcott's manager, was suspended in New York for having a criminal record. "If I lose to Marciano take my name out of the record books," said Walcott, "He is not even good enough to be in Joe Louis's 'Bum of the Month Club.'" As usual, Marciano said little and left the talking to his manager, Al Weill, and trainer, Charlie Goldman.

Marciano and Walcott met in September 1952. In the first round Marciano was down from a left hook, but he was up on the count of two, ready to go crazy. Walcott, however, was skilled in survival and made Marciano look foolish again and again before age and Marciano's ability to absorb punishment started to alter the fight. In round nine Walcott was dropped, in round 10 he looked like the old man he was, and in round 13 a right, an infamous Marciano "Suzy Q," landed and Walcott was down and out.

One ringside journalist said the sickening final punch left Walcott "looking down his own spine with eyes that could not see." The punch is one of the most famous in boxing's history. Walcott never stood a chance. At the time of the knockout he was leading on all three scorecards. A rematch was inevitable and when they met eight months later it was over in one round. There was nothing Walcott could do, he was caught cold. However, Sugar Ray Robinson was critical, saying Walcott "Not only let his people down, he sat on them." He never fought again.

Walcott had been an odd champion. When he won the title in 1951, it was his 21st year as a pro. "Boxing was a mystery to me. When I look back and see what I had to go through to get to the top I find it hard to believe," Walcott reflected after he retired. In his last fight with Marciano, when he was 39, he looked older than any heavyweight had ever done in a championship fight.

For Archie Moore 1952 was the year he had been waiting for. "I should have been champion of the world as a middleweight round about 1940 when I was 23," said Moore, who claimed to be three years younger than his mother said he was. Instead, he had a long wait until he finally got Joey Maxim in the ring. Moore won over 15 rounds. The pair would repeat the

fight and the decision in both 1953 and 1954.

Moore was extraordinary in many ways. After beating Maxim he set his sights on Marciano, taking out ads in newspapers and pursuing the champion in much the same way as Jack Johnson had done with Tommy Burns. Moore wore capes, excessive outfits and twirled canes. Marciano disliked Moore's style but the pair were kept in separate arenas until 1955. Even in defeat Moore was a showman. If he was bruised, cut or sore he would still attempt to entertain. After losing to Marciano he stood on a table at the post-fight press conference: "Gentlemen," he said addressing the press, "I hope you enjoyed that as much as I did."

In the same year, Sugar Ray Robinson made a comeback, but he had been fighting for too many years. He lost his second fight and was on the canvas in another. However, his form improved and he won and lost the middleweight title three times between 1955 and 1960. Many of the fights have a special place in the sentimental archives of all who sought the sacred in Robinson: the two with Carmen Basilio, in particular, are unforgettable.

When the titles were gone, the last fights – often against good young boxers – went on too long. Had Robinson stopped boxing some years earlier he would have undoubtedly become the icon he is today long before he actually lost his last fight in November 1965. He started boxing when Joe Louis had been heavyweight champion for three years and quit when Muhammad Ali was in his second year as champion.

Robinson's last fight, against contender Joey Archer, ended in a points defeat, but Archer was world-class and 12 months earlier had outpointed Dick Tiger. When Archer beat Robinson there was a new middleweight champion – it was Tiger. Robinson was still able to mix with the best in his division when he was 45 years old.

The influence of the gangsters and wiseguys, whose colourful careers had covered roughly the same period as Robinson's fighting years, was also in decline during this time and many were forced to retire early. A Senate Committee Hearing in 1957 found Jim Norris, his associates and the IBC guilty of monopolistic practices. The game was up. In 1959 the Supreme Court ordered the "divestment, dissolution and divorcement" of Jim Norris's International Boxing Club from the sport of professional boxing. Norris's reaction was to offer J. Edgar Hoover a $100,000 salary to salvage the IBC.

For Frankie Carbo and Blinky Palermo, the plot thickened. The two sporting "gentlemen" were eventually sentenced to 25 and 15 years respectively for trying to extort money from a promoter. Carbo had earlier been sentenced to two years in New York for undercover matchmaking. Their departure only justified the years of complaints by Cus D'Amato, a manager who was frozen out as a result of his insistence on independence.

In 1956 D'Amato found himself in charge of the heavyweight division when his fighter Floyd Patterson won the vacant title by stopping Moore. However, D'Amato was only part saviour and he took the heavyweight championship on a tricky journey in the ensuing years.

▼ **MARCIANO'S "SUZY Q"**

Rocky Marciano lands a trademark "Suzy Q" – big right cross – to flatten Jersey Joe Walcott in round 13 and win the world heavyweight title. At the time of the knockdown Marciano was losing on points.

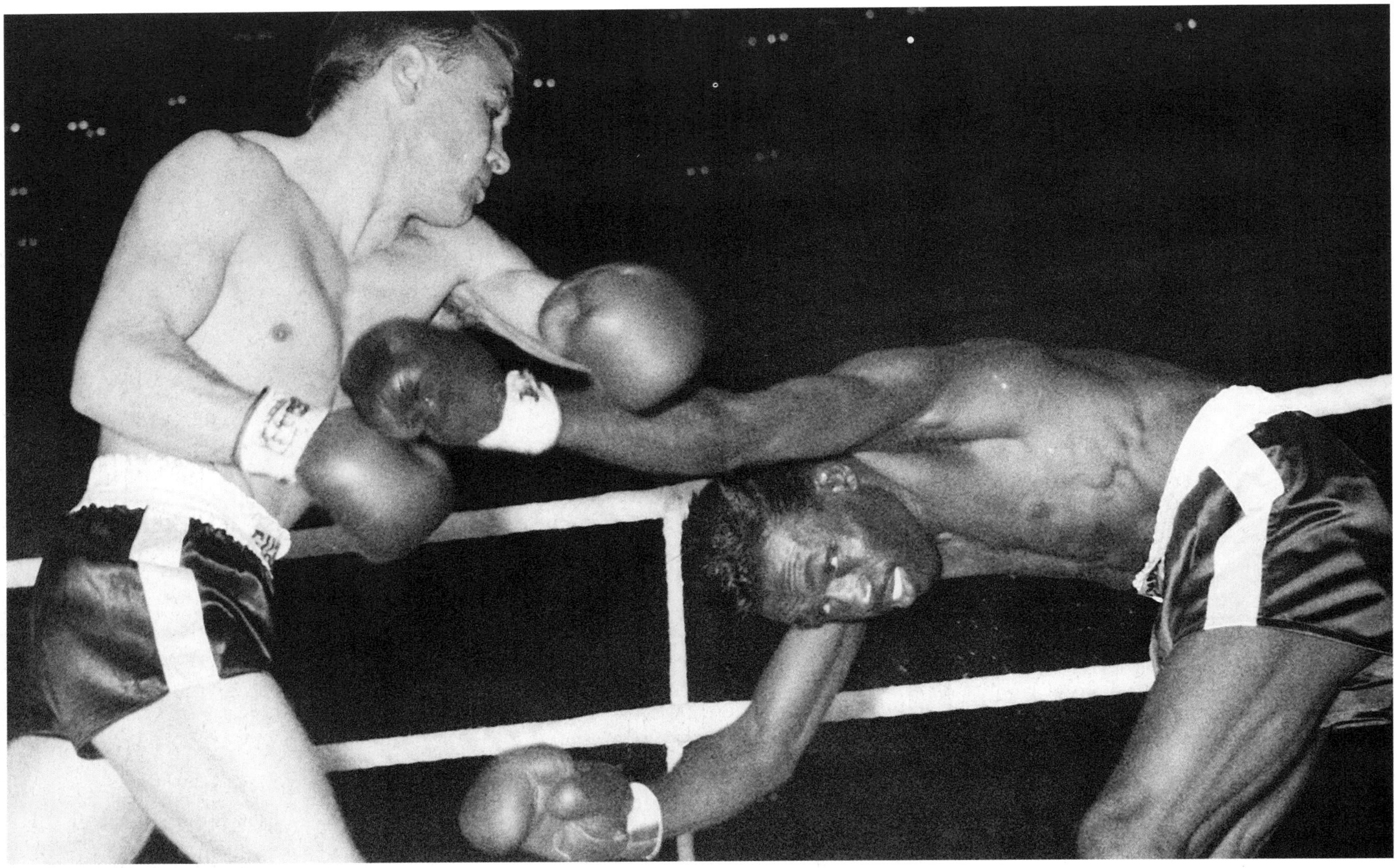

"Just one right hand punch used to break jaws" – Joe Brown

▲ **"OLD BONES" BROWN**

Joe Brown (right) was 30 when he won the lightweight title, 36 when he lost it and 44 when he finally retired in 1970. In 1959 Brown beat Charnley in Houston, Texas, because of a deep cut, and he repeated the victory in their rematch (above).

Joe Brown, like Archie Moore, fought in four different decades. He was known as "Old Bones", which is surely a perfect description of a man who looked old when he was young and yet somehow managed to defy time when he was old.

Brown was a well-connected man. His manager during his world title years was Lou Viscusi, a friend of Carbo. Brown turned professional in 1943 and fought top-ranked boxers from the start, winning the lightweight title in 1956. His wins over Wallace Smith, Orlando Zulueta, Britain's Dave Charnley, Kenny Lane and Ralph Dupas during his six-year reign as champion make him one of the lightweight greats.

When he lost the title in 1962, he passed the championship to another great fighter, Carlos Ortiz, from Puerto Rico. In their televised fight Ortiz was technically brilliant. He knew that trading punches with Brown, who had a knack of finding the type of punch that could put a swift end to fights, would be foolish. Ortiz had won and lost the junior-welterweight title before meeting Brown and although he was young he was a quality fighter and won after 15 rounds. Brown never got another chance but continued fighting until 1970.

◄ **A BLACK DAY FOR BROWN**

Brown made hard work of his rematch with Dave Charnley in 1961 and made just one more defense after it. In 1962 he fell victim to Carlos Ortiz in Las Vegas, in a dignified last act.

▲ **A TRUE PROFESSIONAL**

Brown and Charnley pictured at the weigh-in for their 1961 clash. After losing the title to Ortiz, Brown was back in London in 1963 – this time losing to Charnley in six rounds. By then Brown knew it was over, but he was a true pro – appearing in 41 more fights despite losing 21 of them.

Robinson still tasted as sweet as sugar after his comeback

▲ **SUGAR'S SWEET RIGHT**
Robinson's right damages Carmen Basilio in their 1958 rematch. Basilio's left eye was closed from round six and he lost the title he had won just a few months earlier.

The comeback of Sugar Ray Robinson was amazing. At the end of 1955 he knocked out Carl Bobo Olson with a perfect left hook to win the middleweight title again. The form-book was useless when Robinson's punches were finding their mark.

After beating Olson in a return fight in 1956, Robinson had the most remarkable year of his pro career in 1957; it was certainly hard but it confirmed – not that confirmation was necessary – Robinson's position as one of the true greats. In January Robinson lost his title after 15 rounds to Gene Fullmer. There was a rematch clause and this time Robinson, after studying tapes of Fullmer's fights, devised a plan. He saw a gap for a left hook, he told people. The fight ended in round five with Fullmer on the canvas for the first time in his career: it was the left hook.

Robinson's year was not over yet, however. He was 37 when he defended his title against Carmen Basilio in September 1957. Basilio was the welterweight champion and an uncompromising brawler. The fight was gruesome and when it was over after 15 rounds Basilio was the new champion. One journalist said after the fight: "They may fight again, but they'll never fight any better."

They did meet again and it was as magnificent as the first occasion with Basilio fighting from round six with a swollen eye. At the end of round 15 Robinson was champion once again.

◄ **STYLISH IN TRAINING**
Robinson looking slick in training before his points defeat to Terry Downes, in 1962. He lost three of his six fights that year, and fought in America, Trinidad, France, Austria and England before finally quitting the ring in 1965.

▼ **A SWING OF WILD FURY**
Basilio sways from Robinson's vicious right uppercut early in their second fight. It would be the last world title victory of Robinson's career.

GIANTS OF THE RING

ROCKY MARCIANO

1923–1969

Rocky never officially lost a professional fight. He came close but his sheer guts, combined with the help of the officials on several occasions, saw him through. When it was time to go he left with a perfect record of 49 wins in 49 fights, including 43 by stoppage.

He had the presence of mind to recover when hurt and an instinct that allowed him to get through drastic moments. He also had, in his favored right hand, a single punch finish. He was not, by any means, a perfect fighting machine but neither was he the "master of no defense," as he was often unjustly dubbed. His reach was 14 inches less than Ali's and even an old Louis had caught him clean. But as a champion he beat the men in front of him and that is all that matters, even if some were not the best available.

ROCKY MARCIANO

Rocky was the Last Fairytale Prince

▼ EZZARD WEIGHS-IN
Rocky Marciano leans forward to listen to a word of advice from his manger, Al Weill, at the weigh-in for his second fight with former champion Ezzard Charles in 1954. Charles was stopped in eight rounds. In their first fight, three months earlier, Marciano won on points after a bloody brawl.

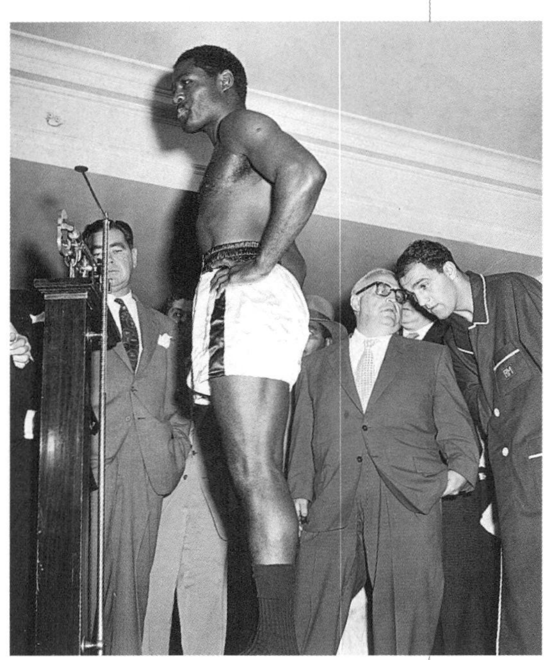

Marciano never took risks as champion. He beat the right men, at the right time and at the right weight. He also used tactics that were to his advantage. After beating Walcott for the second time Marciano met Roland La Starza again. Their first fight in 1955 had been dubious. The judges were divided and the referee had a draw, but the winner was determined by an odd system – where rounds won were compared to rounds drawn – and Marciano was given a split decision.

Before the return contest La Starza was calm. "Every fight is won and lost during heavy training. This fight is probably over now," he said four days before the fight. The rematch – in front of a crowd of 44, 562 at the Polo Grounds in New York – once again saw La Starza avoiding most of Marciano's often crude punches in the early part of the fight. Despite this, Marciano's perfection of illegal and borderline punches soon started to swing the fight his way and Marciano stopped La Starza in round 11.

Next was former champion Ezzard Charles in June 1954. Marciano had been out of the ring 10 months but had sparred nearly 200 rounds. Charles went 15 rounds and Marciano ended up cut and hurt. He kept his title but a rematch was made. It was the last chance for Charles, who has only recently started to receive the credit he is due. There were moments when Charles, a stylish boxer, was able to move and counter with ease as Marciano missed. Charles had been a quality fighter since the early 1940s, but by the time he met Marciano he was past his best. Marciano said that it was his hardest ever fight.

"Don't get me wrong, I would like to have been beaten only to know what the feeling is like," said Marciano after the first Charles fight. The rematch ended in round eight with Charles down for the count. Charles continued to fight and was knocked out four times before retiring in 1959. Notoriously bad with money, he died penniless in 1975.

There were other heavyweights waiting for a chance at Marciano but his manager, Al Weill, was always one step ahead of the contenders. In 1954 Nino Valdes, from Cuba, knocked out Tommy "Hurricane" Jackson in an eliminator. In 1955 Moore won a fortunate decision over Valdes and in 1954 Moore knocked out top contender Bob Baker; Moore was in pursuit of Marciano.

After Charles came the massacre in San Francisco against Britain's Don Cockell. The fight was a dirty one, but Cockell was brave. Had he just fallen over like most of Marciano's opponents there would have been no need for the list of infringements. In round one it was kidney punches and in round three Cockell was hit after the bell; he was butted in the fourth, before being hit low in the fifth (three times after the bell); and in the seventh he was repeatedly butted and hit low. There was, the irate British press corps screamed, never a single warning. It must have been fearsome to watch. Cockell's courage was praised but when it ended in round nine after two knockdowns his career was effectively over. He fought just twice more and was stopped on both occasions.

There was a vacant look on Cockell's bloody face when the referee finally intervened. "I hit him harder than I have ever hit anybody," said Marciano when the fight was finished. There would be just one more Marciano title fight, a finale to his career against Moore. "I think Moore will come at me fast. I'm a slow starter and he is a quick thinker but I will be warm and ready."

▲ **A RELAXED ROCKY** *Marciano was an honest pro with a simple fight ethic that endeared him to thousands of fight fans.*

Marciano leaves a sport in turmoil

▲ MOORE LANDS WITH A LEFT
Archie Moore strikes out at Marciano in the fifth round of their fight, having already had him over in the second. Before the fight Moore had predicted a quick finish if Marciano was dropped. "Walcott made a mistake when he had Marciano out – I will not make the mistake," he said. However, Marciano got up off the canvas in round two to finish Moore in the ninth.

◄ ROCKY SHOWS NO MERCY
Moore slumps for the final time in round nine, the black scar from his ulcer operation clearly visible. Marciano had been forced to listen to Moore's poetry, pleas and accusations for over a year, and revenge must have been sweet.

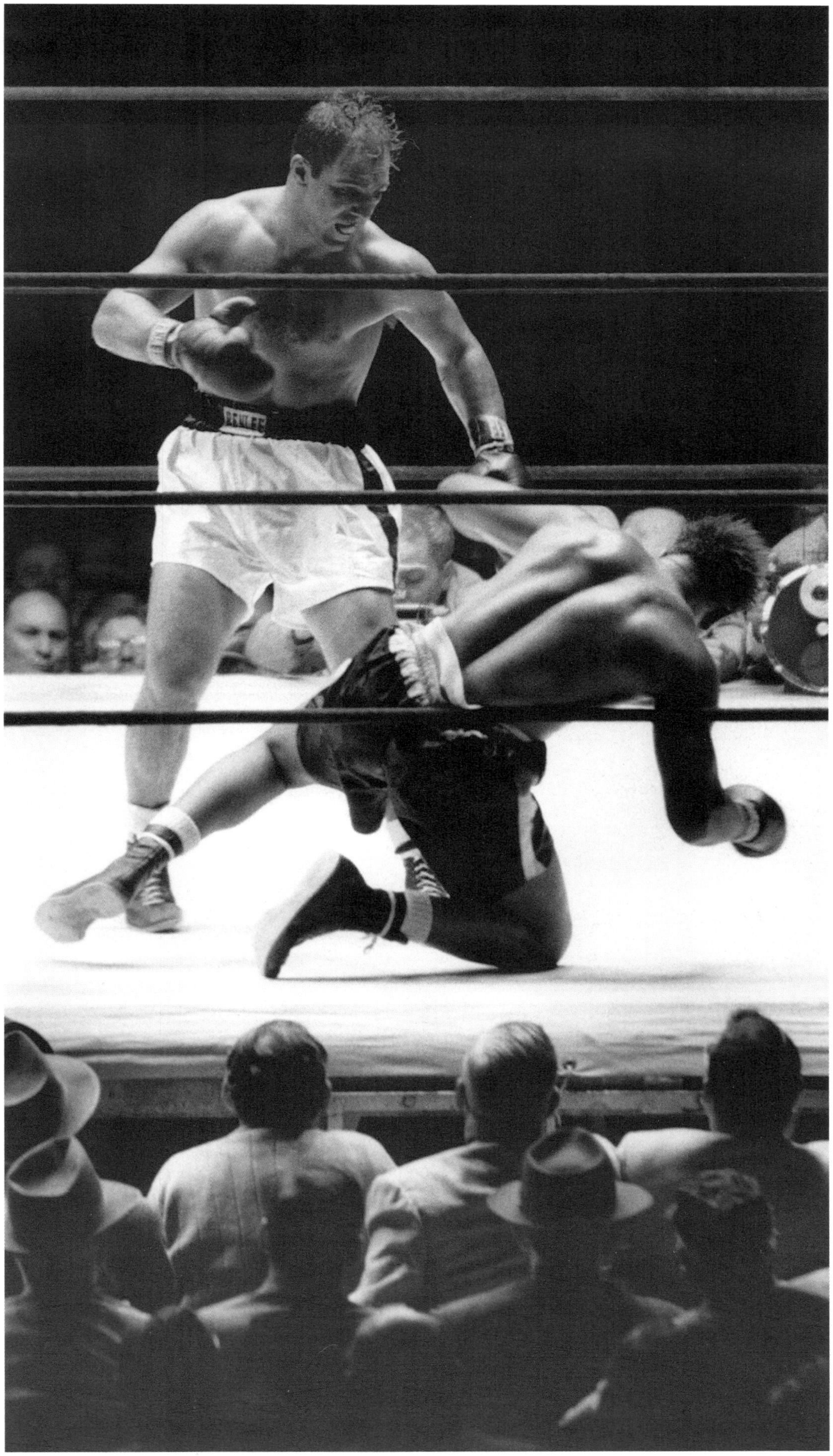

▶ **THE END IS NIGH**
Marciano talked of retirement after beating Moore, seen here going down in round six. "My wife wants me to, my mother wants me to: I just might retire," he said. His manager, Al Weill, hurriedly tried to reassure everyone in the changing room that the champion was not serious, but Marciano was true to his word. He quit the ring the following year.

The last fight of Rocky Marciano's career took place in September 1955. His opponent was Archie Moore, who had stalked the champion and used a press campaign to get his shot. There had been "Wanted" posters with Marciano's face on them and weekly bulletins about Marciano issued by Moore. The champion was not impressed.

In the second round Marciano was down. It was a good knockdown. He climbed up at the count of four, but was clearly dazed. At this point the referee, Harry Kessler, should have let Moore win the title. He didn't, he forgot that championship rules in New York at that time excluded compulsory eight counts – Kessler gave Marciano an eight count. At the end of the fourth round Marciano waited for the bell to sound and then whacked Moore one more time. Moore hit him back and pushed him. Marciano walked away smiling. The crowd of 61,574 at Yankee Stadium roared their approval. When the fight ended with a knockout in round nine Moore had been on the canvas five times. "My legs were not what they once were," he lamented. Despite this he continued to fight.

In December 1955, Bob Baker, a former Golden Gloves champion from Pittsburgh, outpointed Nino Valdes in an eliminator for Marciano's title. In April 1956, Marciano announced his retirement. "I'm tired of having to introduce myself to my daughter," he said. The title was vacant and Cus D'Amato's protected fighter, Floyd Patterson, and Moore were matched for the championship.

▶ D'AMATO THE SAVIOUR?
When Floyd Patterson won the heavyweight title in 1956, Cus D'Amato effectively took control of the sport. He ignored his critics, of which there were many, and raged against his enemies during a period of great transition.

▲ VALDES THE OUTSIDER
Archie Moore knew enough to beat Cuban-born Nino Valdes in the ring. Meanwhile, champions Marciano and Patterson knew enough of the right people outside the ropes to keep his challenge at bay and ensure his career stayed on the periphery of success.

Cus D'Amato takes control and ends the big carnival

Despite the fact that Archie Moore was 43 and Floyd Patterson just 21, there were many experts who believed Moore would win. However, the fight ended in round five and Patterson became the youngest world heavyweight champion. Moore later claimed that he had overtrained. "A fighter can still do things in the ring after 40, just by moving his head and shoulders," he explained. Moore still held the world light-heavyweight title but was stripped of it in 1962.

Patterson and D'Amato took control of the heavyweight division at a time when the old regime of Norris, the IBC and the gangsters were in trouble. Patterson had fought for the IBC when he beat Hurricane Jackson before the Moore fight, but D'Amato had taken the $45,000 and ran from the "bad elements in boxing."

Patterson beat Jackson in a rematch in his first defense, then Pete Rademacher (an Olympic champion who was having his first fight), followed by Roy Harris and, against the British Boxing Board of Control's wishes, Brian London, a jovial doorman from the north of England. All four fights were decisive. D'Amato was doing an exceptional job as manager for his fighter by getting the greatest fee for the least amount of risk, but there were many who felt that he was ruining the credibility of the sport.

In June 1959, just 56 days after beating London in a dreadful mismatch, Patterson was set to defend against Sweden's Ingemar Johansson. It looked like another flop for boxing and a victory for D'Amato. Meanwhile, Bob Baker, Nino Valdes and the mean Sonny Liston couldn't get a look in.

◀ **LONDON CALLING**
Brian London, seen here in training, caused uproar when he fought Patterson in 1959. The British authorities were against the contest, and London famously remarked, "I feel like a prawn (sic.) in the game." Patterson stopped him in 11 rounds, and in his next fight Valdes took him out in seven.

▶ **INGEMAR UNDER FIRE**
Floyd Patterson lands with a left to Ingemar Johansson's body during their heavyweight title fight in June 1960. Patterson won the contest with a fifth round knockout to regain his belt.

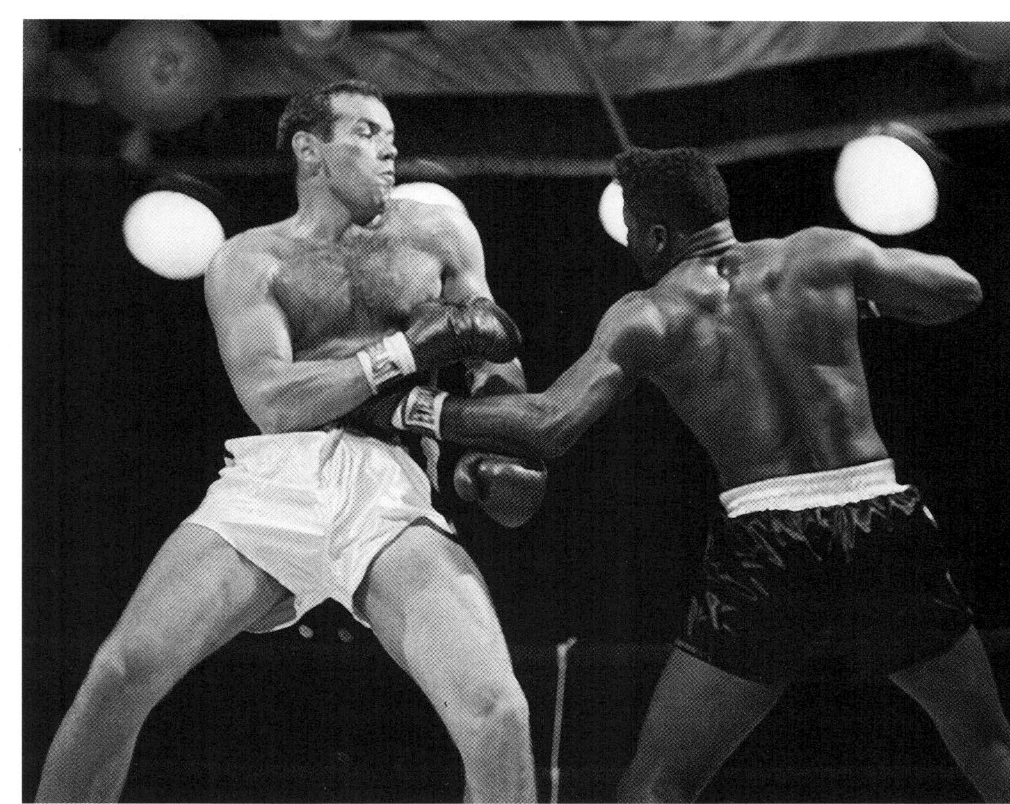

THE OTHER SIDE OF BOXING

DEATH IN THE RING

The tragic death of Benny "Kid" Paret, following his 1962 welterweight championship fight against Emile Griffith at Madison Square Garden, led to calls for boxing to be banned. The fight was broadcast live on television and the final moments when Paret slumped into his corner will remain as one of boxing's most tragic images.

It was the third meeting between the pair for the title. Griffith won the first and Paret the rematch. Just four months before their third meeting, however, Paret had been badly beaten and knocked out in 10 rounds in a world middleweight title fight against Gene Fullmer. He should not have been in the ring.

Paret never regained consciousness and died in the hospital on April 3, 1962. News, a year later, that his widow was destitute was a sad indictment of a sport that so often neglects its former champions. In such situations the difficulties faced by the other boxer are often overlooked too. Griffith decided to continue. "What else can I do?" he asked. Other boxers in the same situation have asked similar questions.

PATTERSON V JOHANSSON

Ingo's Bingo Ruins D'Amato's Babe

Gus D'Amato was an angry man who mistrusted the world. Before the first of Floyd Patterson's three wild fights with Sweden's Ingemar Johansson he harangued the press and Patterson's persecutors one more time. "Patterson beats a fellow, and they say whoever it may be is a bum. Maybe he is a bum, but they ought to say he is a bum that was ranked the leading contender until Patterson made him look like a bum." Well, to all intents and purposes Johansson looked like a bum.

▲ **TOO CALM FOR THE STORM** *Patterson is just hours away from losing his world heavyweight title to Sweden's ever-smiling Ingemar Johansson, in June 1959. "He couldn't punch, he was too frail a caliber," said Johansson after his third round win. Patterson, however, would restore parity with a fifth round knockout of Johansson the following year.*

The Swedish fighter had beaten contender Eddie Machen in one round in his previous fight, but was best known for his dismal display in the heavyweight final at the Helsinki Olympics, when he was thrown out for holding, running and not trying against the American Ed Sanders. At the same Olympics, Patterson had won the middleweight gold. Johansson was not given a chance of winning. His first round win against Machen was considered a fluke. "I knew I had done my best in preparing for the fight," Johansson stated.

The fight, in June 1959, started cautiously enough but in round three Johansson landed his right and Patterson was down for the first of seven knockdowns. It was all over, the title was gone and Patterson disappeared into the night. Describing the event a year later Johansson wrote: "He was reachable with my left and he was not not cunning or fast enough. He pushed away my left and the right followed automatically. It landed smack on his face – if it had landed on his jaw the match would have ended at that moment."

Rocky Marciano was due to make a comeback to fight Johansson but D'Amato had a return clause in the original contract, and 12 months later the rematch was on. The fight, at the Polo Grounds, took in over two million dollars, including film, television and radio rights. There was a shift of opinion in Johansson's favor as many believed Patterson's state of mind was wrong. After the first fight he had not left his house for a month and in preparation for revenge lived in a near-derelict building to try to get his hunger back.

Patterson confounded the critics, however, when two left hooks sent Johansson sprawling unconscious on the canvas – it took 10 minutes to get him up. Patterson had made history with his fifth round knockout and was paid over $100,000 more than the champion. A third fight was made between the two, leaving no gaps for leading contenders such as Sonny Liston, Zora Folley, Cleveland Williams and Eddie Machen – a murderer's row of formidable fighters!

In March 1961 Patterson and Johansson were back in the ring. Patterson was over twice in round one and fell over at the start of round two. However, Johansson could not finish him and by the end of round two Patterson had worked his way to safety by using his jab and vanishing behind his gloves. In round six the fight came to a sudden halt when Johansson, who was cut above the right eye and was moving slowly, was dropped by three punches – the last, a short right, delivered illegally to the back of the Swede's head. The trio of fights was at an end.

Patterson made one more defense before he was forced to meet Sonny Liston – a farcical contest against Tom McNeeley in 1961. McNeeley crashed to the canvas 10 times before the pointless slaughter was ended in round four. The lasting memory from the fight is the awful image of the blood smeared over the face of McNeeley's wife, Nancy, as she kissed his battered face.

▲ **INGEMAR FEELS THE PAIN** *Patterson lands with a crunching left lead to the face of Johansson on his way to victory in 1960.*

Sonny Liston had a face that bore the strain of a lifetime's hardship

▲ A SOLEMN SONNY

Sonny Liston had to wait a long time to prove himself in the ring. But for the politics outside the ropes he would have met Patterson in the 1950s. "I could see what was happening," said Liston "I just had to find the patience to wait." When they did eventually meet in 1962, Liston needed just 126 seconds to win the title.

Sonny Liston was bad news. He had spent time in prison for armed robbery before he was a boxer and served time for assaulting a policeman when he was a boxer. There were many, including former champion Jack Dempsey, who believed he needed to prove himself a worthy citizen before getting his chance at a title. He had already proved himself in the ring.

He should have been given the chance to knock Patterson out in 1960 or 1961, but had to beat Valdes, Machen, Williams and Folley to keep busy. His chance finally came in Chicago in 1962. It was rumored that Liston was part-owned by Blinky Palermo and Liston was and still is referred to as a "mob fighter." The connection motivated D'Amato to keep Patterson as far away from him as possible. Patterson had been through reform school and Liston through jail, but there the similarities ended.

On the night the pair met at Comiskey Park, it took Liston just two minutes and six seconds to get what he deserved. "The left had all of me in it," claimed Liston. "The only time I was hurt was when he started getting up on one knee at the count of nine. I thought he was going to make it before 10, which shouldn't happen to anybody I hit." It never did and Patterson was counted out. Liston, so often a guilty man but also a regular fall guy, had justice on his side at last.

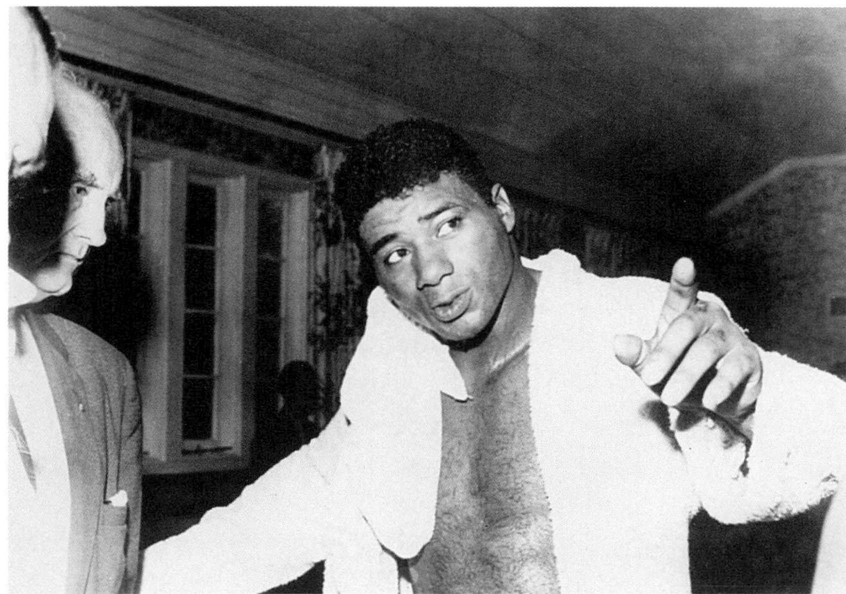

▲ **THE END OF EASY STREET**
Patterson (top) in training for the Liston fight. Liston promised Patterson a mauling. "It will be quick," said the challenger. It was.

▲ **OPEN SLAUGHTER**
Liston (above right) knows that Patterson is out on his feet as yet another right uppercut is about to rattle the senses of the champion.

GIANTS OF THE RING

FLOYD PATTERSON

1935–

Patterson will forever be remembered for two unique records he set. In 1956 he beat Archie Moore to become the youngest heavyweight champion at the age of 21, and in 1960 he became the first fighter to regain the heavyweight championship, when he knocked Ingemar Johansson out in their rematch.

Patterson was 17 when he won an Olympic gold medal at middleweight in 1952. His careful rise from amateur star to world champion – there was only a slight problem when he was narrowly outpointed by veteran Joey Maxim – set the standard for the future and angered many of the old purists whose early careers had been much tougher. It was the end of the old days, when long apprenticeships and hard fights eventually led somewhere. After Patterson came Clay and he needed even less time and fewer fights before he won a world title.

The young upstart Clay was the permanent voice in the background

▶ THE LATE BLUES OF LISTON

Liston arrives in London, with his wife Geraldine, for an exhibition bout. He always wanted to be a popular champion. "I want to reach my people. I want to reach them and tell them: 'You don't have to worry about me disgracin' you'. I know that the better class of colored people were hoping I'd lose, even praying I'd lose," said Liston after beating Patterson for the first time.

When Cassius Clay performed a shuffle above the crumpled form of Archie Moore in November 1962, he sent a clear message to boxing's past and future. His speed, defiance and brilliance were impossible to deny. Clay embraced Moore when it was over.

The previous year Clay had dazzled in sparring sessions with Johansson in Miami, before the Swede's third fight with Patterson. He was the permanent presence in the background and when the rematch between Liston and Patterson was made for Las Vegas, Clay arrived in town and performed a ritual that he would repeat whenever he wanted people to notice him, until he finally retired nearly 20 years later.

Liston had promised to knockout Patterson in a repeat of their first encounter. He did it again in one round and needed just four more seconds. "I'm only disappointed that they let him have a couple of eight-counts to clear his head," said Liston. He had predicted a quicker ending. Liston spoke about Ali after the fight: "It would take me two rounds – one and a half rounds to catch that young thunderjaw and the other half to knock him out."

Clay, who had been in a suite at the Dunes for the week of the fight, had appeared at the craps tables when Liston, who often had Joe Louis with him, was playing. He was becoming impossible to ignore. There were days, before the second Liston-Patterson fight, when people believed Clay's mouth would get him a beating for free. He created the impression he wanted, but it was not necessarily the impression that veterans of the fight game wanted to see.

◀ THE LOUISVILLE KID

Clay returned with a gold medal from the Rome Olympics in 1960. He later threw it away after being refused service in a restaurant because he was a negro. He was given a replacement in 1996, at the Olympic games in Atlanta.

▲ **CLAY DANCES OVER MOORE**

It was Archie Moore in four rounds for Cassius Clay in 1962, and a quick shuffle after the first knockdown. "Archie's been living off the fat of the land. I'm here to give him his pension plan. When you come to the fight, don't block the aisle and don't block the door. You will all go home after round four," said the audacious Clay.

A KID *called Clay*

1964-1971

Peter Noble

▲ **THE PERFECT SHADOW**
Cassius Marcellus Clay was born in Louisville, Kentucky in 1942. "I'm going to be the perfect champion – like the young Joe Louis. I'm clean living, I haven"t got a prison record. I think you've got to be an idol for young people,' said Clay in 1963.

◀ **THE "LOUISVILLE LIP"**
Previous page: Clay in London for his fight with Cooper in 1963, predicting a fifth-round knockout.

His predictions were so often right. When Cassius Clay started to tell the truth the world of boxing was stunned. He was so pretty and so fast that the best were reduced to watching him in disbelief. "He can beat Liston now," said Archie Moore in 1962. He was right.

PURE ALI

Boxing changed forever in 1964. When Cassius Clay beat Sonny Liston, the Big Ugly Bear, the sport was revitalized, never to be the same again. The morning after his victory, Clay became Cassius X.

After winning a gold at light-heavyweight in the 1960 Rome Olympics, Clay turned professional with the help of a syndicate of businessmen in his home town of Louisville. Known as the Louisville Sponsoring Group, the LSG consisted of 11 white men aged between 25-70; 10 were millionaires and they contributed $2,800 each, while William Faversham, the organizer, contributed just half that amount. Clay received a $10,000 signing bonus.

At first Clay stayed in Louisville where he was trained by Fred Stoner, a black man he had known for years. After his pro debut at the Freedom Hall, Louisville, however, the LSG decided they needed someone with more experience in Clay's corner. Clay wanted Sugar Ray Robinson but he was sent instead to Archie Moore in San Diego.

At Moore's gym, The Bucket of Blood, the young fighter and the old fell out over many things. Clay, for instance, refused to sweep the floor when asked. The pair were from different worlds. Moore had come through hardships that Clay would never have to know and still slept with his watch and wallet under his pillow. Clay left just a few months after arriving. When the two men eventually fought two years later, Clay had clearly matured and instantly comforted Moore at the end of the bout.

Clay was then sent to Miami to work with Angelo Dundee. The pair had met a few years earlier in Louisville when Clay had pestered Dundee and world light-heavyweight champion Willie Pastrano. Dundee remembered the young kid. When Pastrano and Dundee had been in Louisville in 1957 for a fight they let Clay and his brother, Rudolph, visit their room. "He just started telling us he was gonna do this and do that. He was gonna win the Olympics – which he did – he was gonna win the world title – which he did. They stayed for few hours and we mostly talked about boxing," said Dundee.

On December 27, 1960 Clay won for the second time and his relationship with Dundee started. The trainer accepted $125 a week; a deal that lasted until the second fight with Liston, after which he negotiated a percentage deal.

Clay won 19 fights before he met Liston. Some, like the dull and disastrous television appearance against Alonzo Johnson, were fights that continued to raise questions about his temperament and his punch. "Gaseous Cassius," Budd Schulberg called him. Other writers were not so kind and a spiteful cult of Clay, and then Ali, detractors started. There were some fight reports that defied logic and some that were just

plain unfair. Others were racist. With hindsight, the blindness of the men who wrote at the time in the face of such brilliance seems quite astonishing.

In Clay's first New York appearance in 1962 he was dropped by Sonny Banks. He recovered to stop Banks as predicted in round four, but he was on the floor and the cynics laughed. He beat Moore, his old trainer, in 1962 and survived another knockdown when he traveled to London to fight Henry Cooper. Cooper's manager, Jim Wicks, responded to a suggestion that Cooper would be meeting Liston in a title fight: "Meeting Liston? I wouldn't let Henry meet him going down the bleedin' street." Wicks and Cooper had more confidence about beating Clay, however.

On that night at Wembley Stadium Clay was criticized for his showmanship. The British press, like most of their American counterparts, simply refused to accept what they were seeing. Instead of concentrating on Clay's skill, they attacked him for his crown and robe outfit.

In round four Clay was down from a left hook when the bell sounded. While Clay was sitting in his corner, Dundee discovered a small tear in the left glove. The timekeeper, Stan Courtney, claimed the break was only one minute 40 seconds between the rounds. The gloves were not replaced, but spares were ready for the end of round five. There was no need, as Cooper was rescued from Clay's fists with lacerations on the left side of his face, and with his left eye a purple mess. The next fight was Liston, and what was for many purists the death of boxing.

Since Floyd Patterson had stopped Moore to win the vacant heavyweight title in 1956 the division had lost a lot of its glamor. Clay was its saviour. Even Liston, who for so long waited patiently as Patterson fought mediocre fighters, seemed intent to just sit and wait for paydays when he beat Patterson. All of Liston's brilliant non-title victories in 1959 and 1960 should have been title defenses.

The middleweight, welterweight and, at the end of the 1960s, the light-heavyweight divisions had some of the greats in action against each other. Emile Griffith, Dick Tiger, Bob Foster, Jose Napoles and Carlos Monzon all came through as Gene Fullmer, Paul Pender, Jose Torres and Joey Giardello were finishing their careers. The rivalries and competitive fights at this time match any period in boxing history.

▲ **DOWN BUT NOT OUT**
Clay recovered from Cooper's left hook late in round four of their bout at Wembley Stadium in 1963. The bloody fight came to an end in the following round with Cooper being rescued from Clay's fists.

By the end of the 1960s it had all gone horribly wrong for Ali. He was out of the ring from March 1967 until October 1970 because as a Muslim he refused to be inducted for the draft and was disowned by the sport's governing bodies. In early 1964, though, nothing else mattered in boxing but the prospect of Sonny Liston silencing Cassius Clay, the Louisville Lip, in Miami. There appeared to be far more at stake than just the heavyweight championship of the world.

Clay arrived with predictions and taunted the experts

▲ **ONE ENCHANTED NIGHT**

"Eighth round he'll be dazed, he'll be frustrated, he'll be tired and nervous," predicted Clay before the first Liston fight in 1964. He promised "a total eclipse of the Sonny" and he delivered.

It was the wildest weigh-in ever. Clay was pronounced "scared to death" by Dr Alexander Robbins. Liston looked bored on the eve of his second defense of his title against the "thunderjaw" who had been stalking and annoying him for far too long.

The fight was in Miami on February 25, 1964. Clay was just 22 and Liston was mean and malevolent. Liston's age was not expected to be a factor but when it was over he suddenly looked older than his years. Nobody really knew exactly how old he was, although his daughter was 17.

Clay played with him. It's that simple. Liston refused to come out of his corner for round seven and Clay was the new heavyweight champion.

"I'm still pretty, the prettiest man alive. But go look at that Liston. He's gone to the hospital with his face all cut. Don't ever call me an underdog again. I'm the greatest champ who ever lived. I cut him to pieces," said a jubilant Clay.

Liston claimed to have injured his shoulder, but few believed him. He looked like a man with a shattered soul that night as he sat forlornly in his corner. He must have known there was nothing he could do.

The next morning Clay became Cassius X Clay, and announced his conversion to Islam. At the conference his voice was low. On March 6 he was given the name Muhammad Ali by the leader of the Nation of Islam, Elijah Muhammad.

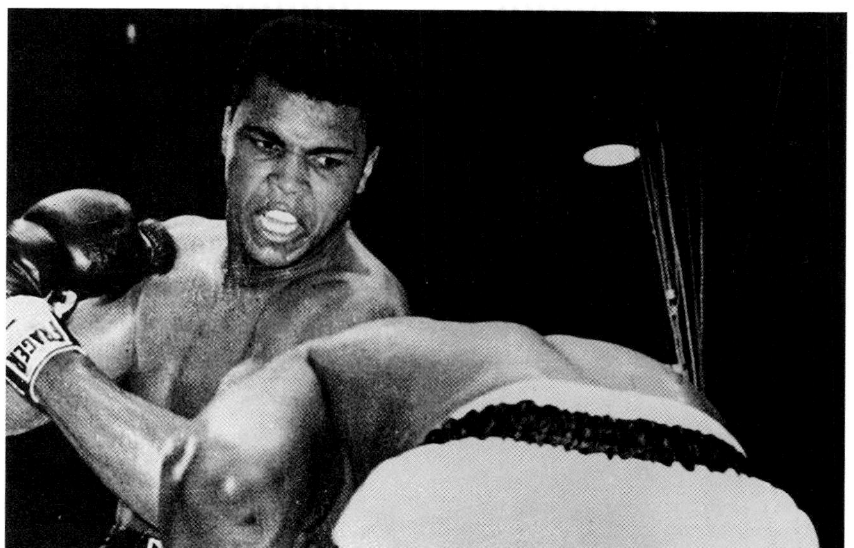

◀ **NO REFUGE FROM THE PAIN**
Liston tries to duck below Clay's punches but it was no good. There was no solace for the champ anywhere in the ring.

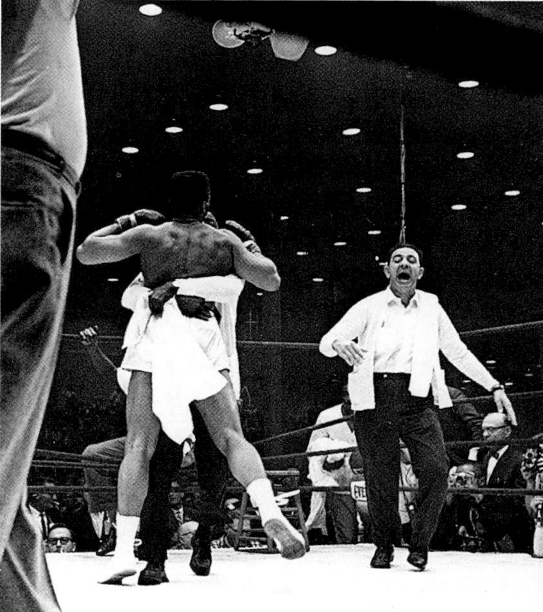

▲ **MOMENTOUS MOMENT**
Dundee is all smiles when the news of Liston's injury surrender is known. Clay is the champion, the champion he said he would be.

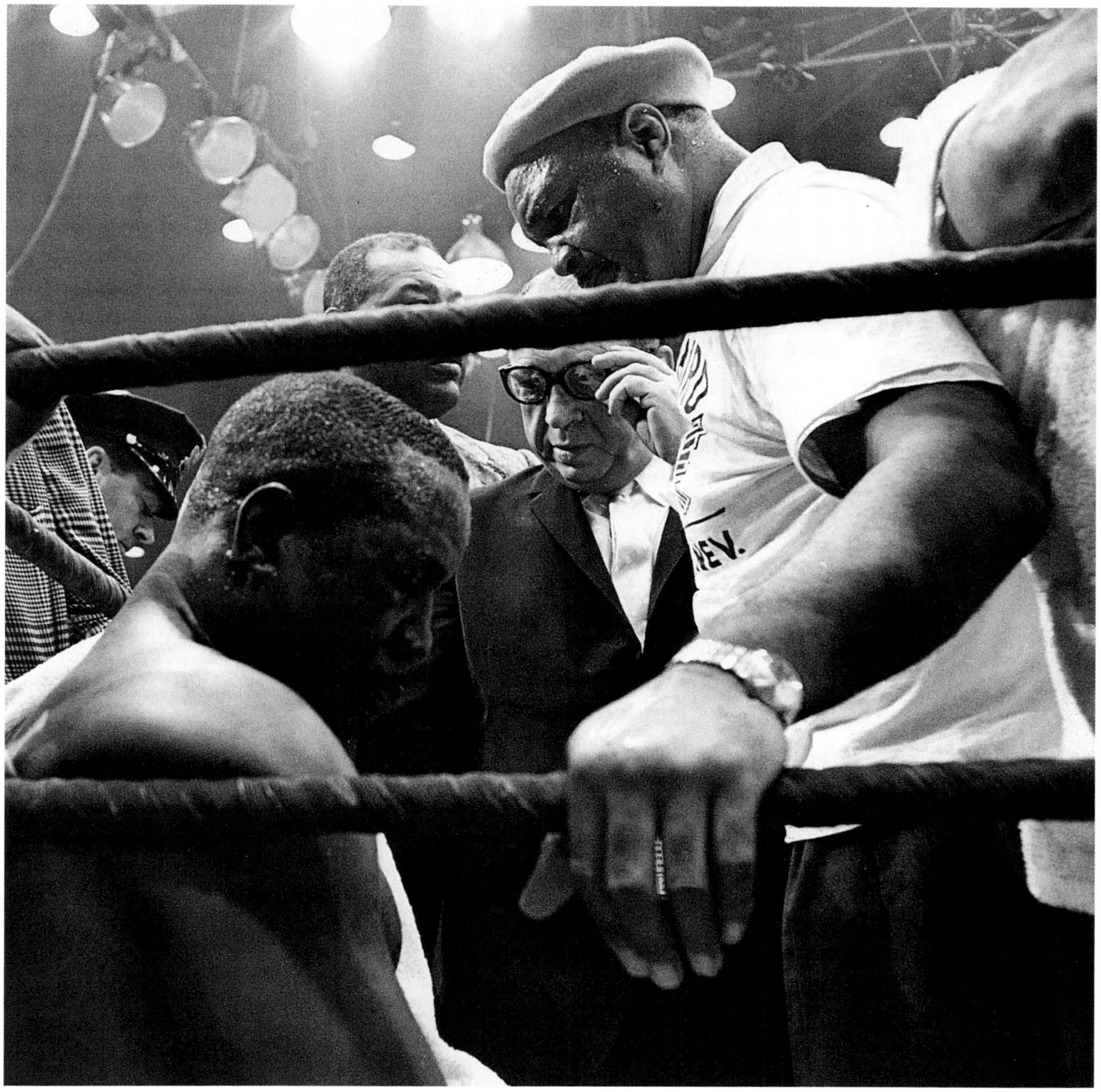

◀ **WHAT HAPPENED?**
Joe Louis looks on in stunned confusion. What went wrong? Nobody really knew. "In the ring Sonny was a killing machine. I seen him knock guys out with a jab, just one jab. Bang," said Liston's loyal friend Johnny Tocco.

"Get up sucker and fight. Get up and fight" – Ali to Liston

▶ THE END APPROACHES
The chaotic final moments of the Ali-Liston rematch, when the referee, former world champion Jersey Joe Walcott, lost control, lost the count and rushed in to save Liston when he regained his feet. "Sonny was in no fit state to continue boxing," said Dundee. Sadly, most people disagreed.

The rematch between Ali and Liston was postponed when Ali had a hernia operation two days before the original date. The fight was then switched from Boston to Lewiston, Maine, and just 2,434 people showed up on May 25, 1965. What they witnessed was one of the most controversial fights in heavyweight history.

"He was in terrific shape, and then lost it," claimed Liston's cornerman Milt Bailey. On the scales Liston's body looked flaccid – Ali had won the mind game. "Liston was scared," claimed Al Braverman.

Before the fight Dundee had the 16-foot ring exchanged for a 20-foot ring. It would have made no difference because when the first bell sounded Ali landed twice with light taps before the third and final punch of the fight, a glancing right, caught Liston high on the cheek. He went down in a weary heap. There were moans of disappointment from ringside and the punch, a brilliant counter, was immediately dubbed the "Phantom."

"Get up and fight you sucker," Ali screamed as he hovered over Liston gesturing with his right hand. The referee, Jersey Joe Walcott, lost control and the count went on and on before Walcott finally waved it off. Walcott later admitted he missed the count. Both fighters were booed. "I never quit – I just didn't get the count," claimed Liston. Others claimed it was a fix. In Washington, Senator John Tower called for a Congressional Investigation.

At the end of the fight Ali remained in the ring for 20 minutes. The look of disgust on his face when Liston first collapsed had gone and he was smiling. "I want Patterson," he kept repeating.

THE FIRST AND FINAL ROUND

Ali smashes a left into Liston in the opening moments of the rematch. The venue was switched at a late stage and as a result few people turned up to watch the slaughter.

LISTON STAYS DOWN

Liston claimed he could have gotten up, claimed he was nervous that Ali would hit him before he was fully up. There was confusion and Walcott was out of control. Liston always denied he took a dive.

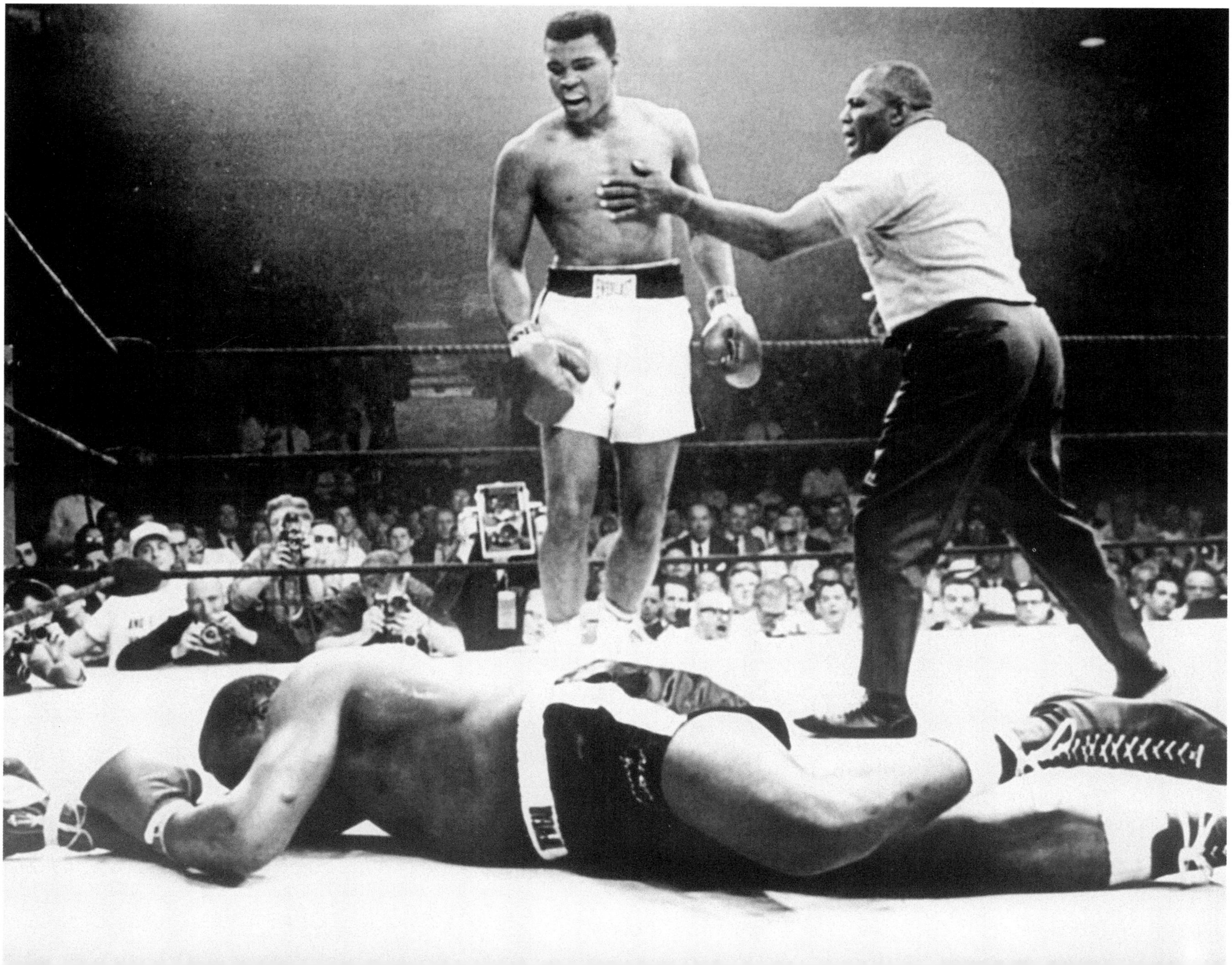

Ali was one man in a ring paradise creating hell for his opponents

Ali got Patterson in Las Vegas in November 1965. It was arguably the first of his many cruel performances and when it ended in round 12 the public had a clearer picture of the boy from Louisville. "Let's not call this a fight. It was a public humiliation," wrote George Whiting, in the London *Evening Standard*. Ali had promised a sacrifice and he delivered.

After Patterson came the brave Canadian George Chuvalo, in Toronto in 1966. At the same time as the fight was taking place there was a grand jury investigation into Ali's postponed defense against leading contender Ernie Terrell. There were allegations of gangster involvement. Ali would ruin Terrell the following year.

Ali was superb against Chuvalo and won the fight on points. His next three contests were too easy but he had other troubles. The FBI was monitoring him and the specter of his enlistment in the American forces loomed ever larger.

In London, in May 1966, he cut Henry Cooper again and it was over in round six. In August he was back in London and this time he needed less than three full rounds to knock out Brian London. In September he was in Frankfurt for another defense against southpaw Karl Mildenberger. It went 12 rounds before it was called off. The Mildenberger fight provided a ray of hope for the Ali detractors, who incurred the champion's wrath by still insisting on calling him Clay.

"If he leaves his head open against Cleveland Williams he could be in real trouble," warned Joe Louis. The fight with Williams turned out to be another brutal display. In Europe, Ali had not been so vicious.

◀ **STYLE WAS HIS ANSWER**
Ali fighting German, Karl Mildenberger, in 1966. It was his third easy victory on an obscure and lonely tour of Europe.

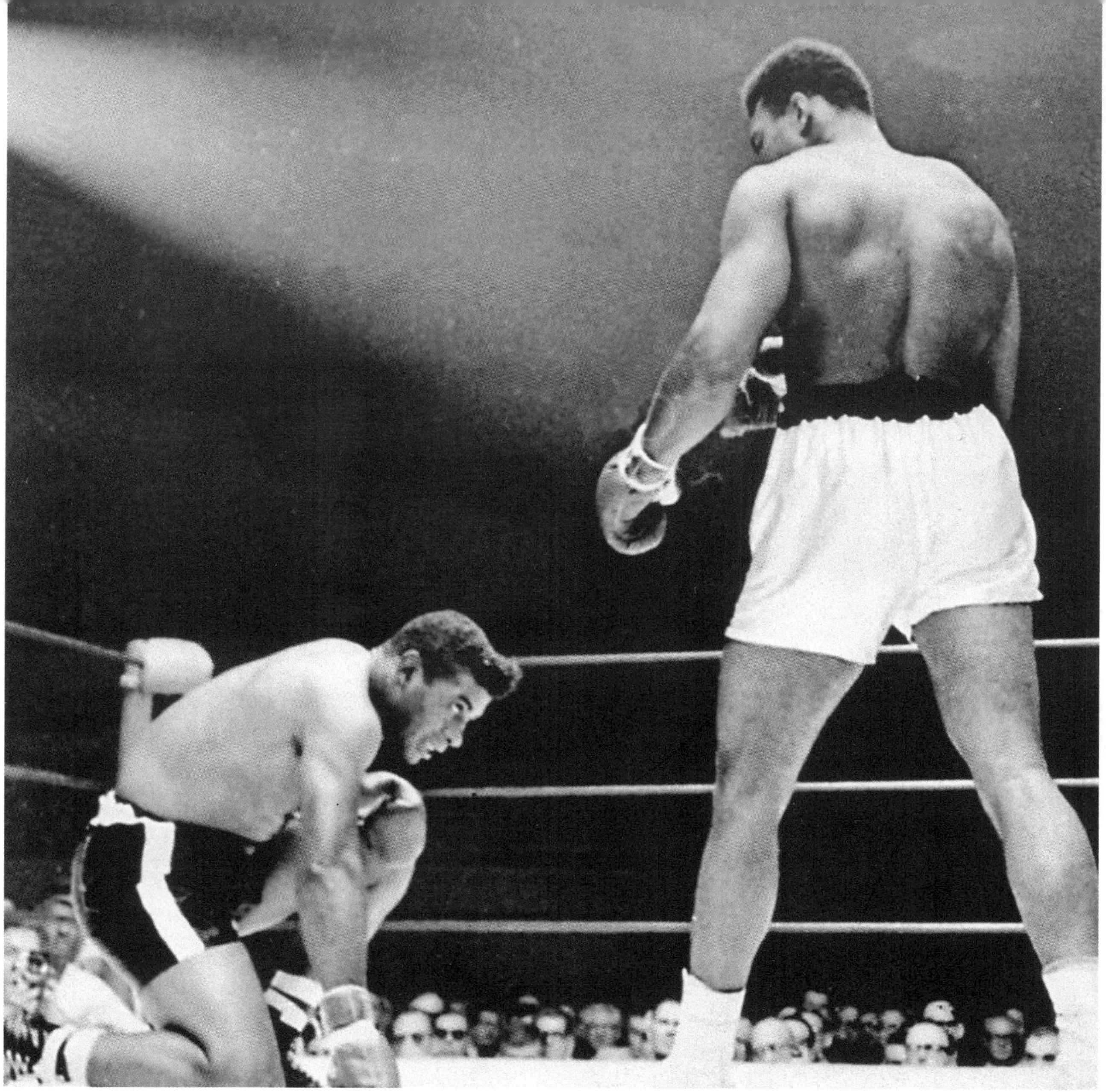

▲ **AVOIDING EYE CONTACT**
Floyd Patterson faces defeat in his 1965 match with Ali. Patterson had a back injury and Ali was cruel – Patterson never stood a chance.

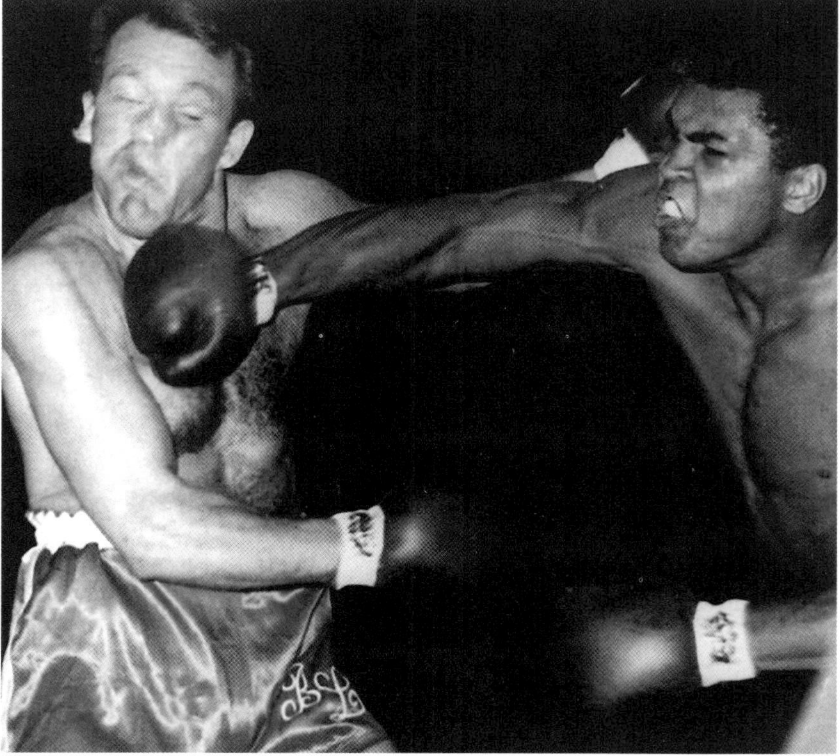

▼ **UNLAWFUL CONTACT**
Ali and Brian London shake hands before their 1966 fight. The British Board of Boxing Control objected to the fight but it went ahead anyway.

◀ **ONE PAINFUL NIGHT**
"I could hit him, but he could hit me and he hit me more than I hit him, and I tell ya, whoever said he can't hit was telling a lie,' said London after his fight with Ali.

The price of victory was too much for Cooper in the rematch

▲ **THAT CRIMSON CURSE**
Henry Cooper tries in vain to make his punches reach their target. "The blood was in my eyes, I couldn't see a thing," said Cooper. His two defeats at the hands of Ali made him a hero in Britain.

Henry Cooper is still considered one of Ali's greatest supporters. His two fights against the American secured a special place in the hearts of all British boxing fans for the man they called "Our 'Enry." A crowd of over 44,000 people paid to see the fight at Highbury, the home of Arsenal football club.

After a good first round, Cooper was beaten to the jab and caught by sharp rights. His face started to turn purple from the opening round. Ali was a different fighter to the young boy who had fought Cooper three years earlier. When the cut appeared in round six the blood formed a crimson arc that soaked both fighters. It was a fresh wound and Cooper must have known that his world title hopes had just vanished. "I told the ref to stop the fight," claimed Ali. "There was too much blood and I didn't want to hurt him anymore." Cooper, however, insisted the cut was the result of a butt.

The deep gash needed 16 stitches – four below the surface and 12 to close the wound. Ali's slashing

▶ **COOPER'S DREAM**
"If only I had caught him with that left hook a little earlier I might have licked him," said Cooper after his first fight with Clay.

▼ **THE CUT THAT ENDED IT**
"It was one of the worst cuts I have ever seen," said Mickey Duff after the second Ali-Cooper fight was over.

rights had done the damage. "Ali respected me in the second fight but it was a physical thing. My weak skin let me down," said Cooper.

When Ali was denied the right to box and stripped of his title, Cooper was matched with Jimmy Ellis in a WBA championship fight. However, the British Boxing Board of Control refused to sanction the contest and it never took place. Cooper relinquished his British heavyweight title in protest. His friend, Ali, would have approved of his stand.

MILESTONES OF BOXING

MUHAMMAD ALI WINS WORLD HEAVYWEIGHT TITLE

FEBRUARY 25, 1964, MIAMI BEACH

CONVENTION HALL

The fight was the shock of the decade. Clay, as he was still known, started fast and kept the action at a pace that poor, lumbering Liston could not match.

In the fourth and fifth Clay was temporarily blinded by the liniment that was smeared all over Liston's shoulders but by the end of the sixth Liston was finished for the night. Clay had taken his best shots and was still talking, still dancing and still landing jabs.

"I was hit on my left shoulder in the first round and it kept getting worse," claimed Liston, whose purse was stopped pending an investigation. At the time of the stoppage the fight was even on the scorecards.

ALI and DUNDEE

Happy Cornerman, Happy Fighter

Angelo Dundee taught himself to be a trainer by watching the legends of the corners at Stillman's gym in the 1940s. Initially he slept on floors and cleaned up blood and spit, but by the early 1950s he was making a name for himself. He worked with Carmen Basilio during the early days and was first seen in the ring, with one of his distinctive swabs hanging from his mouth, when the tough onion farmer stopped Johnny Saxton to regain the welterweight title in 1956. But Dundee is remembered for the boy Cassius Clay, who became the man Muhammad Ali.

Their professional relationship started in December 1960, after Ali's short spell with Archie Moore. "Before I was hired, there was a conference about his future. He (Ali) was a serious subject. I had never heard a fighter discussed the way Ali was discussed," said Dundee, who had been a guest of Clay's sponsors at his debut against Tunney Hunsaker.

▼ ALI'S MAIN MAN

Dundee was with Ali through his best years in the ring. "With Ali everybody wanted a little piece. People everywhere wanted an Ali story, a moment they shared with him to share later with their friends. I have too many pieces, too many remarkable days and nights," said Dundee.

Dundee had other fighters when he first starting working with Clay. In 1963 he trained four world champions – Ultiminio "Sugar" Ramos, Luis Rodriguez, Ralph Dupas and Willie Pastrano. In the late 1960s and 1970s he worked with world welterweight champion Jose Napoles and in the late 1970s was in the corner for Sugar Ray Leonard. However, it is Ali that people remember when Dundee's name is mentioned.

Dundee met Clay from the train in Miami in December 1960. The fighter trained at the 5th Street gym and lived in a one-room apartment. The atmosphere in the gym (now sadly torn down and replaced with a parking lot) was a little crazy. "When Clay came it just got worse," said Dundee. From that point until Ali's last controversial loss to Trevor Berbick, in the Bahamas, in 1981, the pair were together. The only time Dundee was not in Ali's corner, he was in the opposite corner with Jimmy Ellis in their 1971 North American Boxing Federation title fight. "With Ali I was part of the team, with Ellis I was the team. Ali understood when I explained that to him," claimed Dundee.

"I always believed in him from the very start. When he said he was the greatest I believed him. I told people long before people accepted him. There was a time when people would simply not accept what their eyes were watching," said Dundee. "I remember watching the first Liston-Patterson fight with him in Chicago and I knew he could beat Liston. Nobody believed me but I knew and Muhammad knew."

According to Dundee there were never problems with Ali in the gym: "He was alert to ideas but he had to be shown what to do in an indirect way. I would sow the seeds and let him believe he had thought of it. What I called kiddology. I could get him to do something twice without having to ask him once by making him believe it was his idea."

In the corner between rounds during the Thrilla' in Manila, the pair reached perfection. It was not always that way, though. In other fights Ali lost his cool and pushed Dundee and Drew Bundini Brown away and told them to "shut up," but in Manila it was just the two of them working a very special kind of magic. Dundee was the only one who could help Ali find that something extra and he did.

In April 1968, when Ali had been out of the ring just over a year he returned to help his Louisville friend, Jimmy Ellis, prepare to meet Jerry Quarry for the vacant WBA heavyweight title. "It was a great feeling to have him back," said Ellis. Two years later millions of fans were saying the same thing.

▲ **PARTNERS IN THE RING** *Dundee tapes Ali's hands prior to his training session. Ali was preparing for his defense against Henry Cooper in 1966.*

"Big Cat" Williams licked in three

▲ **NO SANCTUARY**
Cleveland Williams falls in round three and Ali's grimace tells a story that few want to hear. There is no whimsical twinkle in Ali's dark eyes, just the violence that illustrates the other side of his character.

Cleveland "Big Cat" Williams may have been past his best when he met Ali, but he was still considerably better than the previous trio Ali had fought.

The fight, at the Astrodome in Houston, set an indoor attendance record of 35,460. The fans witnessed a night of genius. Ali was devastating – arrogant, accurate and nasty from the bell. In the second round Ali dropped Williams with a right, after showing him a left. It was the type of simple but masterful move that Ali could successfully use against the best fighters of his generation.

Williams, who had been shot two years earlier by police, survived the round. However, he had a familiar expression on his face: Liston, Patterson, Moore and others had had the same sick look after fighting Ali. It was over in the third round. It was a slaughter, and the final picture from that amazing night is the sight of Williams in total confusion as Ali starts screaming for his next opponent – Ernie Terrell.

The delayed fight with Terrell was set for the same venue on February 6, 1967. Terrell, from Chicago, was the leading contender and had once been a friend of the champion. The build-up to their fight started to turn nasty, however, when it appeared that Terrell

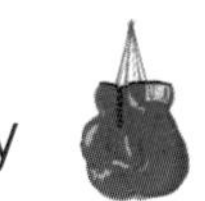

◀ **ANOTHER MAN DOWN**
Williams is down in round two. He managed to get up for one more round, however, before Ali finished the job. Dundee had been fearful as he watched Ali's punches ruin Williams. "I could see the damage as each landed and I knew Cleveland was proud," said Dundee. Ali, however, didn't give Williams a chance to show his pride.

would only call the champion Clay and not Ali – it was not a move that would endear the fighter to Ali.

"What happened was, we were at a meeting and somebody asked me something about the fight and I said: 'Sure, if that's all right with Clay.' I didn't mean nothing by it but Ali, he went mad. I had known him as Clay and it just slipped out and after that I figured I could just keep using it because it was getting him mad," claimed Terrell at the Ali Tribute night in Louisville in September 1997. Terrell's strategy certainly got Ali mad but it was not necessarily a good move on Terrell's part.

▶ **THE MAN ALI WANTED**
Ernie Terrell was no edifying fighter – his ungainly style was at the other end of the spectrum from Ali's. In the run-up to the fight both men taunted each other. "At the time I really didn't think all the talking and shouting would work, but it did. Ali made it work and how it has worked!" said Terrell many years later.

▶ PROVING A POINT
Ali points out that he is not the only one opposed to the Vietnam war. His refusal to be inducted into the army was controversial and cost him his license to box.

Ali knew he was running out of time and running into trouble

Terrell was nicknamed The Octopus by Ali. His style was not easy on the eye but he had beaten Eddie Machen, Zora Folley, Cleveland Williams, George Chuvalo and Doug Jones, a fighter who had given the young Clay a few problems. He was also the World Boxing Association champion and had a jab like a piston.

Before the fight Ali dropped the octopus sobriquet and started to call Terrell Uncle Tom. "What's my name?" Ali began asking before the fight and continued asking during as the two men fought. Terrell always answered: "Cassius Clay."

The action was truly grisly and Terrell was made to suffer for 15 rounds. He took one of modern boxing's most damaging and soul-destroying beatings. Vicious punches altered his face and in his ear he heard the same questioning taunt: "What's my name, what's my name?" There was no twinkle in Ali's eye that night. It was Ali at his most savage.

Terrell claimed Ali had thumbed him in the eye and raked his eyes on a rope but he could do nothing to halt the punches, the taunts and the sneers. At the start of round 13 Ali spat contemptuously at Terrell's feet. When it was over, there were no friendly handshakes. "I made it a great fight with a dull man," boasted the champion.

There would be just one more fight before the government beat him. On March 6, 1967, the National Selective Service Presidential Appeal Board voted unanimously to maintain Ali's 1-A classification. He was officially eligible for induction to the armed forces. As a Muslim he refused, as a black American he refused. "I ain't got no quarrel with them Vietcong," he famously said.

He was due to meet Folley at Madison Square Garden on March 22, but he was rapidly running out of time and had few allies.

◀ NASTY FROM THE START
Ali against Terrell in Houston, Texas, in 1967. Ali was at his spiteful best in front of the 37,321 fans. "What's my name?" Ali demanded. "Clay," Terrell kept foolishly replying.

▲ ALI THE PREACHER
Ali preaches as the guest minister at Frankfurt's Mosque in September 1966. "I believe in Allah and in Peace," said Ali after the first Liston fight.

▶ TERRELL ACCUSES ALI
Terrell blocks a right from Ali. Terrell claimed that Ali thumbed him in the eye and raked his eyes across the ropes. When it was over Ali was treated with indifference by the fans and not admiration.

There were other talented champions around during Ali's reign

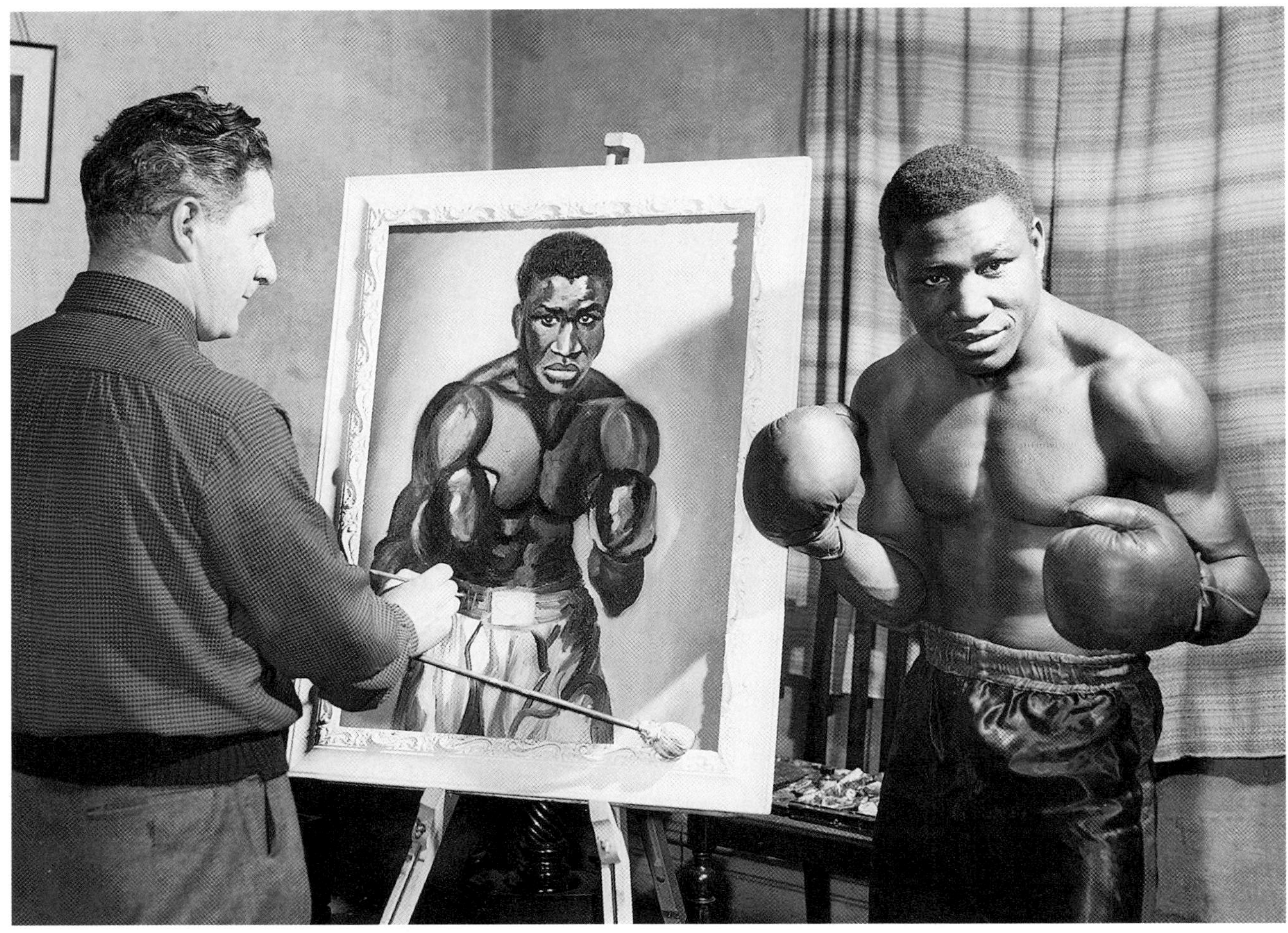

▶ A WORK OF ART
Dick Tiger having his portrait painted by his trainer Maurice Foran in June 1958. Tiger moved to Britain in 1955 and fought anywhere against anybody. In 1962 the Nigerian's hard work paid off when he won the world middleweight title.

In 1962 Dick Tiger took the world middleweight title from Gene Fullmer. To reach that point Tiger had undergone a long and often lonely struggle that involved him moving from Nigeria to England and then battling his way through the ranks for his shot at the title. Tiger never had easy fights but he persevered and it paid off in the end. When his career was over and he had lost and regained the middleweight title and won and lost the light-heavyweight championship, he returned to Nigeria and in 1971 died of cancer in the village he had left 19 years earlier.

Between Fullmer losing to Tiger and the arrival of Carlos Monzon there were incredible middleweight fights. Ali may have dominated the headlines, but the middleweights were also showing their class. Joey Giardello, who turned pro in 1948, beat Tiger in 1963 and in his only defense beat Rubin "Hurricane" Carter, who had knocked out Emile Griffith in one round in a 1963 non-title fight. Tiger won the title back from Giardello in 1965, a few months after beating Carter on points in a non-title fight.

Griffith beat Tiger in 1966, Nino Benvenuti beat Griffith in 1967 but Griffith got revenge inside five months. In 1968 Benvenuti won the title back from Griffith. Most of the fights went 15 rounds. In 1969 Benvenuti lost an overweight non-title fight to Tiger in New York when he was champion.

By the end of the 1960s Carlos Monzon was arguably the best middleweight in the world. He was eventually given a chance to win the title and beat Benvenuti in 1970 in Rome. Monzon held the title until retiring as undefeated champion in 1977.

MILESTONES OF BOXING

A NEW MADISON SQUARE GARDEN OPENS

Legends have retired at Madison Square Garden and some of the most memorable fights in boxing history have taken place there.

The original Garden was built in 1882 and then rebuilt less than 10 years later. In March 1968 the present Garden opened – the fourth in total – with a fight between Joe Frazier and Buster Mathis. Frazier knocked out Mathis to win a version of the world heavyweight title that Ali could no longer defend.

A few years later it was Ali and Frazier in the Garden in the Fight of the Century. The lure of the venue is hard to resist for any fighter or fan but it is no longer a big-fight venue. There are no benefits, no cash incentives comparable with the offers made by the Las Vegas and Atlantic City casinos. At the Garden now there are just memories and black and white images of a past that will never be forgotten.

◀ LA DOLCE VITA
Benvenuti (far left) was a Roman idol, who drank wine and collected works of art. He won an Olympic gold medal in 1960 at welterweight and won and lost the world junior-middleweight title once and the middleweight version twice.

◀ MONZON WINS AGAIN
Carlos Monzon (left) celebrates his victory over Benvenuti in May 1971. Monzon won for the last time in 1977 when he retired as undefeated world middleweight champion.

RUBIN "HURRICANE" CARTER

One Boxer's Hellish Nightmare

The Rubin "Hurricane" Carter story is a tragedy. In 1967 Carter was wrongfully convicted of a triple murder in New Jersey and sentenced to three life terms in prison. Carter was one of the most ferocious boxers in the world. "I think I hold some sort of record for knocking people out of the ring," joked Carter, who always entered the ring wearing a black hooded gown to conceal his shaven head. "He was bad before bad was good," remembers top trainer George Benton.

In 1963, Carter knocked out Emile Griffith but was outpointed by Joey Giardello in a title fight in 1964. The fight with Giardello was delayed and switched from Las Vegas to Philadelphia. There was no disputing the points loss. "I had a bad night," conceded Carter. The first round knock out of Griffith was different. It remains one of only two stoppages in Griffith's career total of 112 fights. "I told Emile to be careful because I knew Rubin could punch but Emile got carried away, listened to Rocky Graziano, and went and got knocked flat with a right," remembers Griffith's loyal trainer Gil Clancy.

▲ **SINGING FOR THE HURRICANE**
Bob Dylan and Joan Baez perform at a benefit evening to raise funds for the release of Carter and John Artis in 1975. Ali was another strong supporter of Carter.

Carter entered his living hell on the night of June 16 when he parked his distinctive white Dodge outside the Nite Spot in Paterson, New Jersey. Twelve blocks away, at the Lafayette Bar and Grill, two customers and the bartender were brutally murdered at about the same time. Carter had not been in the Lafayette, but was stopped as he drove home from the Nite Spot with John Artis, a young track star. The police were looking for two black men in a white car and they fitted the description.

"I thought it was just harassment. They told us to follow them. We did. There were several cars and the police were leaning out through the windows with shotguns pointing at us. We drove to a bar, a bar I'd never even heard of. They told us to get out. There were a lot of people crying and standing around and I started to get a bad feeling. It was like a lynching," remembered Carter.

It was just the start of Carter's problems, the first steps that would lead to him spending nearly 20 years in prison. Carter and Artis were convicted of the crimes. It was a travesty from the start.

"I was isolated a long time before the murders. In 1964 I spoke out after the Harlem fruit riots, when New York police killed a little black child, and I spoke out and said black people ought to have died in the street protecting their children. Instead they were forced to watch by police holding guns on them as the children were shot. On June 17, 1966, they finally put the handles on me," said Carter. There had been negotiations for Carter to challenge Dick Tiger for the middleweight title in early 1966 and 10 days before the murders took place, Griffith had beaten Tiger for the championship.

In March 1976 Carter and Artis were released on bail after a campaign for their freedom. Ali picked Carter up from Trenton State Prison, but on December 22 Carter and Artis were reconvicted.

Artis was released in 1981 and Carter in November 1985. There was no bail. The game was over for the New Jersey officials. In August 1987 the original conviction was thrown out by United States Supreme Court of Appeals. However, it was not until February 1988 that a judge in Passaic county formally dismissed the indictments. Carter has never received a cent in compensation, or an apology. To this day he will not even fly over New Jersey. He left for Canada in March 1988, a free man, and still lives in Toronto.

▲ **A MEAN FIGHTER** *"There was a way that I did things back then that was different ... I went to the ring with the bad intentions of an angry man."*

Folley was a shadow that Ali left floating on the canvas

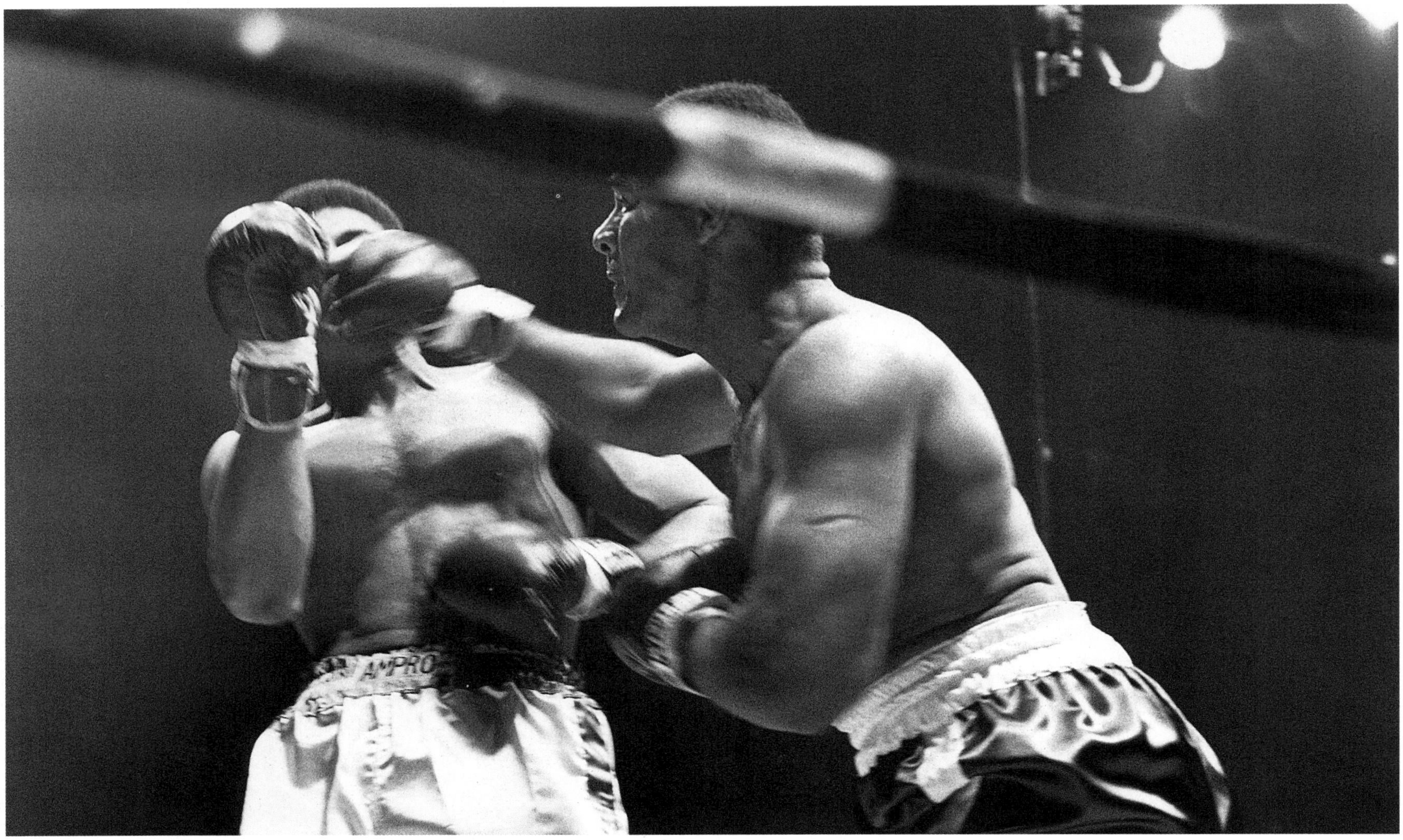

▲ **THE LAST FIGHT**

Ali knew that beating Folley was not his real problem. He won in round seven with a perfect right that stunned the veteran's senses.

Ali had the war in Vietnam on his mind when he sent Zora Folley into oblivion in round seven in front of nearly 14,000 people at Madison Square Garden. The date was March 22, 1967 and Ali would not fight again until October 1970.

He embraced Folley at the end. He liked the veteran. "I don't remember much about the last round, but I don't have to be ashamed at being beaten by a man like Clay – I mean Muhammad Ali," said Folley.

On April 28, 1967, Ali arrived for induction in Houston. He refused to step forward on religious grounds. On May 8 he was indicted by a federal grand jury in Houston and released on $5,000 bail on the condition that he did not leave the United States. In June 1967 the New York State Athletic Commission suspended his license to box. Other commissions followed. Muhammad Ali was still champion, but there was not a ring for him to fight in.

After refusing to be inducted, Ali gave the media a statement that ended: "There is an alternative, and that alternative is justice. If justice prevails, if my constitutional rights are upheld, I will be forced to go neither to the Army nor jail. In the end, I am confident that justice will come my way, for the truth must eventually prevail."

◀ GYM PERFECT

Ali skips in training under the watchful eye of Angelo Dundee. "When Muhammad was in the gym he concentrated on the job. He could still talk, boy could he talk, but he worked and worked," said Dundee. Most training sessions were attended by the press and other members of the public.

▲ A FOCUSED FIGHTER

Ali in training. "Ali is quicker than Marciano, hits as hard as Patterson. All he needs now is a little more brain behind his punches," said Archie Moore in 1963.

▶ A VICTIM OF WAR

Ali acknowledges his fans as he arrives at the Army Induction Center in Houston. He never went to war and he never went to prison, but he did lose what could have been his finest years as a boxer.

"Sweat in the gym, don't bleed in the street" – a sign in Frazier's gym

In the mid-1960s Joe Frazier arrived on the professional scene fresh from Olympic glory. He was not the type of boxer who ever wanted to be in another fighter's shadow, but when Ali was forced out of boxing, there was no other alternative for Smokin' Joe. "He knows I would have fought him then before he lost his title, before the war went and ruined it for me," said Frazier, who had stopped Chuvalo in four rounds one year after Ali had gone the full route of 15. Frazier pulled out of a World Boxing Association tournament involving Jerry Quarry, Oscar Bonavena, Jimmy Ellis, Thad Spencer, Karl Mildenberger, Terrell and Floyd Patterson. In March 1968, however, Frazier landed a chilling left hook to knockout Buster Mathis and win the World Boxing Council and New York version. In February 1969 he landed a similar punch to ruin Ali's old sparring partner Jimmy Ellis, who at the time was the WBA's champion. Ellis, a one-time middleweight who had once lost to Rubin Carter, was pulled out by Angelo Dundee at the end of the fourth.

Ali was still the people's champion, but his exile was in its third year and Frazier was the obvious number-one contender. In late 1969 and early 1970 Frazier spoke out on behalf of Ali to various commissions and the two sanctioning organizations. It was act of kindness that Frazier insists Ali forgot when he was eventually allowed to fight again. It was the start of a bitter and bloody feud between the two fighters that would last many years.

◀ THE NEW CHAMPION

"I had to get Ali back. I needed to beat him to shut him up and get people off my back," said Frazier. He won the title in 1968 but had to wait until 1971 for his chance at Ali.

▲ **JOE'S QUARRY**

Jerry Quarry has his face altered by one of Frazier's famous left hooks. Frazier stopped Quarry in seven rounds when they met for the first time in 1969.

◀ **ALI'S OLD SPARRING PARTNER**

Jimmy Ellis was the WBA champion at one time. When the pair met in 1971, Ali won in the 12th round.

THE OTHER SIDE OF BOXING

THE ALPHABET BOYS DO BATTLE

Jose Sulaiman was first elected WBC president in 1975. "I am a friend of Don King and I say that with respect," Sulaiman commented, but his critics insist the "friendship" has been bad for the sport. There has been a problem with the unification of titles since the birth of modern boxing, and before 1962 world championships were often split. There were years when New York, Pennsylvania or Britain recognized rival fighters as world champions. Disputes are, however, not unique to modern boxing.

In 1922 the National Boxing Association was formed in New York and fighters like Sugar Ray Robinson fought for their title. However, in 1962 the NBA became the World Boxing Association (WBA), followed in 1963 by the formation of the World Boxing Council (WBC). The two organizations remain fierce opponents.

The 1964 battle started between the two sanctioning bodies when the WBA stripped Ali after the first Liston fight, and Ernie Terrell beat Machen for the vacant title. Times have not changed, and by 1997 there were 10 rival organizations sanctioning championship fights on different television networks!

Foster's perfect left hook signaled the beginning of his reign

▲ **FOSTER IN CHARGE**
Dick Tiger lies at the feet of Bob Foster after being knocked out in their 1968 bout at Madison Square Garden. "I knew it was a good shot and I could see that he was not getting up but I still had to look. I was the champion, the new world champion," said Foster.

After a low-key decade the light-heavyweight division was salvaged by the slow, long overdue emergence of Bob Foster. He won the title in 1968 when a perfect left hook sent Dick Tiger to the canvas for the full count in round four.

Foster had been a pro since 1961 and had fought heavyweights to stay busy. He twice stepped in at short notice against top heavyweights, once in 1962 when Doug Jones stopped him in eight and again in 1964 when Terrell needed one round less. He lost a points decision to Folley in 1965 and quit in frustration for a short time.

In 1970, after four defenses, Foster was back with the heavyweights and matched against Frazier for the title. In the first round Foster succeeded in hurting Frazier with a right but two left hooks from Frazier did the damage and Foster was stopped. He got up once but the final one left him out cold. In 1974 Foster retired after a drawn title defense. Sadly, he made a comeback but was stopped twice in 1978 before retiring for good. He was unbeaten light-heavyweight champion for six years and made 14 defenses.

By the time Frazier knocked out Foster in November 1970 his former friend Ali was back in the ring. The two fighters were on a mission.

◄ **A CHALLENGED MAN**
Bob Foster, the champion from Albuquerque, New Mexico, prepares for his fight against Britain's Chris Finnegan in 1972. In 1962 and 1964 Foster had met quality heavyweights and lost.

▶ **THE WEIGH-IN**
Chris Finnegan shakes hands with Bob Foster prior to their 1972 fight at Wembley in London. In 1970, Foster was beaten in two rounds by Frazier in a bold challenge for the world title and in 1972 Ali finished him in eight rounds.

▼ **BATTLE COMMENCES**
Finnegan and Foster slug it out. Finnegan was brilliant but Foster blocked, countered and stayed. In round 14 it was over. "He hit me with something that should be illegal," said Finnegan afterward.

Ali emerged from his exile and people gathered to praise and condemn

▲ **ALI'S COMEBACK**

Ali connects with a right in the first round of his bout with Jerry Quarry. Ali had last fought in April 1967. "No man is sure he does not need to fight again," Ali had commented before the fight.

Ali was at a secret retreat in Atlanta in the weeks before his return in October 1970. After a long and costly campaign to get his license back he was keeping a low profile.

He watched hours and hours of Jack Johnson tapes. He possibly realized that the gap of 43 months would leave him a slower fighter and watching Johnson time his attacks from the ropes must have given him ideas. "At the start we had to learn a little each day with Ali and each fight I saw things. It was the same before the first fight back after the break," remembers Dundee.

There was a public sparring session at Morehouse College, in Atlanta, in September 1970. On October 26 he met Jerry Quarry. The atmosphere in Atlanta was bewildering – Ali was back after so long and there had been so much change. He was now a martyr and hero to millions.

Expectation was high and Ali delivered as he had in the past and as he would countless times during the next decade. He beat Quarry on a third round cut, but the fight was a harsh and hard reminder to Ali that he was no longer young. His legs ached more than they ever had, and his knuckle joints were sore after the shots of cortisone – needed to counteract bursitis – had worn off. The Greatest was back, but he was different, and Joe Frazier was desperate to prove that Ali was all washed-up.

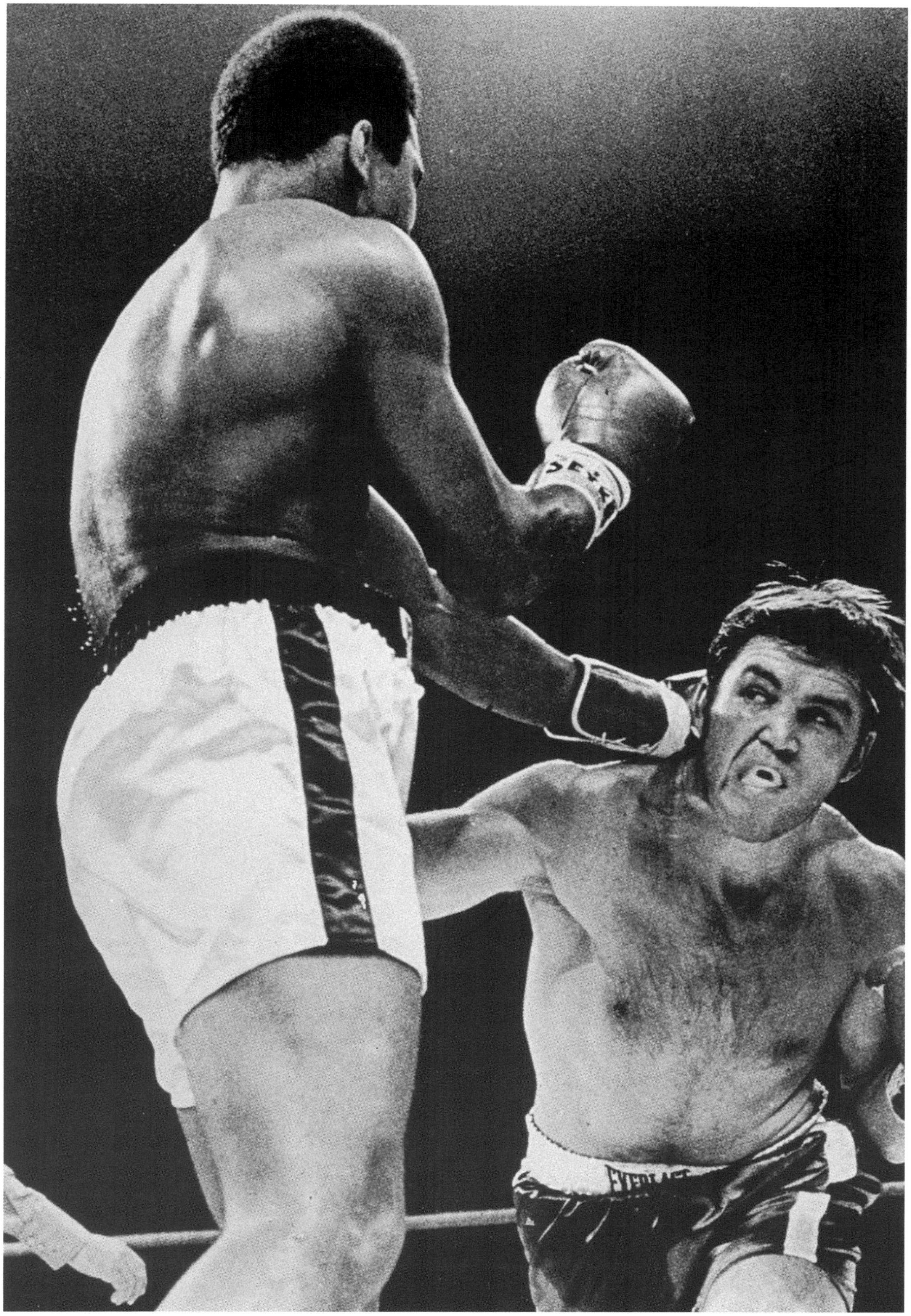

◀ **ALI'S BACK AND ON FORM**
Quarry went down under Ali's relentless assault. In round three it was all over and Ali was back. Many years later Mike Tyson returned to the ring from a very different kind of exile.

▲ **THE GREATEST IS BACK**
Ali had disposed of Quarry in fairly comfortable style, but the real test for him would come the following year, in the first of his three epic encounters with Joe Frazier.

The RETURN *of Ali*

1971-1980

▲ **THE LAST WARNING**
Ali meets with the press at Orly Airport in Paris en route for his fight with George Foreman in Zaire. "You better listen to what I say," he warned. Behind him Don King was laughing.

Muhammad Ali lost to Joe Frazier and George Foreman beat Frazier, but he couldn't beat Ali. "I kept telling him he had no punch, he swings like a sissy and then I knocked him out. I told you all I would and you never listened," said Ali. He was right, few people listened or believed.

FOREVER KINGS

Times changed. After Muhammad Ali returned to the ring against Jerry Quarry in 1970 he met Oscar Bonavena. Ali won both fights but it was a different Ali – a stronger, slower, wiser Ali. Was he better? Critics and fans remain divided. Angelo Dundee maintains that the best of Ali was lost in his three-and-- half-year exile. It makes no difference, because by late 1970 Joe Frazier was the champion and he was clearly more than just a temporary resident.

Ali and Frazier was a natural fight to make. The pair met at Madison Square Garden in March 1971, in a fight that would forever change the position of boxing in society. It was more than just the first heavyweight championship meeting between two unbeaten fighters – it was dubbed The Fight of the Century. Ali's taunting of Frazier helped create the scene.

There was only one winner in the ring on that night and it was Smokin' Joe, but after Ali lifted himself up from the knockdown in the last round he went on to create boxing history again and again. Part of that history would see him go on to beat Frazier on two occasions.

"I couldn't be what I am without him and he couldn't be what he is without me," said Ali, after beating Frazier in the Thrilla' in Manila in 1975. The fight was arguably the best heavyweight bout in boxing's history. It was also the last great performance by either man.

Even before Ali and Frazier fought for the first time, the presence of George Foreman on boxing's horizon proved an ominous sight. The young Foreman, who jabbed and smashed his way past George Chuvalo in 1970, was one of the best heavyweight prospects ever. His jab, a feature of his boxing style so often overlooked by commentators, ruined Chuvalo.

Foreman won the title in 1973 and his raw power came to rule the division and dominate the sport, until one night in the jungles of Zaire, when Ali beat him

◀ **COOL DAYS FOR ALI**
Previous page: The victorious champion relaxes after beating his arch-rival Joe Frazier in January 1974.

and became the Greatest. When Foreman won and again when he lost, Donald King was right there – the best-known unknown, unattached at the time but connected to everybody.

In addition to Foreman, there were other fighters like Jerry Quarry, Earnie Shavers and Ken Norton waiting for their chance. In the late 1970s Larry Holmes, a former Ali sparring partner, and the unfortunate Neon Leon Spinks emerged on the scene. The 1970s was heavyweight boxing's greatest decade.

The 12 top heavyweights that were fighting at the start of the 1980s were talented but, like Neon Leon, many wasted their talents and several ended up addicted to cocaine. They were a lost generation of fighters and a brutal contrast to the men who will remain champions forever. Holmes, who started fighting under the nickname Black Cloud, was the glorious exception and belongs in the company of Frazier, Foreman and Ali.

The heavyweights came close to eclipsing the other weights in the 1970s but the quality of the champions in all divisions was so good that not even Ali could overshadow all the other greats. From Bob Foster all the way down to the fearsome Z-men – Carlos Zarate and Alfonso Zamora – the 1970s produced some of the best pound-for-pound fighters in history. Jose Napoles, Antonio Cervantes, Wilfredo Gomez, Carlos Monzon, Ruben Olivares, Alexis Arguello, Wilfred Benitez and Roberto Duran all won titles during a decade of brilliance. By 1979 Sugar Ray Leonard had won his first title. It was Leonard and his opponents who would shape the next decade.

One fight in 1977 is a perfect example of the type of quality fighter that was around toward the end of the 1970s. In April, Carlos Zarate, the WBC bantamweight champion, met another Mexican, Alfonso Zamora, who held the WBA version, in Los Angeles. Zarate was unbeaten in 38 fights with 37 stoppages and Zamora had a perfect record of 29 wins with 29 stoppages or knockouts. There were no titles at stake, just too much pride and the fight was made two pounds above the limit. Zarate won in four. Zamora was never the same again and lost his title in his next fight. Zarate was stopped the following year when he challenged Wilfredo Gomez for the WBC super-bantamweight title.

The saddest event of the 1970s was undoubtedly the death of Sonny Liston in January 1971. He had been dead for several days before he was found in his Las Vegas apartment. Police reports said there was heroin on a kitchen table and needle marks in his arm. It was the end that many people expected, but loyal friends denied it was self-inflicted. "Sonny hated needles. He never killed himself," insisted Johnny Tocco, the Las Vegas trainer whose gym became one of the most famous in the world. His death is still a mystery. Liston is buried out by the airport in Las Vegas, his simple plot a scene of regular homage.

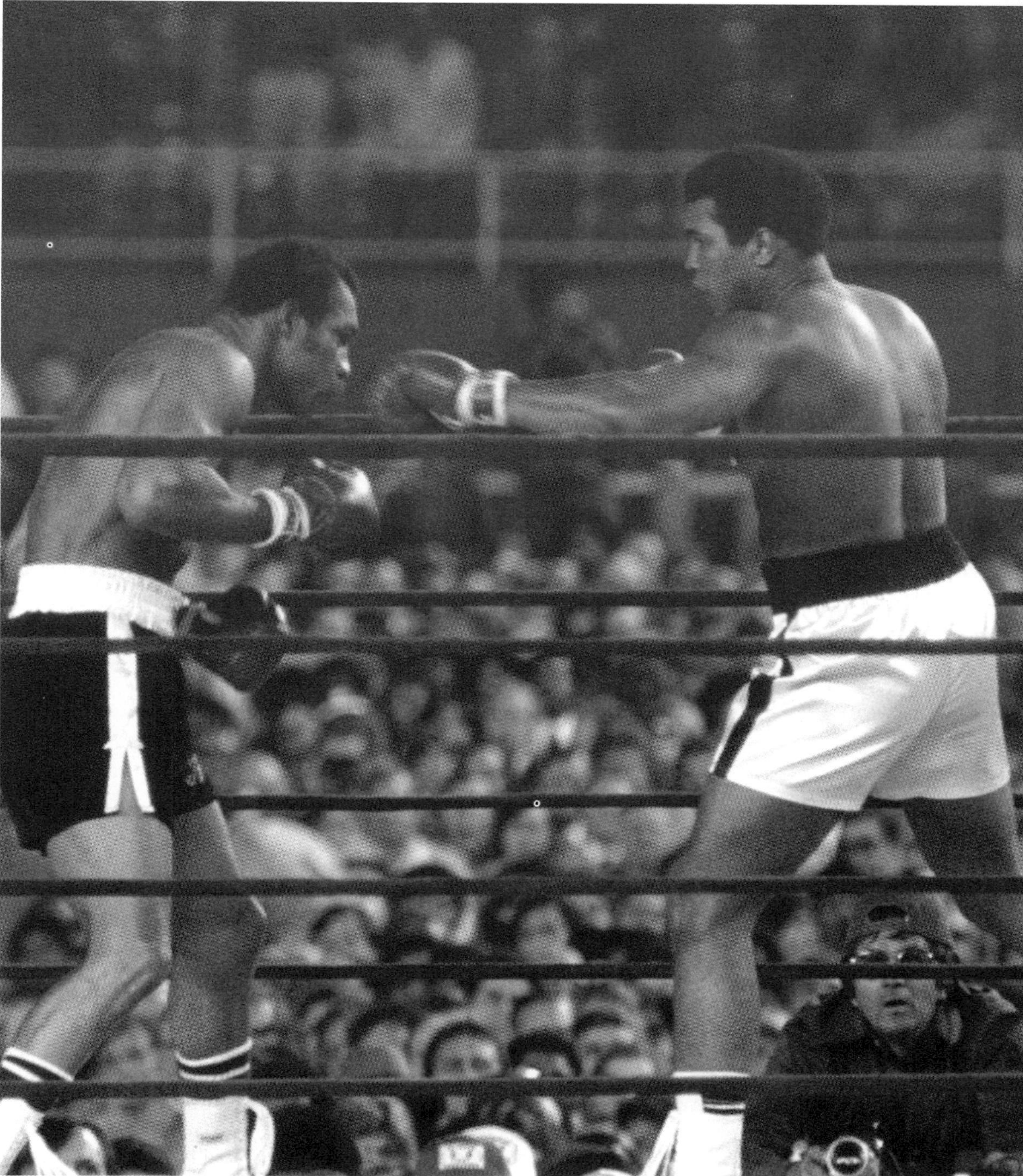

▲ **A TOUGH FIGHTER**

Ali had trouble with Ken Norton. They met three times, went 39 rounds and every round was tight. "I knew what to do and I never listened to his mouth," said Norton.

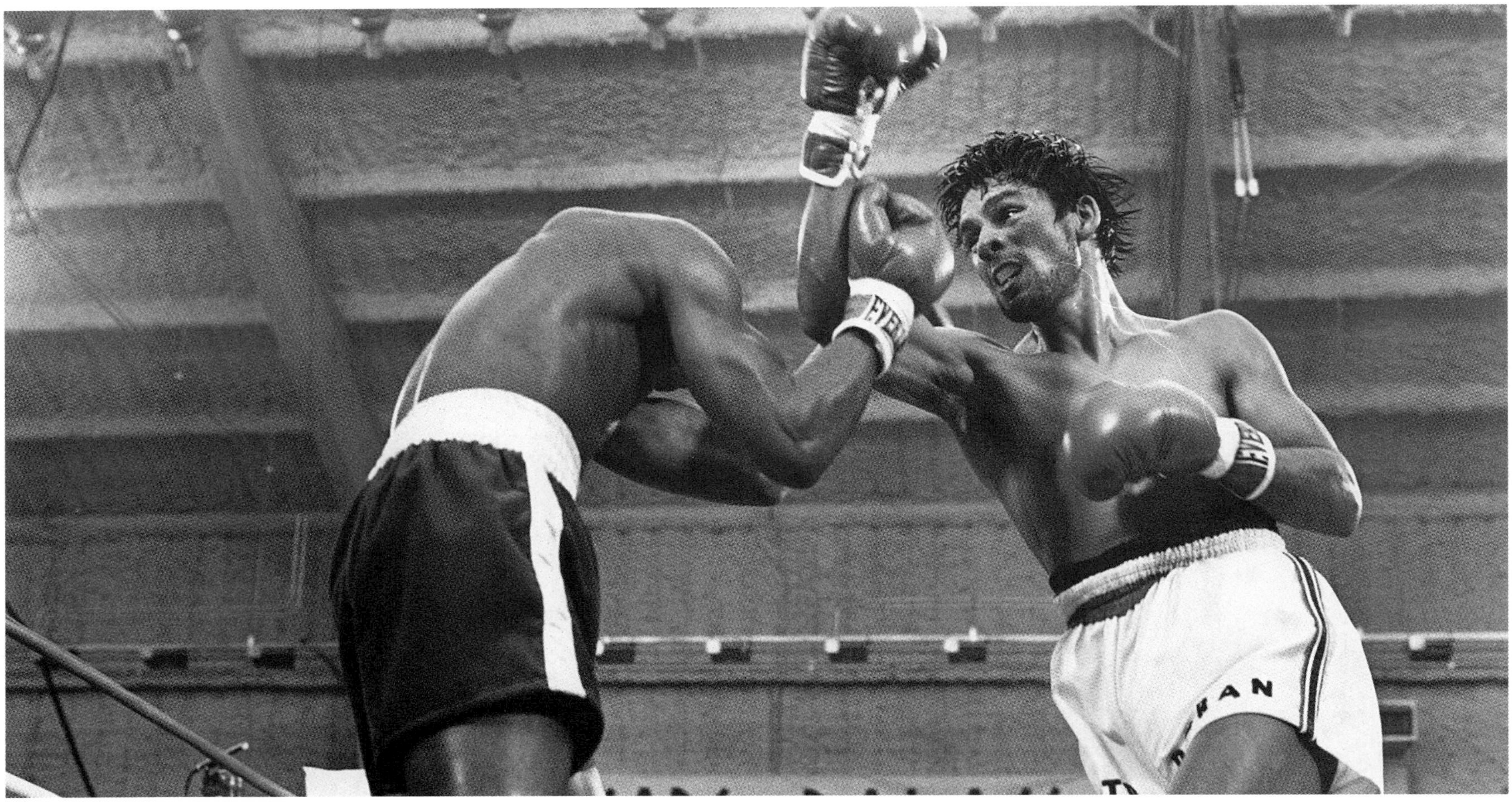

Duran was a born fighter – a hungry kid who had a talent for boxing

▲ **THE PERFECT FIGHTER**
Duran has Esteban De Jesus under pressure in their 1978 unified world lightweight title fight. De Jesus had beaten Duran in a non-title fight in 1972, but it was eight years until Duran's next loss – in 1980 against Sugar Ray Leonard.

When the Scot Ken Buchanan beat Ismael Laguna to win the lightweight championship of the world, the British Boxing Board of Control did not recognize his victory. However, in New York, the canny Scottish stylist was an Madison Square Garden favorite.

In June 1972 he defended against Roberto Duran, then known as Rocky but soon to be known as Manos de Piedras – the Hands of Stone. Duran was just a street kid from Panama but he was a natural fighter, as trainer Ray Arcel found out when he started to work with him. Arcel was in his fifth decade as a trainer. "I never had to tell Duran how to fight," he said.

Before the fight at the Garden was 20 seconds old Buchanan was on the floor from a glancing right uppercut. As each round passed and the bagpipes played in a desperate attempt to stir Buchanan, a classic encounter unfolded. Duran was relentless, but Buchanan was terrific as he tried to keep his boxing together and ignore his challenger's head, which was pushed under his chin, forcing him back in each and every round.

It was over after the bell sounded in round 13 when Duran landed a low blow. It was controversial – still is – but Buchanan was on the canvas and Duran was the new champion. Buchanan told the referee, Johnny LoBianco, he could continue but it was over. Duran went on to become a legend, one of the true greats. Buchanan, on the other hand, ended his career boxing in unlicensed shows in London, still adamant that Duran had robbed him.

◀ THE AGONY IS CLEAR

Ken Buchanan holds his groin in agony after a low punch from Duran. Buchanan never forgave Duran and Duran never forgot Buchanan. "He was my best opponent," Duran always claimed.

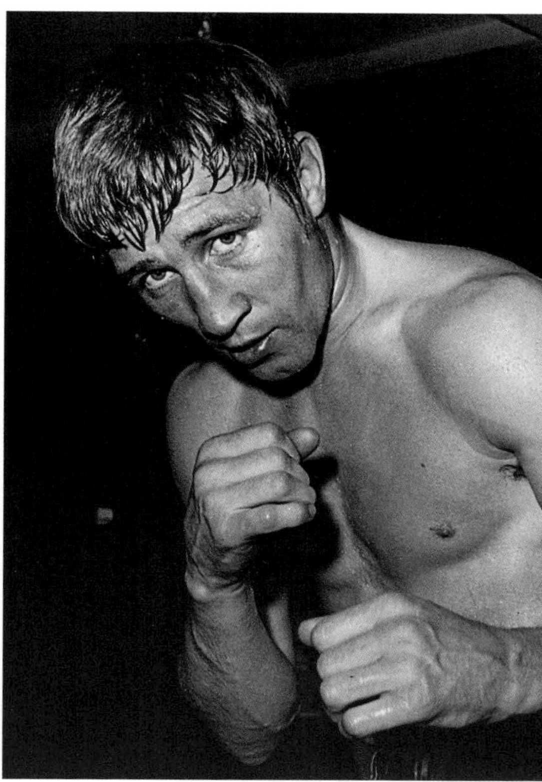

▲ A NEW YORK FAVORITE

Buchanan remained popular in New York after the Duran loss, but there was no rematch. In 1975 Buchanan lost on points in a challenge for Guts Ishimatsu's WBC lightweight title.

Quarry was burdened with the spurious accolade of being a great white hope

▶ POPULAR QUARRY

Jerry Quarry was praised by the men he fought and the men he missed. His slow decline and his many sad comebacks have tainted the achievements of his early career, when he was one of the best.

When Jerry Quarry lost his unbeaten record to Eddie Machen in 1966, Rocky Marciano left the ringside before the decision. Marciano had planned to pay $100,000 for Quarry's contract.

Quarry kept fighting and became one of the best white heavyweights. His wins are not as impressive as some of his defeats – he lost twice to Ali, twice to Frazier and once to Norton. In 1973, however, he knocked out Earnie Shavers in one round.

"Jerry was the best fighter in the world who never became a champion," claimed Foreman. In 1973, when Quarry should have fought Foreman, he was rated fourth in the heavyweight division behind Ali, Frazier and Norton.

Life with Quarry was never dull. He fought and lived the same way, on the precipice with his heart out on his sleeve. The night he knocked Thad Spencer all over the ring before taking him out in 12 was typical gutsy Quarry. Spencer had beaten Ernie Terrell and this made the win even sweeter.

It was easy to predict that Quarry would fight too long and take too many punches. After a comeback in the 1980s and one fight in 1990, it was revealed in 1996 that he was in a dreadful state. His brother, James, cares for him and he survives on $560 a month in welfare payments. The story of his brave battle was not a shock to anybody who witnessed Quarry's earlier bravery in a division touched by greatness.

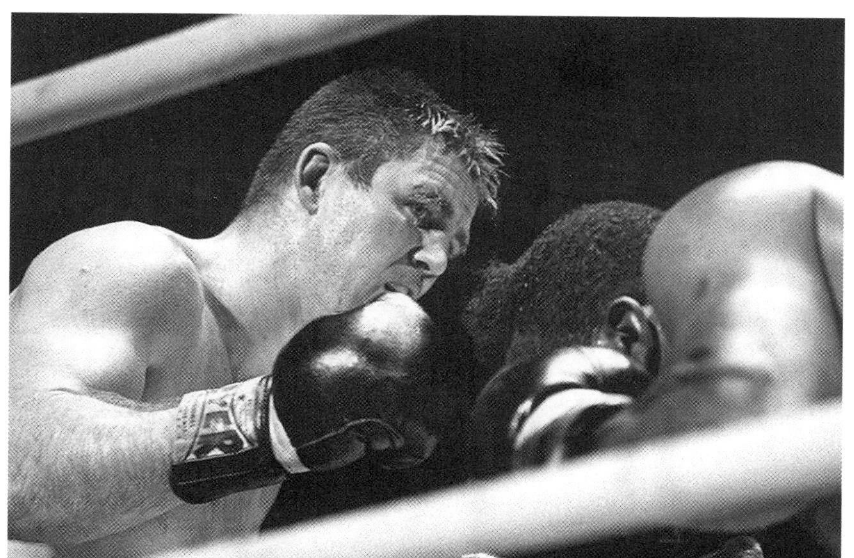

◀ NEVER AN EASY FIGHT

Quarry was cut on his right eyebrow in the first of his two fights with Floyd Patterson in 1967. The first was a draw and Patterson won the rematch.

▼ANOTHER BLOODY CUT

Quarry protects his cut right eye from Joe Frazier's punches in their 1969 title bout at Madison Square Garden. The cut continued to open and the fight was finally stopped in round seven. When the two met again in 1974 Frazier stopped Quarry in the fifth round.

▲ HARD TIMES

Quarry would tell people that his life was like fiction. "It is the Grapes of Wrath – we had nothing," he said.

"It was a privilege to ... be associated with the fight" – ref. Arthur Mercante

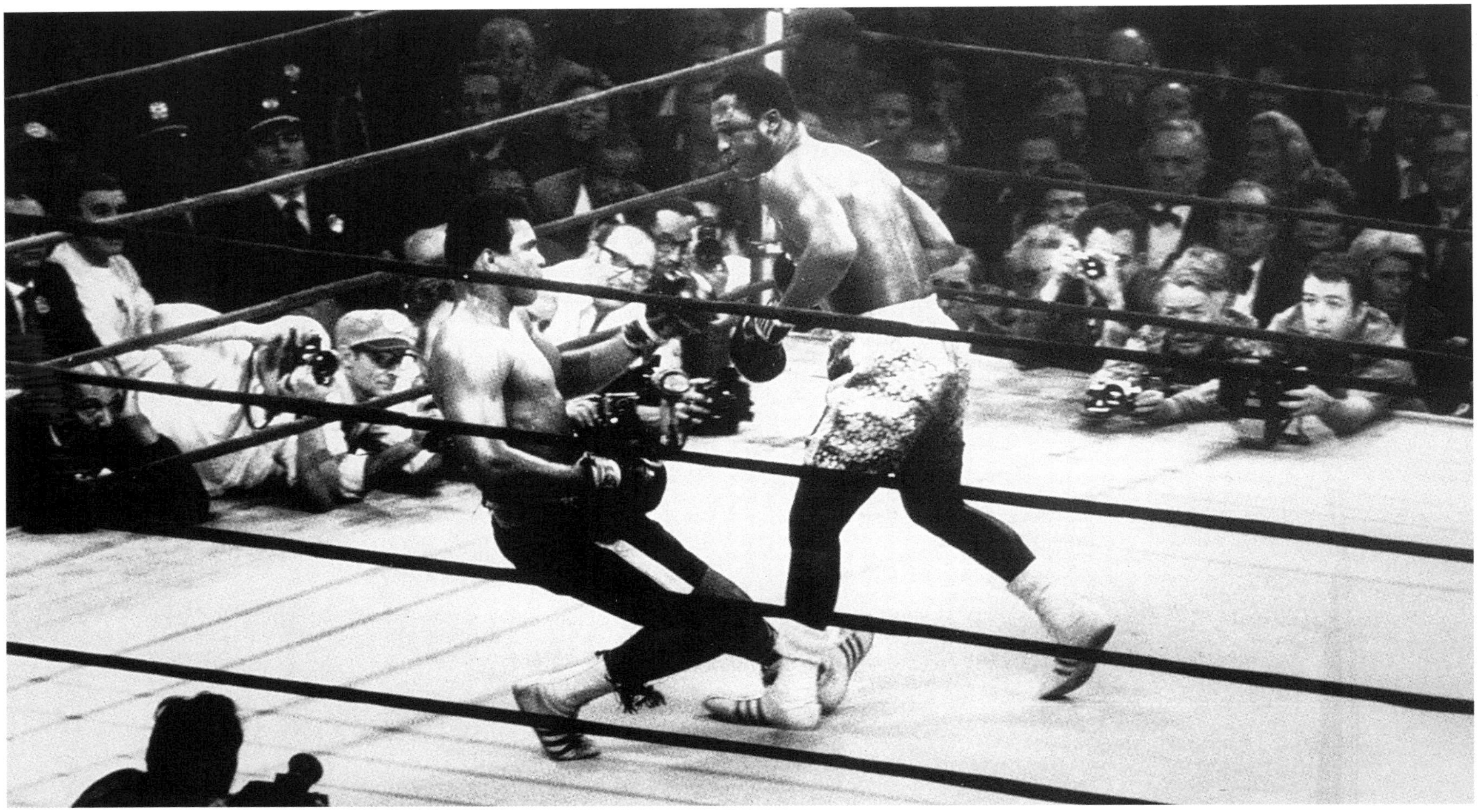

▲ FRAZIER'S TRIUMPH

In round 15 Frazier's left hook connected and Ali fell to earth for a moment. "I thought Ali underestimated me, and that in part cost him the fight," said Frazier. "Joe kept all the pressure inside before the fight," claimed Eddie Futch.

The venue was Madison Square Garden, the date March 8, 1971 and the two men making history were Joe Frazier and Muhammad Ali. It was quite simply The Fight of the Century.

In the months before the contest Frazier was guarded by 12 detectives following death threats and on the day of the fight the crowds outside the Garden were so big that Ali remained on the premises after it was all over. Frank Sinatra took pictures at ringside for *Life* magazine. It was an event that changed boxing and sport in general.

"On the night Joe was a machine of destruction," said Eddie Futch. He was. In round 11 Ali was caught and hurt. He rallied, as he would do so many times during the remainder of his career. "I don't know how he survived the 11th round. It was remarkable," said Dundee. But in round 15 of the most incredible fight ever seen, a precise left hook landed flush on the side of Ali's jaw and he was over. He regained his feet, survived until the bell but he was no longer the champion. What an end.

Frazier's blood-smeared lips parted and a malevolent grin crossed his face as he walked away from Ali after the punch dropped the former champion.

The two fighters had entered the ring with perfect records: Frazier had won 26 and Ali 31. The numbers changed during the 15 rounds, but it was the impact of the occasion that would forever link the two boxers with an event that changed the way people viewed the sport of boxing.

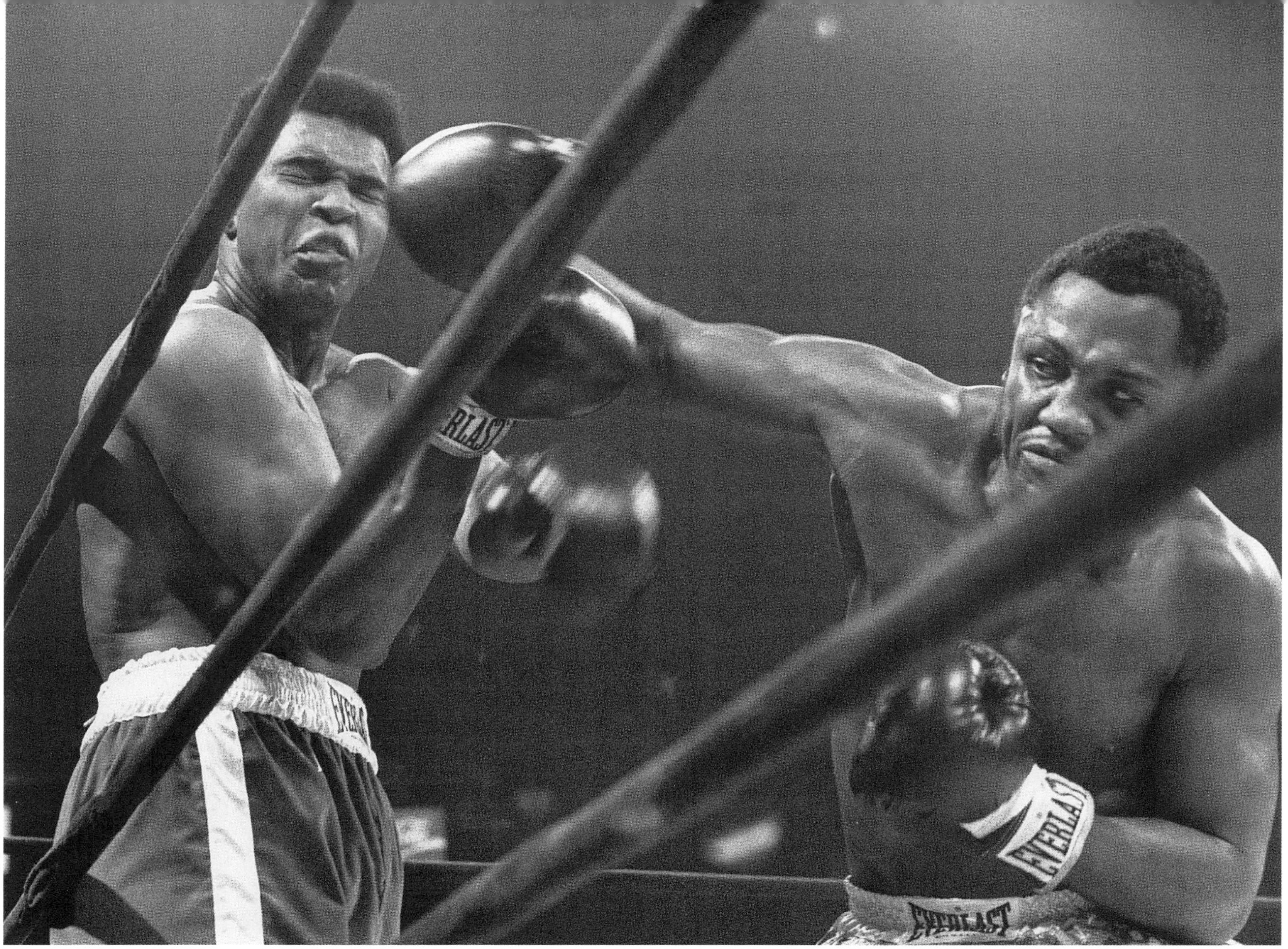

▲ AGAINST THE ROPES

With Ali on the ropes, Frazier connects with a right. "He must be crazy to stay against the ropes like that. It was foolish and it didn't make any sense," said Frazier. Three years later Ali used a similar method against George Foreman, but with much more success.

◄ SIMPLE PLAN IGNORED

"I would have preferred it had Ali moved about the ring and jabbed as everybody knows he can, but you know him, he always does what he likes," Dundee said after the fight.

JOE FRAZIER

Frazier's Dark Mood Rules his Head

▼ A NORMAL DAY IN THE RING
Frazier's left eye is closed after beating Britain's Joe Bugner in London in 1973. Frazier was chasing the title he had lost to Foreman six months earlier.

Joe Frazier remembers the moment he made Ali stop dancing. It was in round four after a left, and from that moment until the final bell, including the three seconds Ali was on the floor in the 15th round, boxing changed.

Joe has never forgotten. Today he lives in a luxury apartment above the gym on North Broad Street in Philadelphia that he used to prepare for all the important fights of his career. It is the same gym where Ali and Frazier first argued during a publicity photo-session for their fight.

The resentment between the two men is as fierce as ever and during an impromptu appearance at the Atlanta Olympics, Frazier was in an angry mood. His days as an apparently willing dummy to Ali's often loathsome mockery are at an end. "He (Ali) only cares about himself," Frazier said in Atlanta. "All I ever wanted that man to do was apologize to me. Just me and him in a room, man to man. He told my son Marvis that he never meant what he said about me but he never told me. He never did, he never told me sorry even after the last fight in Manila," said Frazier.

In Manila, Frazier was pulled out at the end of round 14 by Futch who uttered the memorable line: "Sit down, son. It's all over. No one will ever forget what you did here today." Futch was right.

However, it was the first fight with Ali that Frazier is best remembered for and the main photograph at the gym on North Broad Street is of Ali falling to earth during that first fight and Frazier, his own face bloated from punishment, starting to move to a neutral corner. The picture is possibly the most powerful image from boxing's finest hour.

The gym is a brick sanctuary for Frazier, a place full of his memories and illustrated with beautiful and unusual photographs of fighters. Frazier, the curator, calls it an "oasis on the street" but "not an answer to the streets." One photograph, measuring six feet by about 10, features Frazier and a dog running on a cold frosty morning. It is quite breathtaking, but the most alarming spirit in Frazier's fistic temple is Ali. His ghost is everywhere.

"Calling me gorilla and saying I'm the white man's champion. Hey, look in my corner; I got black men. Look in his corner and what you see? White men. Perhaps it was Ali had the problem. If I was a Tom for anybody, I was a Tom for Ali – I helped get him the license back. I was asked (by the sanctioning bodies) if they should give him his license back and I said 'Yes, I can beat him.' People can't tell me how I feel or what I feel. I was there dealing with it at the time," remembers Frazier.

When their first fight was over referee Arthur Mercante, who along with judges Arthur Aidala and Bill Recht, scored for Frazier, said by the closing seconds both fighters were obviously physically and emotionally drained.

"I had to be very careful," said Mercante, "or we would have finished the fight with both men on the floor. They held on to each other like drowning men. Had I separated them with vigor, both would have collapsed. I never before saw two heavyweights suffering so acutely from dual exhaustion." Ali was released from the hospital that night after checks on his jaw but Frazier later spent time in a Philadelphia hospital suffering from exhaustion.

▲ **THE YOUNG SAVIOUR** *After Frazier beat Ali his manager Yank Durham wanted him to quit. "Joe has done all that he wanted to do," he said.*

Foreman wins The Sunshine Showdown

▲ THE STARING MATCH
Frazier and Foreman size each other up at the weigh-in prior to their 1973 fight. Looks can be deceptive, however, and when the fighting started Frazier lost concentration and was punched round the ring by Foreman.

Joe Frazier was not a great champion after beating Ali. In 1972 he blasted Terry Daniels and Ron Stander, but they did not constitute real opposition.

In early January 1973 Futch arrived in Jamaica and found chaos in the gym in the weeks before Frazier's defense against Foreman. "I knew there was something wrong. Joe was sparring with Norton and there was no desire," said Futch, who gave Norton the rest of the time off. Frazier was treating the camp like a vacation. In another part of town Foreman and his trainer Dick Saddler, cousin of legendary featherweight Sandy, were in austere surroundings preparing for a real fight.

The Sunshine Showdown was one of the most savage heavyweight title fights between two quality boxers. The fight should have been far more even, but when the bell sounded Frazier looked lost. Foreman pushed him viciously from corner to corner and whacked away with powerful punches.

Frazier was over six times in less than two rounds. He fell, he crumpled and on one occasion the effects of two left hooks and a right uppercut lifted him clean off the canvas. Seldom has a deposed champion looked so sad and pathetic in defeat.

It was a stunning win and Foreman was carried from the ring by a triumphant group that included Don King, who held his head. King was not the promoter, just a fixer at the time, but he would famously recall how he had arrived with the old champion and left with the new one.

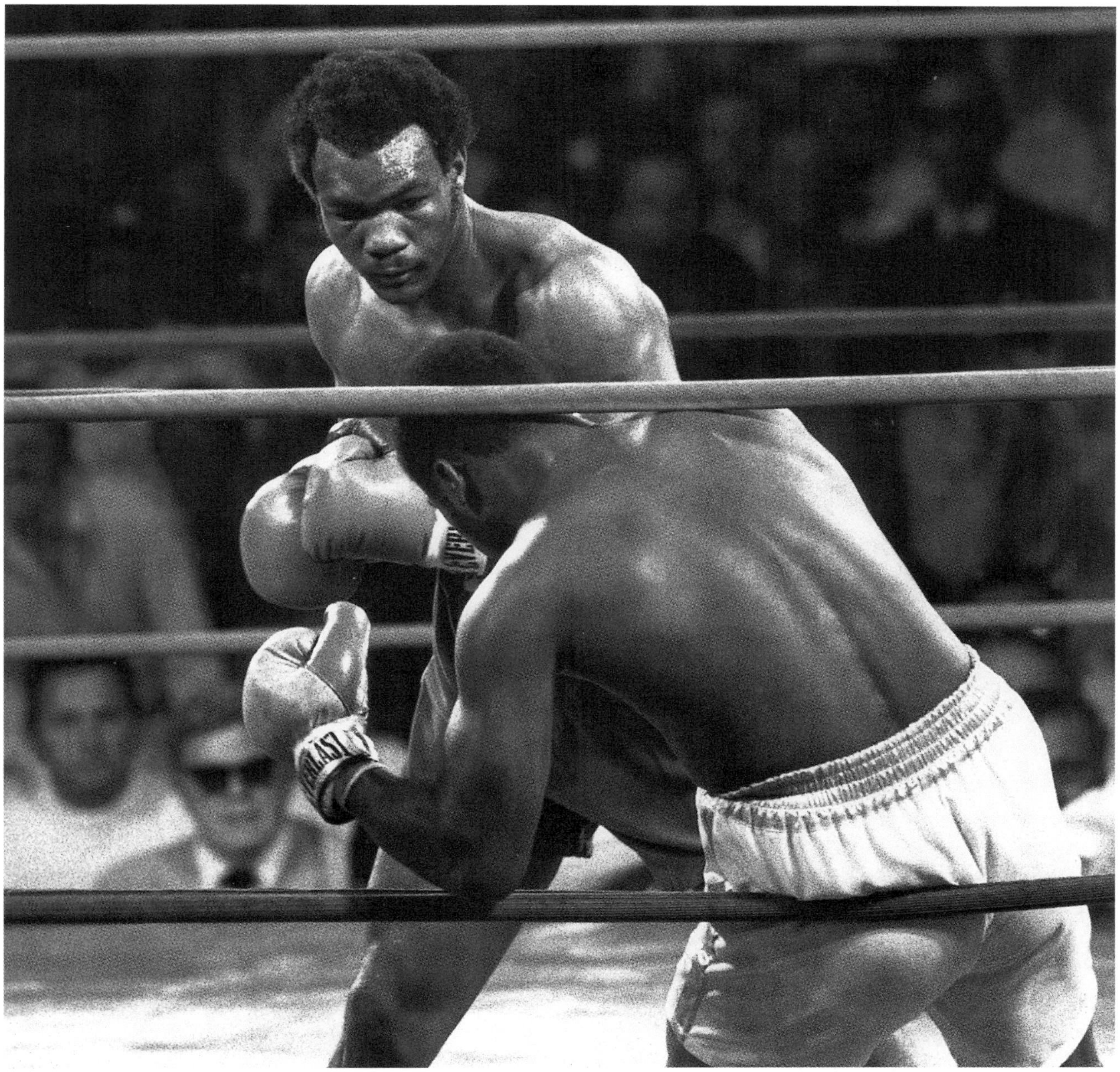

◀ **FRAZIER WAS HELPLESS**
Frazier's knees buckle in round two. "I fought a dumb fight," Frazier later admitted, "I kept getting up." During the final moments of the fight in round two Foreman shouted in desperation: "Stop it or I'm going to kill him."

▶ **THE MAN BOUNCED**
Frazier reels from one of Foreman's punches. "I could see that George had too much power and every time he landed Joe was in trouble and there was no way out from George's punches. No way," said Archie Moore, one of Foreman's cornermen.

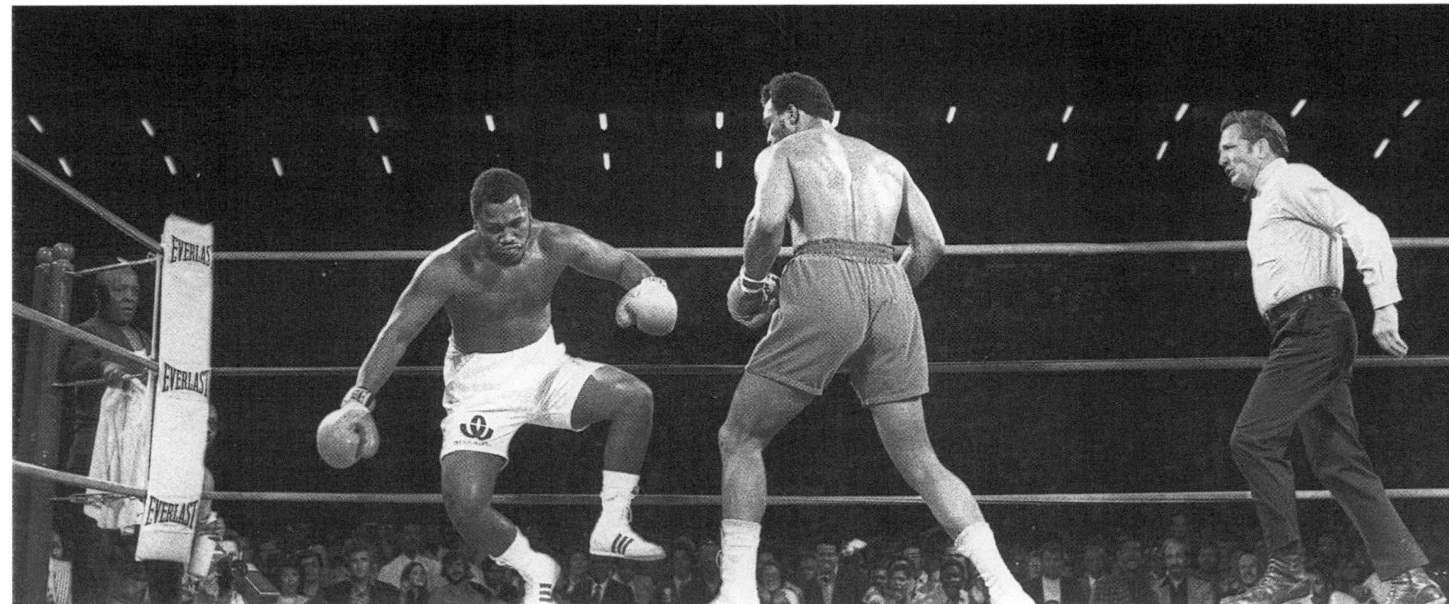

Other great fighters were ignored because of Ali, Foreman and Frazier

In late 1970 Jose Napoles briefly lost his welterweight title to Billy Backus because of a cut eye. When he won it back in the 1971 rematch, Backus's face was so badly swollen the doctor called the fight off. Napoles had a knack of making his punches look light when in reality they were powerful and accurate.

Napoles decided to step up in weight and fight Monzon for the middleweight title in 1974. It was risky, but it was a fight that he could possibly have won. Monzon was untouchable and stopped the Cuban-born fighter at the end of round six.

When Napoles finally lost his welterweight title to London's John H. Stracey in 1975 it was in Mexico City, where he had lived since leaving his wife and small baby in Cuba in 1961. In his two reigns as champion he made 13 defenses, including one against Emile Griffith, and ranks as one of the best welterweights in boxing's history. Just a few years earlier or a few years later and Napoles would have undoubtedly proved his class in a division that was in a slump during his peak.

Like Ken Buchanan and light-heavyweight champion John Conteh, whose career is one of the tragedies of modern British boxing, Stracey ended his boxing life with little more than memories from his moment of glory. His win over Napoles is one of the best ever by a British fighter, even if the champion was at the end of a great career.

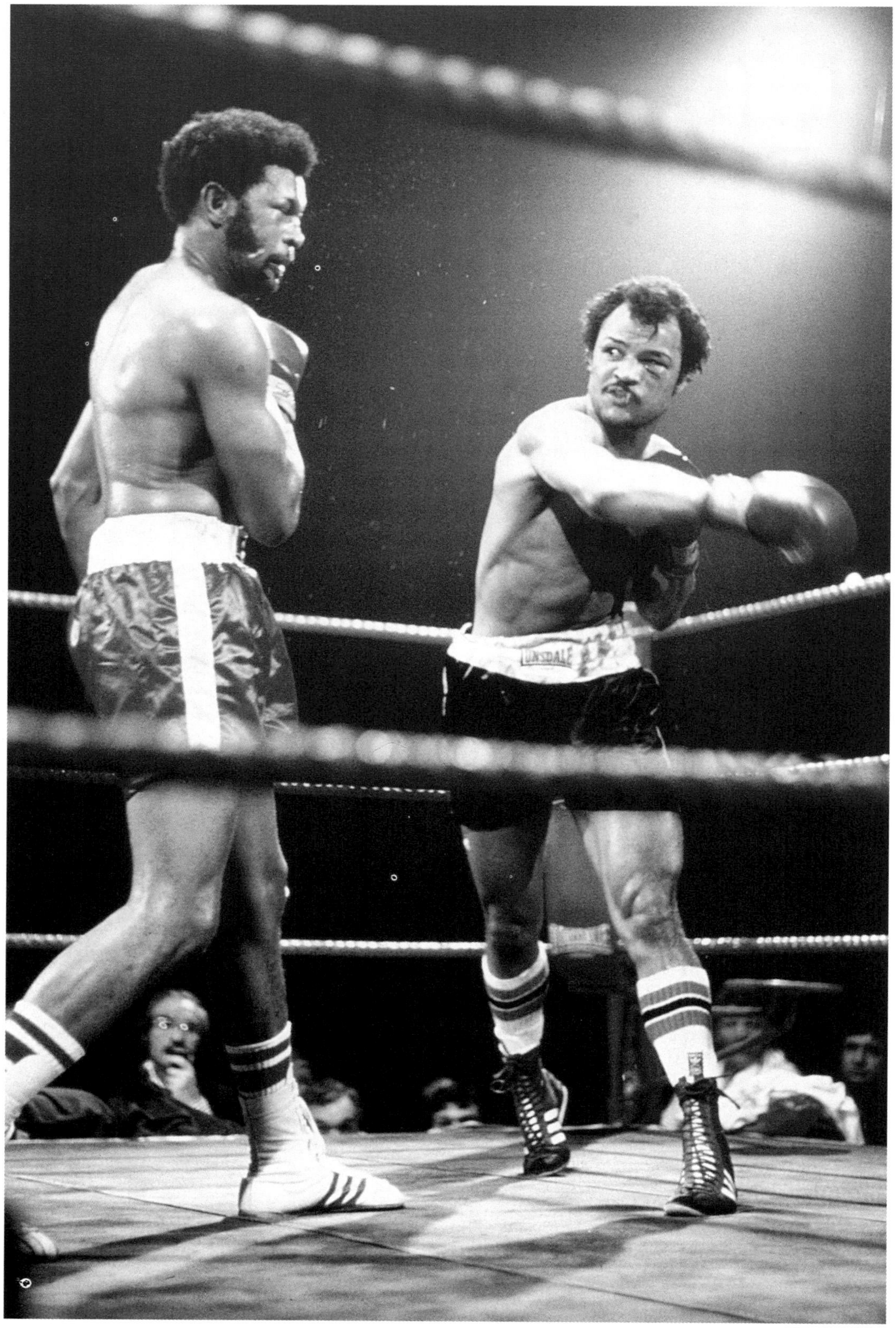

▶ **A BAD END**

John Conteh swings a right at Joe Cokes. Before Conteh won the world light-heavyweight title he acted like he was determined to wreck his career and ruin his life. "I did some stupid things, but had some great times," he said.

◀ THE SAD BOXER

Jose Napoles looks subdued, despite having just won the world title. Napoles had to leave behind his wife and child in Cuba and move to Mexico to continue his boxing career.

▼ A MEAN RECORD

Carlos Monzon never missed a beat in the ring. He lost just three times in 101 fights over a 14-year period.

▲ THE BULLRING STUNT

John H. Stracey took the welterweight title from Napoles in Mexico City in 1975. "I could hear the people chanting his name before I saw them. The fight was in a bullring and the fans had come to see Napoles tame me. They left unhappy, I'm pleased to say," commented Stracey.

Beneath the sunlit sky in California Olivares was a Mexican idol

▶ **NO EASY DROP**
Japan's Kazuyishi Kanazawa falls after a left from Ruben Olivares in their 1971 fight. Olivares retained his bantamweight title, knocking Kanazawa down three times in the 14th round.

▲ **CALIFORNIAN FAVORITE**
"When Olivares was in a fight at the Forum the word spread. He was loved by the people in Los Angeles," said promoter George Parnassus. The majority of his world title fights were in California.

When Ruben Olivares, the darling of the Mexicans in California, defended his WBA featherweight title against Nicaragua's Alexis Arguello in Los Angeles in November 1974, the Inglewood Forum was packed with nearly 14,000 hysterical fans.

A classic encounter was predicted. Olivares had twice held the world bantamweight title and Arguello had narrowly failed to win the featherweight championship in February 1974.

The fight lived up to the fan's expectations. Round seven was one of the best rounds and from that point Olivares started to come back until, by round 13, 22-year-old Arguello needed a knockout to win. At the end of round 12 Arguello was trapped in a corner and it looked like another title fight too early for him. In round 13, however, he landed his left hook – the shortest in boxing – to send Olivares down. The champion was badly hurt but clambered up. A right uppercut, another perfect punch, dropped him again and he was on his knees, trying to get up when the count of 10 was reached. It was one minute and 20 seconds into the 13th round.

Olivares won the WBC featherweight title the next year and fought for the last time in 1988, 19 years after he first won the title. Arguello won the super-feather and lightweight titles and continued to fight until 1995. A handsome boxer whose many early televised matches made him a popular fighter in America, Arguello is one of the sport's true greats, a living legend.

THE OTHER SIDE OF BOXING

JOHN CONTEH

THE BRITISH FIGHTER WHO LIKED TO PARTY

John Conteh was regarded as the best British fighter since Randolph Turpin when he beat Jorge Ahumada for the vacant WBC light-heavyweight title in 1974. Only four months earlier Ahumada had drawn with Bob Foster. Despite his early promise Conteh ended up with nothing. He listened to the wrong people and spent too much time in pursuit of pleasures away from the ring.

In 1977, after just three defenses, he was stripped of the title for pulling out of a fight. However, he narrowly lost a challenge to get it back when he was outpointed by Mate Parlov in 1978. In 1979 he lost another title fight, this time a desperately close decision to Matthew Saad Muhammad for his old belt in Atlantic City. Both Parlov and Muhammad were saved from defeat by dubious substances that healed their cut eyebrows. There was a rematch with Muhammad, but it ended in four rounds and Conteh's career was over.

WEIGHT TAKES ITS TOLL
Rafael Herrera blocks a punch from fellow-Mexican Olivares in March 1972. Herrera won by an eighth-round knockout. Olivares had difficulty making the bantamweight limit and two years later won the featherweight title.

THE RUMBLE IN THE JUNGLE

Don King's Mad Dream

Ali knocked Foreman out in round eight to regain the heavyweight championship of the world in Kinshasa, Zaire, on October 30, 1974. It was the fight nobody believed would ever take place and an ending nobody thought possible.

The year before, the proposed bout dominated the hearts and minds of boxing's best hustlers. Foreman was champion and Ali was being ignored.

In early 1974, Don King, whose name never appeared on any posters or tickets for the fight, worked for Hank Schwartz, president of Video Techniques. King first persuaded Ali to fight Foreman for five million dollars but Ali wanted to see Foreman's name on a contract before he agreed to sign.

▲ **ALMIGHTY DON**

Promoter Don King was responsible for setting up the Rumble in the Jungle. A roadside sign in Zaire read "Ali-Foreman – you are our brothers. Let the best man win." King certainly won; it was the fight that established him.

King then pursued Foreman, who at the time was training for a defense against Norton at a gym in Oakland, California. King ambushed Foreman in the parking lot and after 90 minutes of dialogue Foreman signed three blank pieces of paper. Later the same day, Foreman's lawyers and King filled in the spaces. The fight had to be overseas because Foreman was in the middle of an expensive divorce.

King was in control of the chaos. He was brilliant. At that point, with both signatures on the contract but no venue and no money, the fight was still in doubt and time was running out before the first payments of $100,000 were due on February 15 and February 25. A letter of credit for 2.3 million dollars was due by March 15 and the final 2.5 million was due 90 days before the fight. The fighters could pull out if any deadline was missed.

In February 1974 Schwartz met with John Daly, a British film producer, in London. A bizarre series of events started to unfold as men like Fred Weyner, an international fixer who managed the Swiss bank accounts of Zaire's homicidal president Sèsè Sèko Mobuto, emerged at meetings. There was also Mobuto's other financial adviser, Modunga Bula, who was an exile in Belgium. The money was found through a company that was chartered in Panama, called Risnelia, but run in Zaire by Mobuto.

In March 1974 Foreman knocked Norton senseless in two rounds in Caracas. The Rumble in the Jungle was announced the next day. Ali was not thought to stand a chance. In the weeks before the fight, when the distant isolation of the setting threatened to drive everybody mad, Ali watched tapes of Foreman's disappointing points win over Gregorio Peralta.

Ali took Cus D'Amato's advice and hurt Foreman early in the fight. Foreman was tired by round seven. His punches had missed their target, Ali having absorbed the majority of them from his position on the ropes – a style instantly dubbed rope-a-dope. If Foreman had a plan, it was over by the start of round eight. He had no power left and when Ali taunted him Foreman lunged at him and found himself on the receiving end of a left and then a right to the head. When Foreman started to fall Ali was walking away, looking back in relief at what he had achieved.

Gene Kilroy, Ali's facilitator, remembers the mood on the night: "I went to see Foreman's hands being taped and he said: 'Tell your man he is going home in a body bag.' Archie Moore was there saying 'I smell death in the air'. I went back to Ali and he said: 'What that nigger say?' I told him and he just carried on smiling. Ali believed, even if we never. Ali believed, he knew." It is a boxing fairytale.

▲ **THE UNTHINKABLE HAPPENS** *An exhausted and demoralized Foreman is counted out in round eight of the Rumble and Ali is king again.*

The day after the miracle in the jungle Ali was singing "I'm the greatest"

Ali made quick defenses, beating Chuck Wepner – the Bayonne Bleeder and the inspiration for the Rocky movies – on a 15th round stoppage, taking Ron Lyle out in 11 rounds and outpointing Britain's Joe Bugner for the second time.

He was ready for the third fight with Frazier and the Thrilla' in Manila, as it is always known, took place in October 1975. The pair had fought for the second time in New York in 1974 and Ali won clearly. The rubber was made and the heat was on.

When it was over Ali called it the "Closest thing to death." Nobody has ever disagreed. The fight ended when Futch pulled Frazier out after 14 rounds. Ali was winning on all three scorecards but he was exhausted and near collapse himself.

There were some who lost their cool in the heat of the night and criticized Futch for saving Frazier with just one round left. Futch's reply was perfect: "I'm not a timekeeper. I'm a handler of fighters," he gently told his critics.

Ali took five months off and came back with an easy fight against a Belgian called Jean Pierre Coopman, who lasted until Ali blasted him in round five. Frazier took a far more hazardous risk and agreed to fight Foreman for the second time at the Nassau Coliseum, Uniondale, New York, in June 1976.

▲ **A CUT TOO FAR**

Chuck Wepner takes a wild swing at Ali in their 1975 title fight. The battle scars on Wepner's face were evidence of some hard fights. In 1970 when he lost to Sonny Liston – it was Liston's last fight – he needed 57 stitches.

◀ A REAL THRILLA'

Frazier is ducking, weaving and avoiding Ali's punches in round 13 of the Thrilla' in Manila. Ali's victory signalled the end of a truly remarkable series of fights with Frazier.

▼ A FEROCIOUS BATTLE

Frazier is caught with another right early in the fight. The Thrilla' was finally over in round 14 when Futch performed a kind act and saved Frazier from himself.

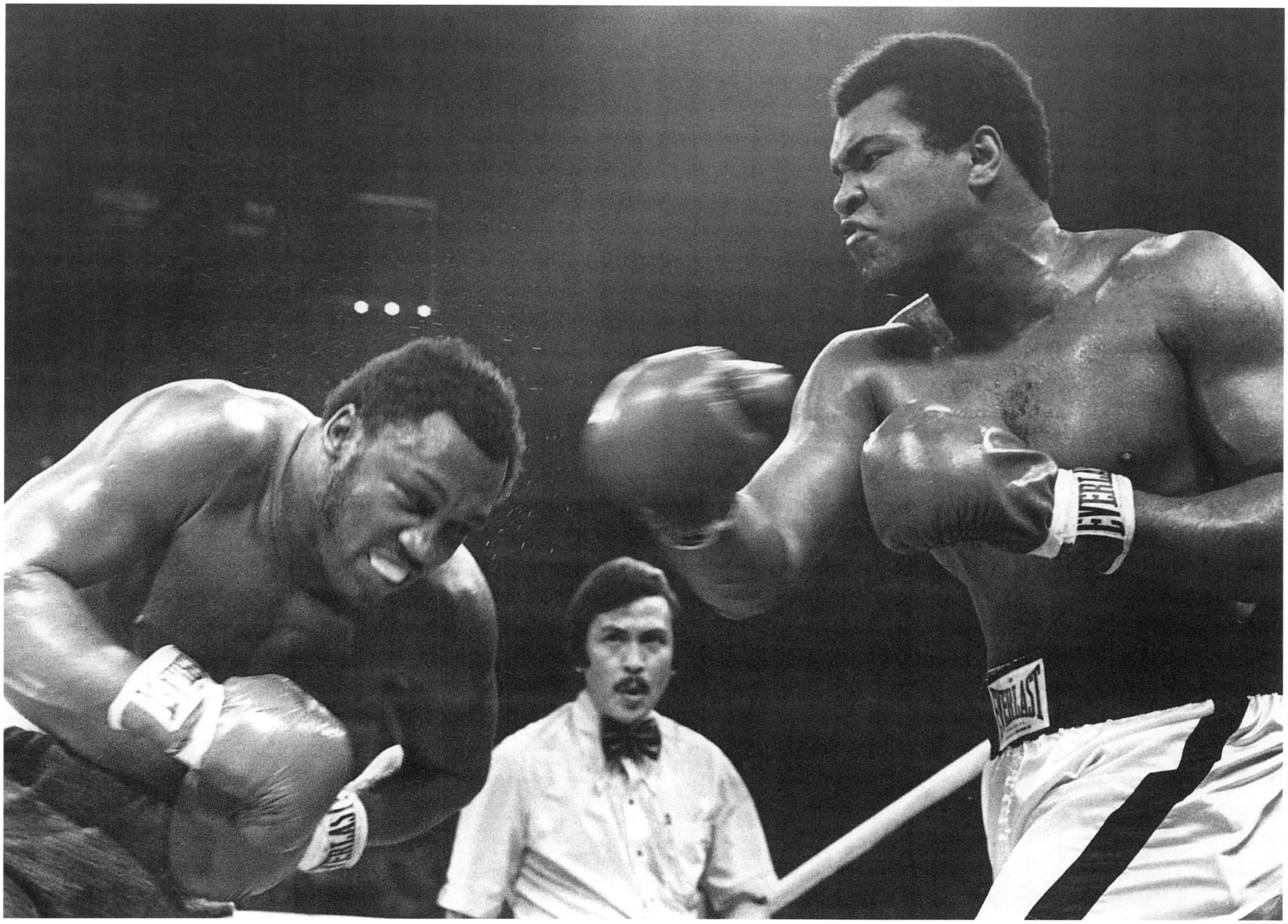

Foreman was not the sort of boxer to wait for a chance to fight

▶ **TAKING ALI 15 ROUNDS**
Ali avoids Joe Bugner in his 1975 defense in Kuala Lumpur. The fight went 15 rounds with Ali retaining his title on points.

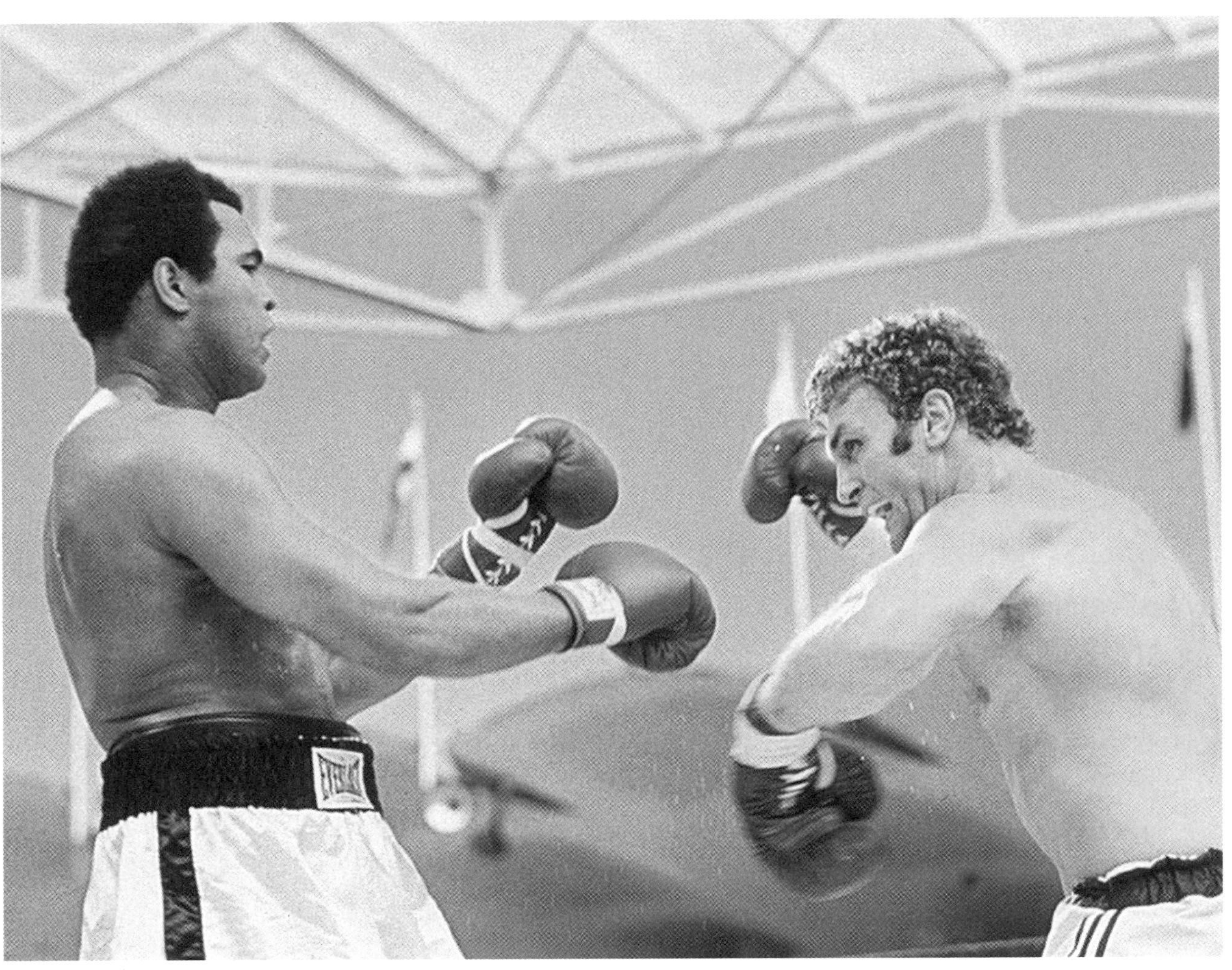

▲ **BIG JOE'S OPINION**
"I have been in and out of the business of boxing and I can say that there are places that are wretched hives of scum and villainy," Bugner once said. He retired several times but was still fighting in 1998.

Frazier never looked relaxed. There was often a disturbing and uneasy look on his face that suggested Smokin' Joe was not his old self. After four one-way rounds Foreman trapped Frazier on the ropes and the brutal fight ended in round five.

Ali should have fought Foreman around this time. Instead, he was busy defending his title against easy options like Richard Dunn and Jean Pierre Coopman. There was a defense against Joe Bugner, a fighter who looked better than he was, but was far better than most people at the time claimed. In 1975 Bugner took Ali 15 rounds in Kuala Lumpur. They had fought 12 rounds in Las Vegas in 1973, the same year Bugner had an excellent fight with Frazier in London.

Bugner is often criticized for his negative style, but during the 1970s he was one of the best heavyweights in the world. His downfall was possibly the tight decision he received when he outpointed British boxing icon Henry Cooper in 1971. He moved to Australia, but came back and fought for Frank Warren when the money was right. Bugner quit in 1987 when Frank Bruno stopped him, but it was not his last retirement and he returned several times.

Frazier retired and came back for a draw in 1981. Foreman won three more times after beating Frazier and then lost on points to perennial contender Jimmy Young in March 1977. He retired but made a comeback in 1987.

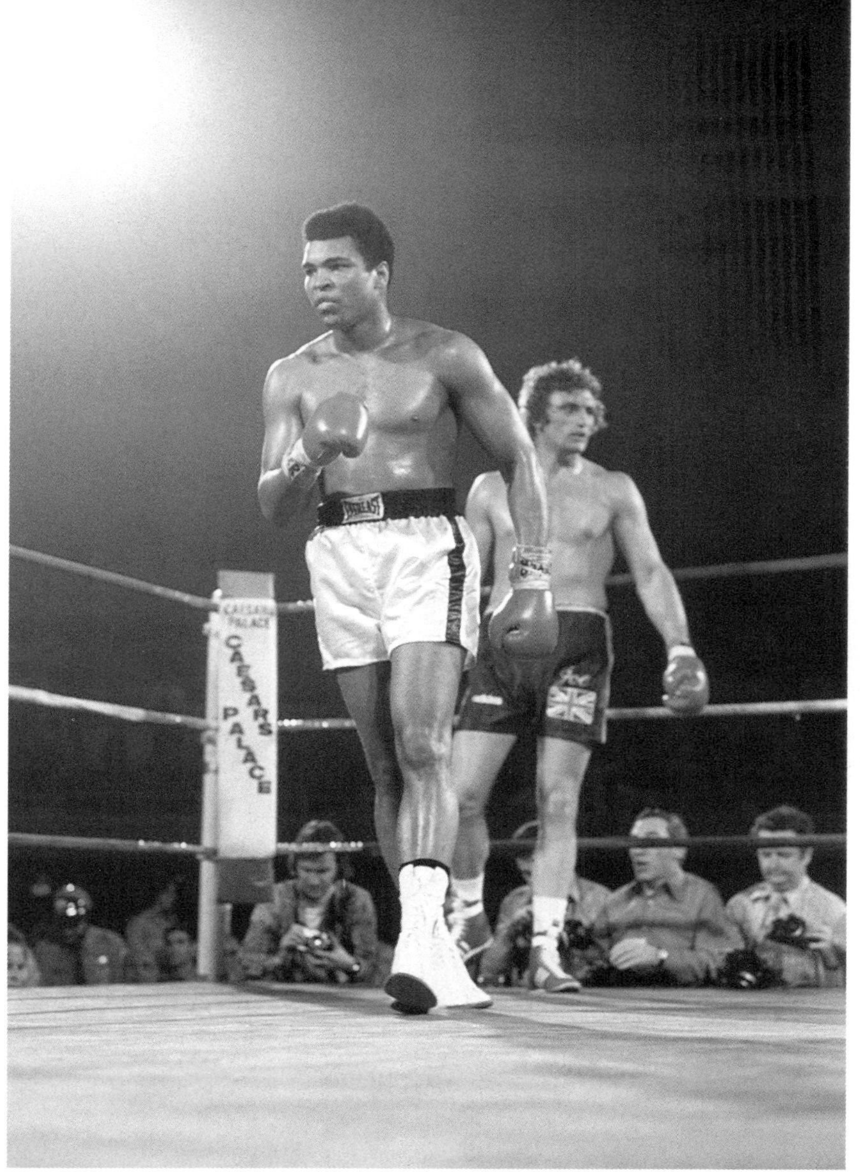

◀ **A DUBIOUS PERFORMANCE?**
Bugner was criticized for his performance against Ali. "He is the bloody best heavyweight ever mate, don't tell me what I should have done," was Bugner's response.

▲ **BUGNER LOSES IN STYLE**
Bugner and Frazier shake hands prior to their 1973 eliminator at Earl's Court in London. Bugner, who was down briefly, survived until the final bell in round 12.

MILESTONES OF BOXING

• • • • • • • • • • • • • • • • • •

THE BIG FIGHTS

THE FIGHT OF THE CENTURY, THE RUMBLE IN THE JUNGLE AND THE THRILLA' IN MANILA.

They are the three fights that raised the profile of the sport to a new level. And three fighters – Muhammad Ali, Joe Frazier and George Foreman – were responsible.

In the first fight, Frazier overcame the jibes and fought perfectly to beat Ali at the Garden in 1971. When the two met again four years later in the Thrilla', Frazier had nothing left when his trainer, Eddie Futch, saved him from himself and Ali's fists after 14 rounds.

When Foreman started to tire in the Rumble, the impossible looked possible and in round eight he stumbled and fell after a combination and a right connected. Ali was champion for the second time.

The days of glory started at the Mexico City Olympics in 1968

▲ **THE LAST AMERICAN**
Tyrell Biggs celebrates after beating Lennox Lewis on his way to winning the Olympic title in 1984.

Both Joe Frazier and George Foreman were Olympic heavyweight champions, but since Foreman controversially waved the stars and stripes in Mexico in 1968, just one American has taken gold in the heavyweight division at the top amateur tournament – Tyrell Biggs in Los Angeles in 1984.

In 1968 Cuba won their first medals and at Munich in 1972 they won their first gold, when Teofilo Stevenson won the first of his three consecutive gold medals at heavyweight. Stevenson beat Americans Duane Bobick, in 1972, and future world champion John Tate in Montreal in 1976. He would have done the same to James Broad in 1980 if the US team had not been withdrawn as part of a political boycott. As it was, he beat Pyotr Zaev of the Soviet Union.

The Cuban team missed the Los Angeles games but in 1986, when Biggs was chasing professional glory, Stevenson won the world amateur championship in Nevada. In the 1970s he was offered several fights with Ali and Foreman. He refused and remains a Cuban hero and close friend of Fidel Castro.

The Cuban teams have dominated the amateur scene since 1972 and their coaches have helped bring success to other nations. However, by the end of 1995 there were increasing numbers of defecting boxers. In Atlanta in 1996 the Cuban team won four gold medals compared to just one, by light-middleweight David Reid, that the US could manage. Even so, few inside the fiercely proud Cuban boxing scene were satisfied with the haul, which also included three silvers.

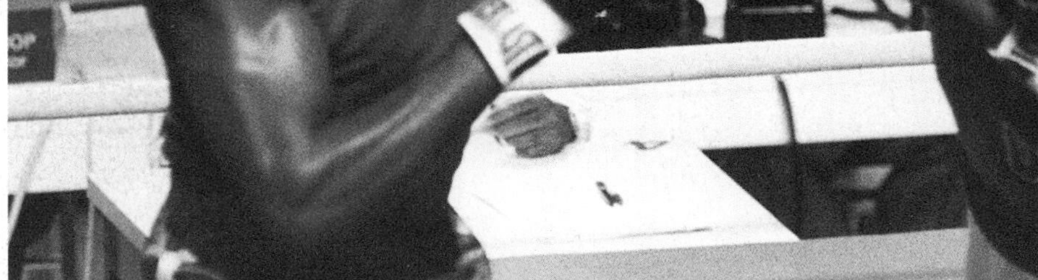

▶ **THE CUBAN HERO**
Teofilo Stevenson hits American John Tate with a left during their semi-final bout in the 1976 Montreal Olympics. Stevenson ruled the amateur sport for 15 years and won three gold medals.

▶ THE PERFECT AMBASSADOR
Stevenson was at the 1996 Olympics as part of the Cuban delegation. "I talk to the boxers, inspire them and remind them what they are fighting for," said Stevenson.

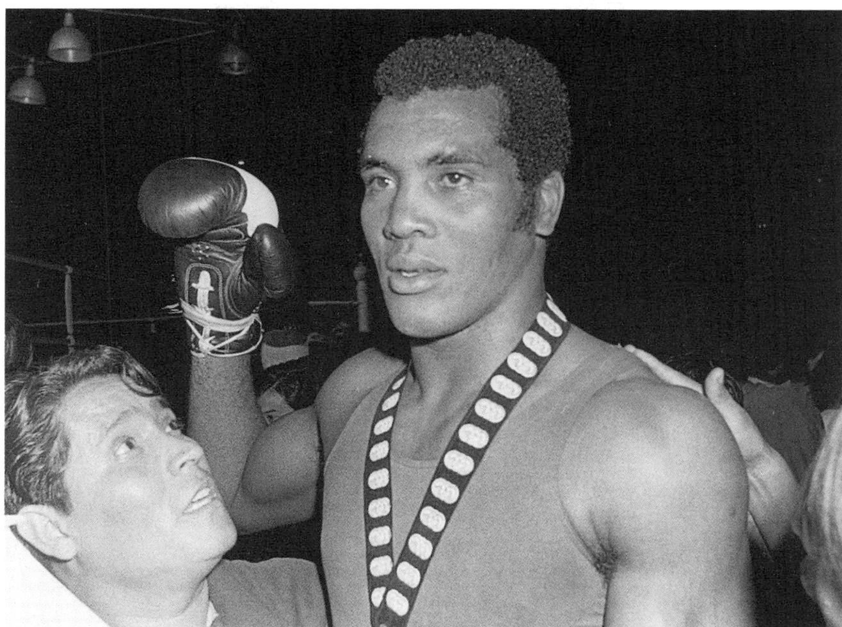

▼ THE PERFECT GENTLEMAN
Stevenson in action against Nigeria's Solomon Ataga at the 1980 Moscow Olympics. Stevenson knocked his opponent out in the first round and then helped him back to his corner.

Leonard and the Spinks brothers made Montreal magic

▲ **THE FINAL GOLD**

Sugar Ray Leonard – seen here beating Valery Limasov of the Soviet Union at the 1976 Montreal Olympics – was the man many thought would replace Muhammad Ali. Within two years of winning the light-wlterweight gold at Montreal, Leonard had fought on all the major TV channels and was rapidly becoming a star attraction.

For Americans, the Olympic ring has never been as blessed as it was in Montreal in 1976. It was the year Sugar Ray Leonard, and Michael and Leon Spinks won gold. It was also the last year the US beat Cuba.

In the finals four Americans beat Cubans in fights that went far beyond the usual importance of the event. The light-heavyweight final between a weary Leon Spinks and Cuba's Sixto Soria was one of the most exciting in Olympic history. In addition to the Spinks brothers and Leonard, flyweight Leo Randolph and lightweight Howard Davis also won gold. Cuba still had three gold winners, including Stevenson.

In 1978 when Soria won the world championship, his former opponent Leon Spinks was the heavyweight champion of the world, having outpointed Ali in February 1978. By the time Soria was back in Havana in late May, his future secure, Spinks was on a self-destruct mission. Ali won their rematch in September 1978 but Neon Leon had lost his way in the champagne haze that had begun to shroud his chaotic life.

Watching Stevenson perform his duties as a sporting ambassador at the 1996 Olympics and then catching a glimpse of Leon Spinks, his face an expressionless mask, at ringside when Lennox Lewis, another Olympic champion, defended his WBC heavyweight title against Andrew Golota, in October 1997, was a harsh reminder of professional boxing's cruel tendencies. In 1978 it was oh so different.

▲ **AN UNEXPECTED VICTORY**

Cuba's Sixto Soria is knocked down by Leon Spinks in the 1976 final for the heavyweight gold medal. Soria was brilliant and Spinks was expected to lose. "I heard he was the man and that just made me wanna do the thing. I had him hurt and I never stopped hurting him. I forgot how tired I was, I just wanted to hear 'Leon Spinks Olympic champion'," said Spinks later.

MILESTONES OF BOXING

ALI'S THIRD CHAMPIONSHIP WIN

Muhammad Ali made history by winning the heavyweight championship for the third time in his rematch with Leon Spinks in 1978. "I did it before and now I have done it again. Against Liston you said no, against Foreman you said no and against Spinks you said 'The champ's too old,' well I done it and I might just do it again," said Ali.

It is possible, however, that at this time Ali was not the best heavyweight in the world. Larry Holmes had won the title three months earlier when he beat Norton. "I knew I could have beaten him then but how could I shout my mouth off. He was my idol and I just had to wait and see what happened," claimed Holmes.

Ali was back in the ring to try and "do it again" in 1980. He failed, when in one of sport's great tragedies, he was easily stopped by Holmes.

MUHAMMAD ALI v LEON SPINKS

Neon Leon Unprepared for Ali Rematch

It went wrong for Leon Spinks before it started to go right. No other heavyweight champion crashed so heavily, so quickly. In February 1978 Spinks, then just 24 and on his eighth fight, won a split decision over Muhammad Ali in Las Vegas. Six weeks later the WBC had stripped him of their portion for refusing to defend his title. He also found himself being sued by a motel and a past landlord for unpaid bills. In the seven months before the rematch in September, Spinks was arrested six times. He was out of control.

In the first Ali-Spinks fight George Benton was able to persuade Spinks to jump all over Ali. It worked. As the months passed and troubles outside the ring increased, Benton was starting to wonder if the same result was possible. "When I got back in camp I could see the influences starting to get to Leon and his mind was in turmoil," said Benton.

"I'm still learning," Leon proudly announced before the rematch. However, there were days when Benton waited in vain for the champion to turn up for training. After long nights, Leon often spent his days recovering. Meanwhile, Dundee was smiling more and more each day – he'd heard the rumors about Spinks. Everybody knew about the stories of Spinks's drug-taking, but he denied any responsibility. "People just keep giving them to me," he pleaded in defence.

"My man will just go out and do his thing", promised Dundee. In the gym Ali looked slimmer – although he was actually only four pounds lighter – and was far better prepared. Ali may have been 12 years older, but Leon was ageing fast.

The New Orleans Superdome held nearly 70,000 on the night of the fight. There was one less after five rounds when Benton left the champion's corner in disgust at the amateur antics of the others in Leon's corner, and walked back to his hotel. The pair never worked together again and Benton claims never to have seen the rest of the fight.

Unlike Leon, Ali's mind was right and, as Dundee promised, he moved well. He was up on his toes messing Spinks about from the first bell until the final one at the end of 15 rounds. "It wasn't my best fight," said Ali, "that was the third fight with Frazier. But this was my most satisfying."

When it was over, Ali was a clear winner and world heavyweight champion for the third time. It was the type of performance that a champion should retire after, but people had said the same thing after the Thrilla'. In June of 1979, however, Ali did the right thing and called it a day.

"The championship brought me a lot of problems", admitted the unfortunate Leon. Also, in June 1979 Leon was stopped in one round by South African Gerrie Coetzee in Monte Carlo. The fight was an eliminator for the title and in November 1979 Coetzee lost on points to John Tate for the WBA championship. It was just over a year after Ali had beaten Leon but the title was in the first stage of decay.

Despite the setbacks, Spinks kept trying and in 1981 Larry Holmes beat him in three and in 1986 he was stopped in six rounds by Dwight Qawi, in a WBA cruiserweight challenge. He fought for the last time in 1995, when he lost on points. It was his 17th defeat in 45 contests.

▲ **MAN AND WILD BOY**

Ali and Leon Spinks announce their intention to fight in February 1978. "I told him he was crazy and that I would never fight him," joked Ali before the fight. The fight was no comedy – Ali lost his title and looked old and finished.

▲ **RETURN OF THE GENIUS** *Ali gives Leon Spinks something to think about in their 1978 rematch. Ali was focused, while Spinks was out of condition.*

Holmes stays on top as the new boys begin to emerge

▲ **A STORM IN THE PALACE**
When Holmes fought Norton at Caesars Palace in Las Vegas the crowd witnessed one of the best fights of the 1970s. Holmes won and held the title for seven years.

Larry Holmes beat Ken Norton to become the WBC heavyweight champion in 1978. Holmes was still fighting for versions of the heavyweight title 19 years later, a relic from a previous time, a survivor of the decade when champions were forever. He was as remarkable back in 1978 as he is now.

Marvelous Marvin Hagler was like Holmes. Neither were glamor fighters. When Hagler declared 'I'm black, I'm a southpaw and I'm good,' he was acknowledging a debt to Ali. It was Ali who had helped give all fighters a voice, even if sometimes his own fell silent when he should have been able to simply say "No".

Hagler drew with Vito Antuofermo for the undisputed middleweight title in 1979. It was just another setback for the Marvelous one, who would win the title from Alan Minter in 1980 in London, in a fight sadly remembered more for the mindless violence of the crowd, than the boxing.

It was also in 1979 that Sugar Ray Leonard, the Olympic golden boy, won his first title when he stopped Wilfred Benitez in round 15 to win the WBC welterweight championship.

Duran was looking for more titles, and Tommy Hearns, a tall skinny kid with a sweet right cross, was starting to make people watch. The new-look boxing scene had Hagler, Duran, Leonard and Hearns and Las Vegas wanted them bad.

◄ SO NEAR SO OFTEN

Ken Norton could always be relied upon to put up a tough battle – the fight with Holmes in 1978 was perfect example. Norton had also beaten Ali in 1973 when he broke Ali's jaw, but he lost the rematch the same year.

▲ A TRUE CHAMPION

Larry Holmes shows off his belt at a press conference in London in 1978. Holmes was a great heavyweight but coming in the middle of two such larger-than-life characters like Ali and Tyson meant he never gained the recognition he deserved.

The VEGAS *boys*

1980-1986

It was a generation of the divine. Leonard, Hearns, Hagler, Duran, Holmes and then Tyson all played the Vegas neon. Their fights set the standard and raised boxing to financial heights that Ali and his generation missed. Vegas was the place to fight and a pitiless wave of hopefuls tried their luck.

NEW STARS ARE BORN

▲ **THE SMILING CHAMPION**
Leonard was just too good to be true. In the ring he could rescue fights from oblivion – outside the ring his frailties and problems pushed him to the very edge.

◀ **THE MARVELOUS ONE**
Previous page: Hagler pictured during training in menacing mood.

Muhammad Ali came back. There was no point, but too many people in boxing believe in impossible dreams, and in the past Ali had defied logic so often. The fight against Larry Holmes for the WBC title was in October 1980. It was called the Last Hurrah. It should have been for Ali, but he decided to try one more time, and another pointless payday was organized.

In December 1981 his career was officially over when Trevor Berbick, a Jamaican living in Canada, beat him on points. It had ended as so many other careers had – in one comeback too many and defeat.

Ali had looked in great shape for Holmes but a mistake with medication had caused him to dehydrate in the days before the fight and left him drained. The fight never got started and as the rounds passed a great sadness descended at ringside in Las Vegas. Joe Louis watched the fight from his wheelchair. It was not one of boxing's great nights.

"Ali was my idol, a tremendous fighter, but he stepped out of his time into my time. I know all there is to know about how he fights. Whatever he tries, I'll beat him," said Holmes before the fateful night. Even Ali admitted that it was difficult to upset Holmes outside the ring – it was impossible in the ring.

At the end of the ninth the fight could have been stopped. Ali had taken too much punishment and Holmes looked disturbed at the prospect of hitting his friend any more. "I wanted the ref to save him," Holmes said. So did thousands in attendance at Caesars Palace. The spectacle was awful.

They fought a tenth round, but Angelo Dundee had seen enough and after Ali slumped to the stool at the end of the round, he waved it off. However, Drew Bundini Brown grabbed his shirt and pulled him away from the ref. "One more round, let the champ have one more round," Brown pleaded.

There was a scuffle but Ali just sat dazed and oblivious as the two men who loved him fought in front of his eyes. It was stopped. Holmes was in tears. He had first sparred with Ali in 1973. Holmes had been one of three sparring partners during the weeks in Zaire before the Rumble in the Jungle.

The last fight against Berbick was predictable. Berbick was too young. He had lost to Holmes on points and in 1986 he would briefly hold the WBC title. It was not an easy fight to accept and it is clear Ali saw it as a way back.

"I decided to go with Muhammad to the Berbick fight. When that was over, he knew it was time to retire because he was terrible," Dundee said. Interest in the heavyweight division faded after Ali's final requiem appearances and it was five years before the weight was salvaged from mediocrity by Mike Tyson when he won the WBC title in 1986. In eight months he unified the division.

The heavyweights were in a state of plunder in the early 1980s. They were destroying themselves in matches that made no sense. Good fighters were losing and bad fighters winning. It was a crazy scene that was further complicated by the accusations made against Don King, who promoted many of the forgettable encounters.

Holmes was a constant reminder of better days, but he was denied a place in the history books in 1985 when he lost for the first time in his 49th fight. If Holmes had won he would have equalled Rocky Marciano's record, but he lost a controversial decision to Michael Spinks, brother of Leon.

After the fight Holmes lost his cool. "To be technical," he told reporters, "Rocky Marciano couldn't carry my jockstrap." He apologized for the insult but has never been able to distance himself from the angry remark. Holmes had won 20 world title fights. A rematch with Spinks was made.

The stars of the early 1980s belonged to the welterweight and middleweight divisions. The heavyweights took a back seat, while the men from the lighter divisions took part in a series of fights that kept boxing alive. The super fights started in 1979 when Sugar Ray Leonard beat Wilfred Benitez and continued every year throughout the 1980s.

Leonard, Roberto Duran, Thomas Hearns and Marvin Hagler fought each other in the decade's best fights. Some of the meetings would eclipse virtually any fight in any decade. The Hagler-Hearns middleweight fight in 1985 was particularly special. The second Leonard-Duran WBC welterweight fight in 1980, however, was the scene of bizarre events.

Below the welterweight division there were fighters who added their names to lists of greats. There were also tragic figures like Aaron Pryor, who was destroyed by inner demons when he was on the threshold of true greatness. It is possible that the early death of brilliant Mexican featherweight Salvador Sanchez in 1982, when he was WBC champion, denied him the chance to prove himself as the best in history.

In 1987 Hagler walked away from boxing but he left behind a unique legacy. Hagler was a living great who came from nothing, won and lost fights the old-fashioned way and then, after a dubious drawn world title fight against Vito Antuofermo in 1979, went to London for his night of glory. It turned out to be a night of mayhem and violence outside the ring.

▲ **THE UNSMILING CHAMPION**
Larry Holmes raises his arms in victory but does not appear to be pleased about his victory over Ali after 10 rounds. "How could I celebrate, my idol was finished and it was my punches that did it," said Holmes in 1980. A few hours after the fight Holmes visited Ali's hotel room to apologize.

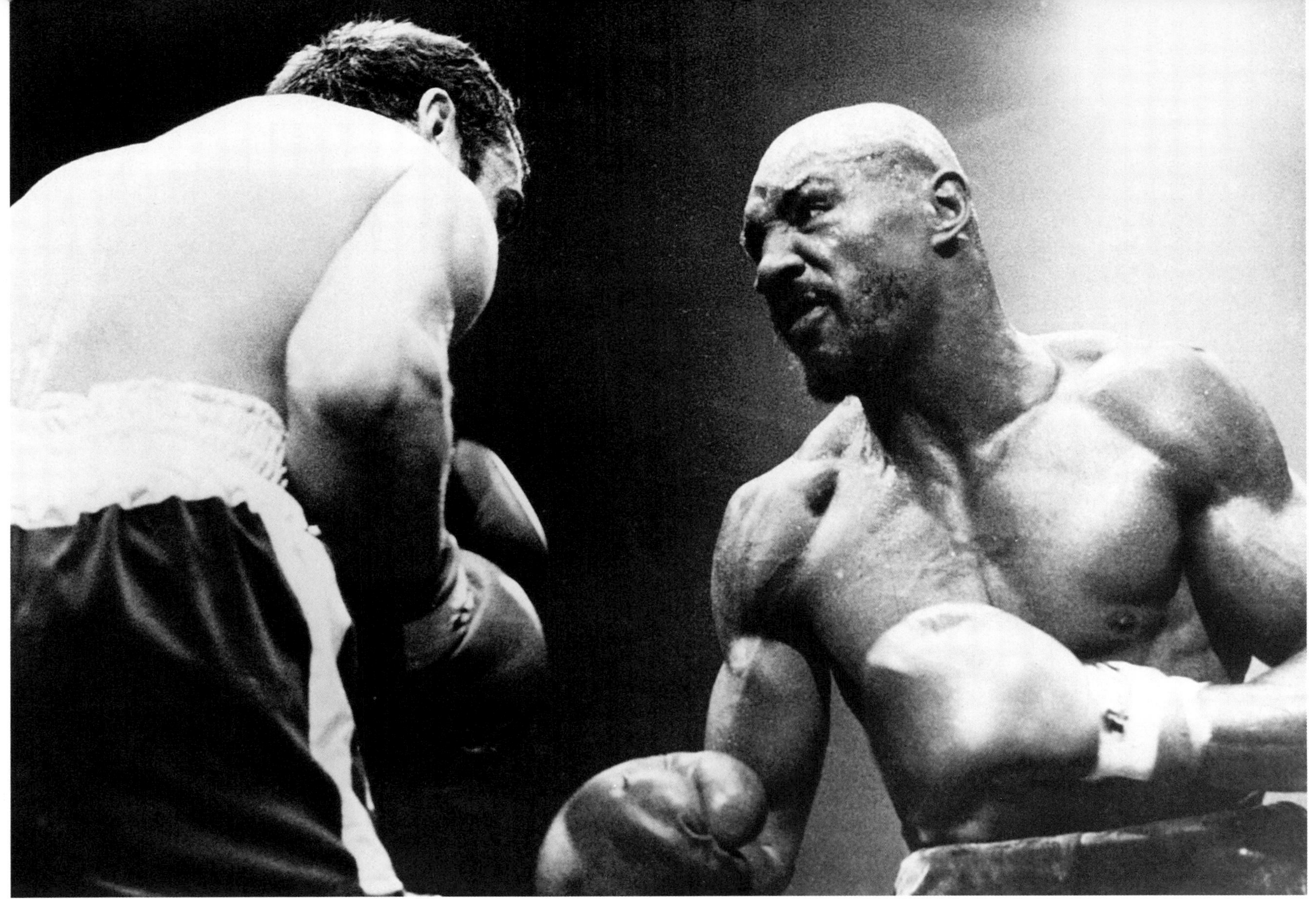

Hagler won the storm in the ring and ran from the mindless violence

▲ A TAINTED EVENING
Hagler (right) cut and beat Alan Minter in three rounds to win the world middleweight title in in 1980. "I just kept taking his face apart," said Hagler.

On the day of the infamous Hagler-Minter fight in 1980, Hagler told his trainer Goody Petronelli: "I can't leave it up to the judges." That night he wrecked Britain's Alan Minter in less than three rounds.

Minter needed 15 stitches – in cuts above and below both eyes – but stood up bravely to the calculated beating Hagler inflicted. Before the fight there were reports that Minter had said he "would never lose to a black man." Minter denied the comments, but the fact that he weighed-in wearing a pair of underpants with the British flag on them was seized upon by some as proof of his guilt!

Minter fought the wrong fight and Hagler did a number on him – his precise, chopping southpaw jabs starting to rip the skin on Minter's cheek from the first minute. When it was over Hagler dropped to his knees in prayer. It was his lifetime ambition and after 54 fights and seven years he was champion.

There was no controversy when it was stopped, no suggestion that Hagler had intentionally butted or used his thumb to open the cuts, but the first bottles landed in the ring when Hagler was still on his knees. More came flying in from Minter's angry fans. "The violence never bothered me. I just kept my head down and then we were out of there," said Hagler. Because of the shameful outbreak, Hagler was not presented with his belt – the ceremony took place later at a restaurant in his home town of Brockton.

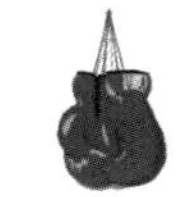

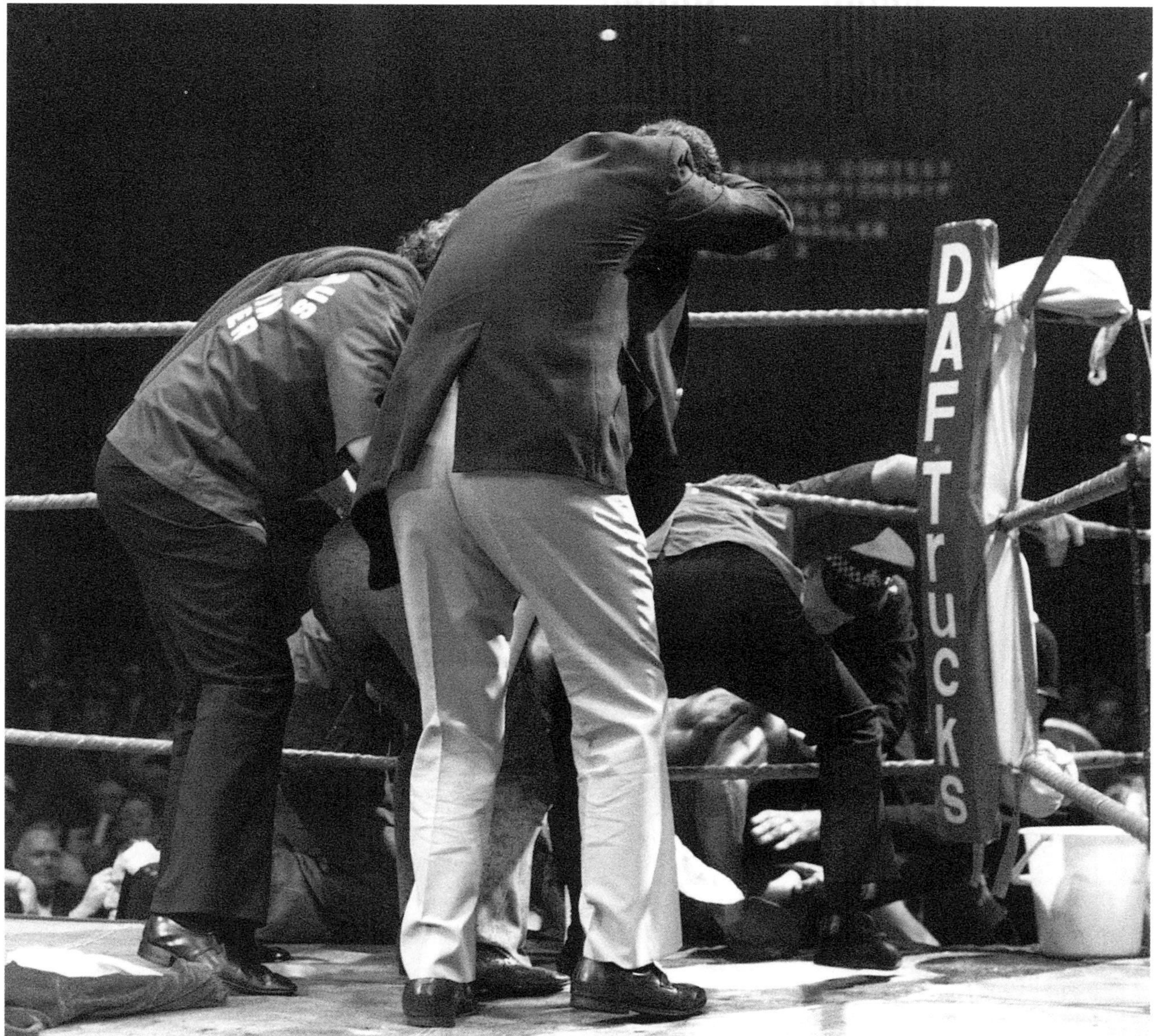

◀ **DELAYED CELEBRATIONS**

Hagler and his entourage leave the ring under a hail of missiles. "When the men leave the corner it doesn't matter where the fight is. I was not afraid of fighting Minter in London and what happened after just delayed my celebrations," claimed Hagler.

▲ **THE FLOWER OF ENGLAND**

Minter won a bronze medal at the Munich Olympics, but he could have taken home a gold. He won the world title from Vito Antuofermo in 1980, and then beat the American in a rematch. Hagler was his next and last defense.

▶ **REGULAR RING RIOTS**

Officials protect Hagler as the bottles fly at Wembley. In Britain several high-profile fights have been followed by riots. In 1991 rival fans fought with police and stewards when Michael Watson was being taken to the hospital for emergency surgery after losing a WBO super-middleweight title fight to Chris Eubank.

From the Kronk gym came a stick-thin fighter who knocked men crazy

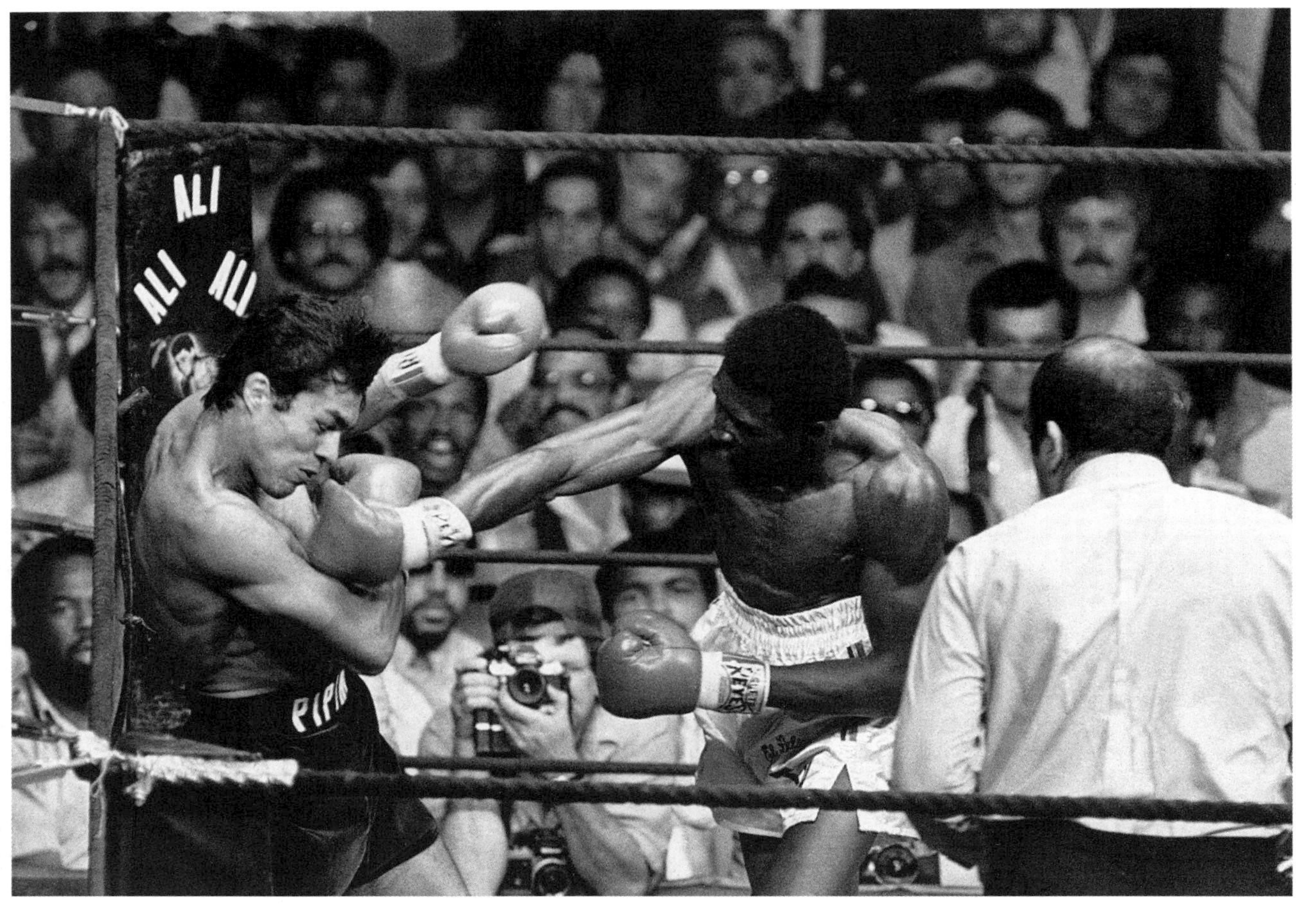

▶ **CUEVAS DEFEATED**

Thomas Hearns lands a right on Pipino Cuevas in their 1980 welterweight bout. Hearns won by a knockout in the next round. Cuevas never looked like he wanted to win and he suffered as Hearns cut him down with sickening rights. Muhammad Ali can be seen at ringside above Hearns's left glove.

▲ **NEXT VICTIM**

Hearns and Cuevas at a press conference before their title fight. Hearns was unbeaten in 28 fights when he challenged Cuevas for the WBA welterweight title in 1980. Cuevas was victim number 29, the 21st in three rounds or less.

Thomas Hearns had a right hand that left boxers in a dreadful state on the canvas. When he challenged Pipino Cuevas for the WBA welterweight title in his home city of Detroit, in August 1980, he was still a kid of 21. Cuevas had held the title since 1976 and had made 11 defenses – 10 had ended early. He was a veteran, but amazingly he was less than a year older than Hearns, having won the championship when he was just 18 years old.

It was one of the super-fights. From the start the outcome looked obvious. Cuevas was never in the fight. His punches were short, he moved without any confidence and looked like a condemned man, not one of boxing's top young fighters. The crowd sensed a quick win and Hearns started to open up with savage crosses.

In the second round Hearns was disdainful. He held his left in position and dropped a perfect right on the Mexican's chin. Cuevas went down, was up at seven but had trouble walking and it was over.

It was the fight that raised the profile of trainer and manager Emanuel Steward, the man from the Kronk gym, who would later train Evander Holyfield.

Hearns was a brilliant amateur, but had lost at the American Olympic trials to future world champion Aaron Pryor in 1976. Pryor had lost a disputed series of fights to Howard Davis, who won gold, but the glamor boy, the often annoying golden boxer from the Montreal games, was Leonard.

In 1980 Leonard managed just one defence of his WBC welterweight title – a knockout of Dave "Boy" Green, a British fighter with a big heart – before meeting Roberto Duran. Their meeting would set the tone for the next decade's fights.

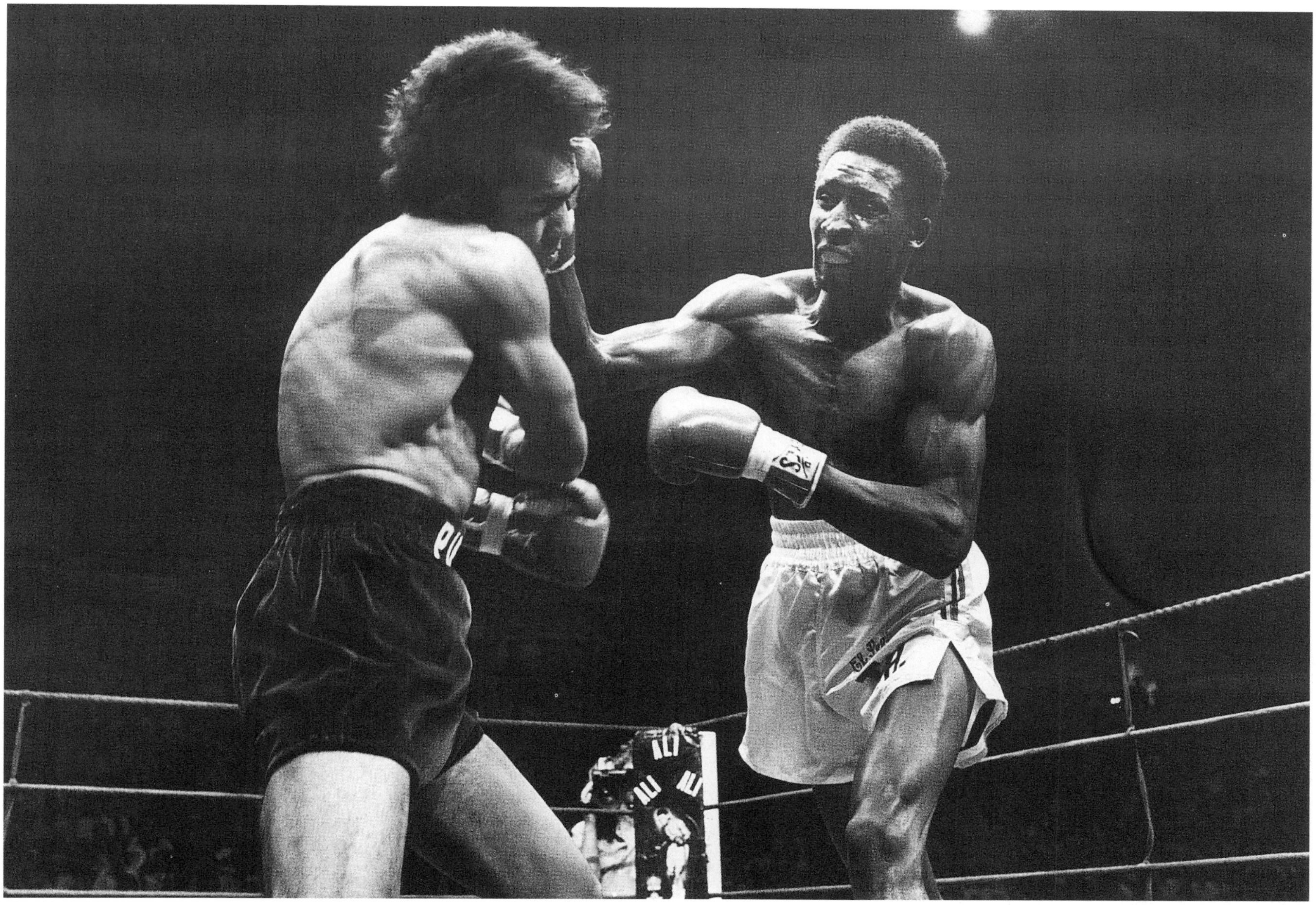

▲ THAT WICKED RIGHT

Hearns catches Cuevas with a right. "Tommy had the skill and the power to take people out with one right. He caught Cuevas again and again until there was no way the fight would last," said Kronk founder Emanuel Steward.

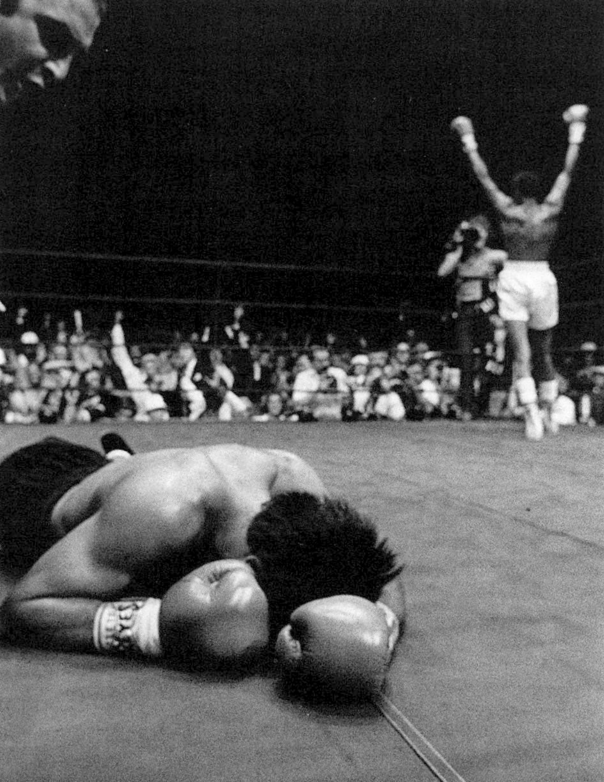

◄ A HORIZONTAL FINISH

The way to beat Hearns was to go out and fight him. Cuevas never tried and he ended up intimate with the canvas. Many others failed, while some like Marvin Hagler were able to predict the pattern of attrition.

SUGAR RAY LEONARD

Leonard was Bitter When Defeat Stained his Ego

Ray Leonard has upset a lot of people in boxing. There is no denying his talent however – he has won world titles at five different weights. Between June 1980 and September the following year he took part in three amazing fights.

Roberto Duran never liked Leonard. He knew he could win against him and the men in his corner – Ray Arcel and Freddie Brown – knew he would win. They had a plan to upset Leonard and Duran was angry.

In June 1980 the two men met in Montreal for Leonard's WBC welterweight championship. Duran set the pace, chased the champion and refused to stop pushing and shoving throughout the 15 rounds. Referee Carlos Padilla was, according to Arcel, an unwilling dupe in their strategy and let Duran hold, hit and shove.

Duran was the only winner but Leonard started to plan the rematch before he left Montreal. "I knew what Roberto had done. I knew how he had won and I needed my own plan," said Leonard. Preparations for the rematch started and New Orleans in November 1980 was selected.

"I've got to beat him with class, in a rare way, a unique way. Make him look bad. Make him crazy," said Leonard on the eve of the rematch. Duran had lost too much weight too quickly for the contest, but nothing in his 72-fight career (71 of them wins) explained his final act in the bizarre fight. Leonard went for Duran's mind from the start in a dangerous ploy that clearly worked. Rounds three and five were close, but in round seven Duran was publicly humiliated by Leonard, who stood at a distance taunting the Panamanian. It was a wild spectacle and poor Duran let his frustration rule his brain. In round eight, as Leonard laughed and played, Duran turned his back and uttered the two most unbelievable words in the history of boxing: "No mas." Duran had quit, the Hands of Stone decided to wave them in total surrender, rather than throw them in anger. The same Duran had called Leonard's wife a whore.

All excuses for his quitting were ignored, and Duran fell from grace. There are still many people who believe that Duran never recovered from the events of that night, even though he went on to win more world titles. Support for Duran came, surprisingly, from Leonard's corner. "Roberto tried to get to Ray. I thought it was a very noble thing because Ray was undressing him. Duran never quit, a legend never quits, he just knew," said Dundee. However, Arcel never worked with Duran again. "What could I say to the man?" Arcel asked.

In June 1981 Leonard increased his weight to win the second of his five different titles when he stopped Denmark's Ayub Kalule in nine rounds for the WBA light-middleweight belt. He vacated the title the following month in one of several calculated moves that tarnished his achievements.

Hearns, meanwhile, stopped three challengers to reinforce his image as the sport's most explosive puncher. Hearns and Leonard met in Las Vegas in September 1981and fought the type of fight that a man can fight just once in his life. It was a classic.

According to the three judges, Hearns was winning after 13 rounds. Many disagree, however. At the start of the 14th, Hearns caught Leonard but he was weary and a right sent him back to the ropes. His strength was gone and Leonard, whose face was swollen from the Hitman's right, opened up until the referee, Davey Pearl, intervened. Hearns was trapped and exhausted and his WBA title was gone. Leonard was the first unified welterweight champion since Jose Napoles in 1975.

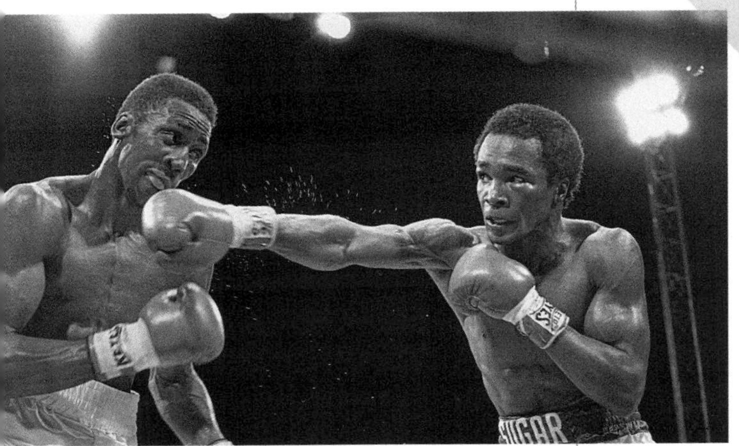

▲ **SOMETHING IN RESERVE**
Leonard's long right reaches its mark. "I told Ray he had to do something drastic and he responded," said Angelo Dundee in 1981. Hearns was in front after 13 rounds but Leonard changed the result, stopping Hearns in the 14th.

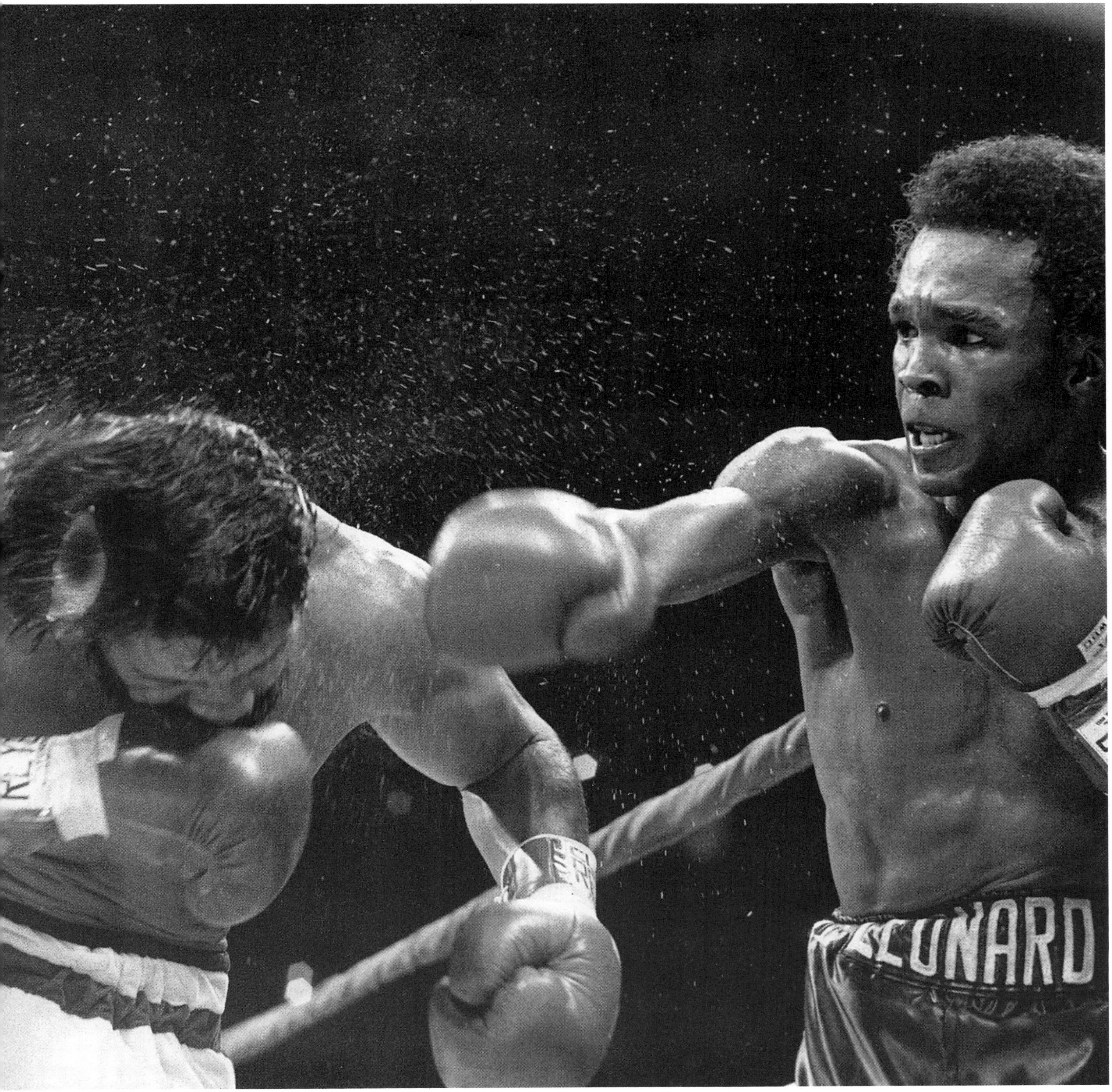

HAOTIC REVENGE *Leonard was cruel and brilliant in the rematch with Duran who quit in round eight with the infamous words: "No mas."*

Nelson's African journey ends in a night of drama at the Garden

▲ **AN UNTIMELY END**

Salvador Sanchez could have become the greatest ever Mexican fighter had he not died in a car crash. He lost just once in 43 fights.

In Bukom, a village in Accra, Ghana, there is a boxing ring in the middle of the main market square. It is rusty, has an uneven surface and becomes wet after storms, but several of Ghana's world champions have used it, including the greatest African fighter ever, the "Professor", Azumah Nelson.

Nelson first challenged for a world title at just two weeks' notice and after 13 fights. The day was July 21, 1982, and the WBC featherweight champion was Salvador Sanchez, who had lost just once in 45 fights, and was making his ninth defense. Nelson arrived in New York for the Madison Square Garden fight and sparred for a few days with a light-welterweight.

At the time Don King was negotiating with Alexis Arguello for a showdown fight. "I wasn't supposed to win. I knew that and Sanchez must have known but my sparring partner warned them," said Nelson.

Sanchez was stretched by Nelson and the fight went longer than many people had expected. It was close and after 14 rounds the judges had it two-to-one in Sanchez's favor. Nelson was 24 but young in boxing years and had never met anybody of the champion's quality. It was a memorable fight and in the 15th round Nelson was saved from his own exhaustion and bravery.

"They saw the next champ that night," remembers Nelson. In 1984 he stopped Wilfredo Gomez, one of the best fighters from the late 1970s and early 1980s, to win the WBC featherweight title. Gomez won a third world title after losing to Nelson and was inducted to the Hall of Fame in 1995.

Sanchez never fought again. He died when his Porsche hit a truck in his native Mexico a few weeks after the Nelson fight. He was 23.

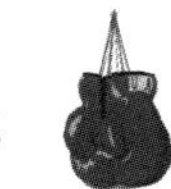

◄ **A HERO IN GHANA**
Azumah Nelson is regarded as the greatest African fighter. "I have to fight for my people each time I get in the ring because they are waiting and expecting triumph," Nelson once said.

▼ **THE STERN CHAMPION**
Nelson retains his WBC belt, having beaten Lupe Suarez in 1988. Nelson always wanted to fight Irishman Barry McGuigan, but the fight never happened. "I would beat Barry. It would be easy," he boasted.

MILESTONES OF BOXING

MUHAMMAD ALI: THE END

After Muhammad Ali lost to Trevor Berbick in 1981 he was lost to boxing. In 1984 the rumors about his health had reached such a peak that a statement was issued.

It confirmed that Ali had Parkinson's Syndrome but stressed he was not suffering from *dementia pugilistica*, commonly known as punch drunk. His condition, claimed his physician, Stanley Fahn, will stabilize with medication. It was a shock to the people who remembered the fluent fighter but many of his associates and former members of his entourage had seen signs of his ailing.

Ali had told the New York press in September 1984 that he felt tired. "Sometimes I have trembling in my hands. My speech is slurred," he added. However, in September 1997, when Ali returned to his birthplace of Louisville for a tribute evening, his speech and his movement were better than they had been for years.

After beating Arguello, Pryor's career and life was on a downward spiral

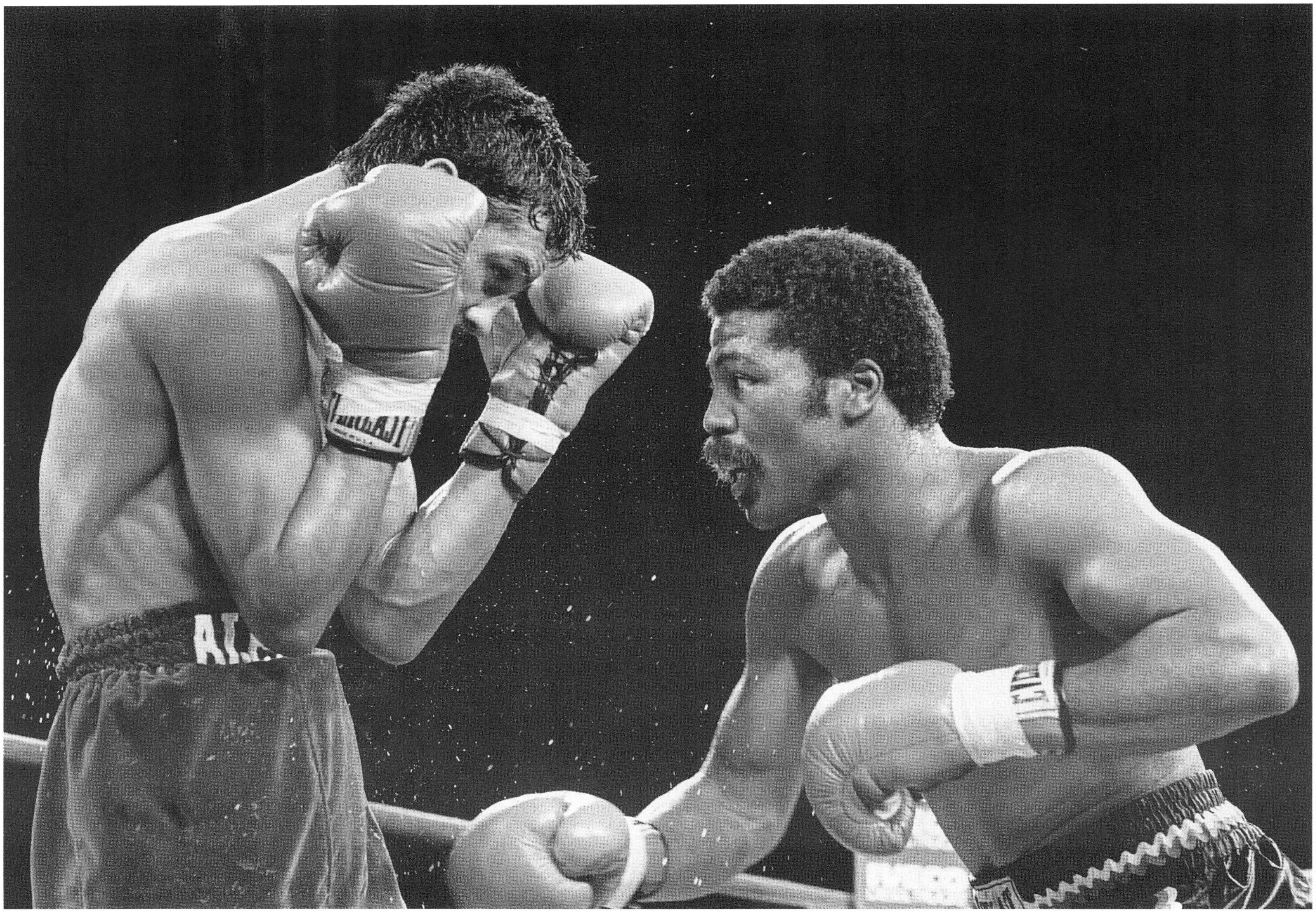

▼ THE COVER UP

Alexis Arguello attempts to block Aaron Pryor's punches in their 1982 fight. Arguello was able to block punches that had left other fighters in tears. "I knew what to do and how to do it – Pryor just kept coming," said Arguello.

When Salvador Sanchez died, another opponent had to be found for Alexis Arguello, who needed a super-fight. It was 1982 and the welterweights had shown the way in a series of thrilling fights that captured the public's interest and netted a lot of money.

Arguello agreed to challenge Aaron "The Hawk" Pryor for the WBA junior-welterweight title. Pryor was undefeated in 31 fights. He had stopped or knocked out 29 opponents and had lost to Olympic gold medalist Howard Davis in the American Olympic trial in 1976. The fight was set for Miami in November 1982.

Pryor received a junior-welterweight record of 1.6 million dollars. He won in round 14 but what a fight it was, considered by many to be the fight of the decade. Pryor never stopped throwing punches.

They had to meet again. Caesars Palace, Las Vegas,

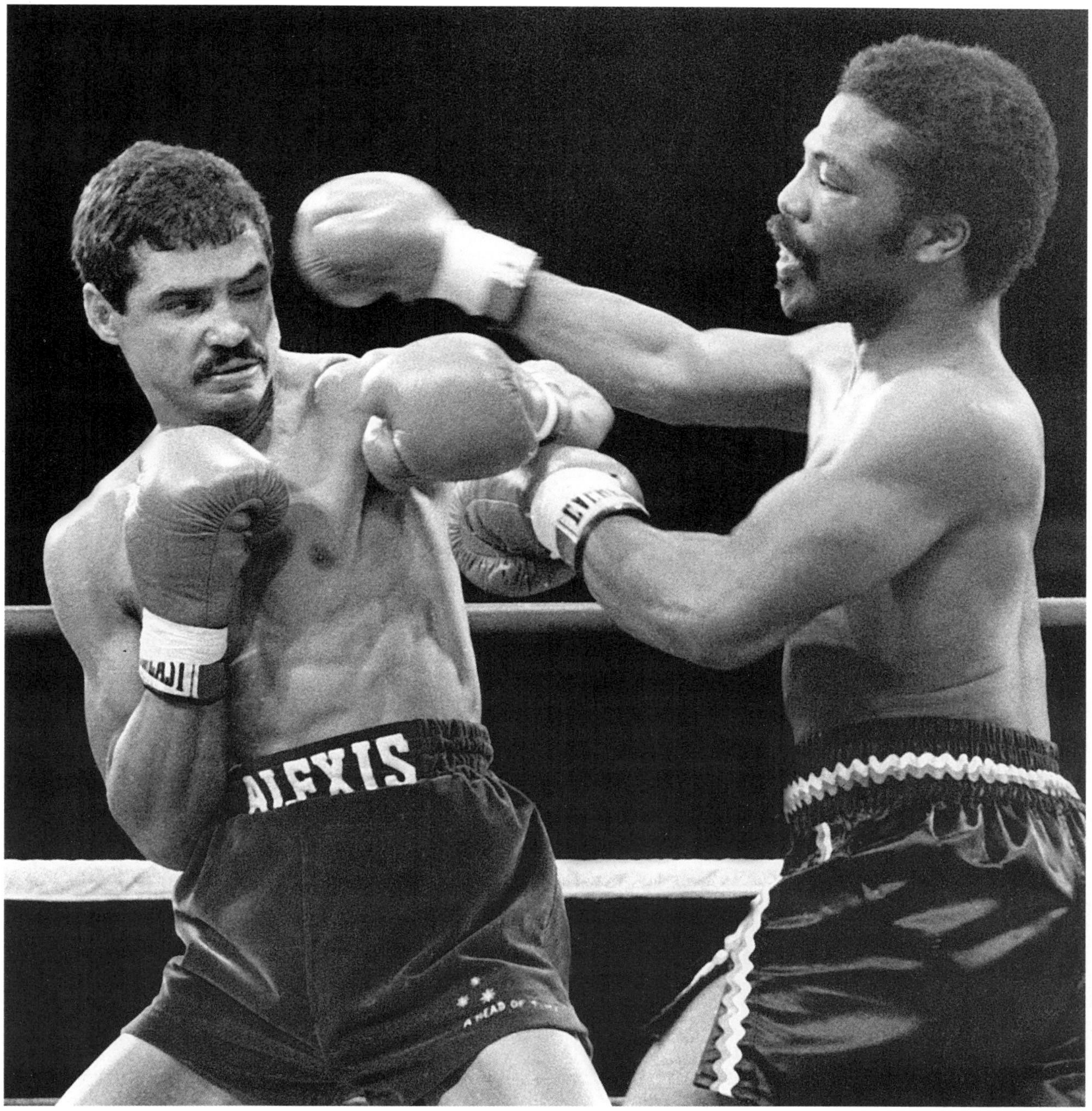

▲ **PRYOR'S DECEPTIVE DECLINE**

Pryor throws a right at Arguello. Pryor claimed that pain was one of his best weapons and his self-destructive tendencies have never been disputed. His descent into the abyss of suffering was initially ignored because he kept winning.

hosted the thrilling rematch in September 1983. Arguello survived knockdowns in round one and four but rescued himself in the 10th by sitting out another count. "I did not want to risk my life," he said later.

After the fight Pryor became a crack addict. He fought on but relinquished the WBA version and in 1984 was given the fledgling IBF's junior-welterweight belt. He made two defenses and gave that up. He was in drug hell by 1984 and during an altercation in Miami he was shot by a Jamaican drug dealer. He last fought in 1990, was imprisoned for drug abuse in 1991 but has now kicked his addiction and is a boxing trainer and church deacon in Cincinnati.

▼ **SITUATION VACANT**

Arguello is out in round 14 of his first fight with Pryor. It was the end of his hope of holding four world titles at four weights. As feather, super-feather and lightweight champion he beat some of the greats from the 1970s and 1980s.

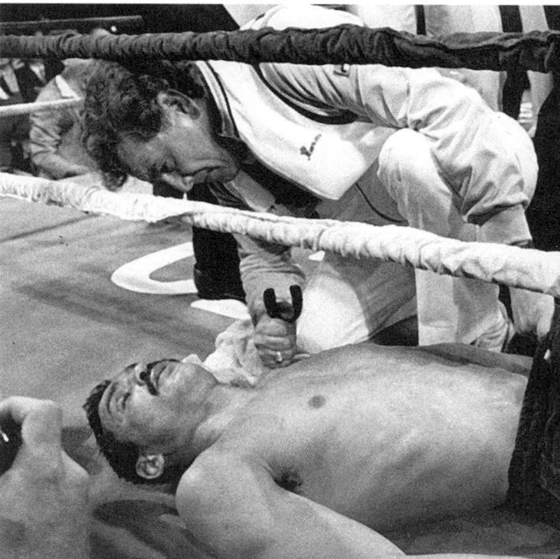

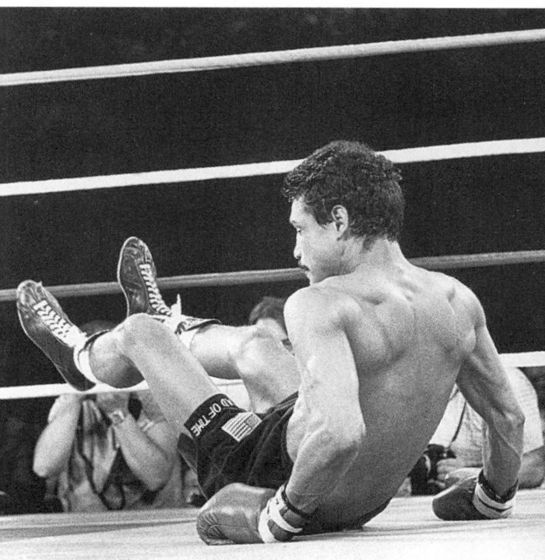

▲ **REMATCH REPEAT**

Arguello is over in the first round of the rematch in Las Vegas in 1983. It lasted until round 10. "I could have gone on and made millions. Instead I wrecked my life and made everybody that loved me suffer," said Pryor.

HEARNS and STEWARD

The Pride of the Man in Yellow

Emanuel Steward has to have total control outside the ring and total conviction in the ring. His fighters need heart. "Greatness comes from inside," Steward claims. When Steward and Tommy Hearns first met at the Kronk gym the trainer was impressed. "Tommy had a strength, I could just see how eager he was to win. He had no fear and heart is a quality I have to have from my fighters. It can't be taught – a fighter has to have it and Tommy did," remembers Steward. "Tommy started as a terrific boxer. He hardly stopped anyone in the amateurs. But then I taught him to punch," claims Steward.

▲ **EMANUEL IN CONTROL**

Steward makes adjustments to Hearns's gloves before a sparring session. "The first fight with Leonard was very emotional for both camps. I almost got into a fight with Ray at one of the press conferences. I kept Tommy cool," said Steward.

The pair turned professional together in late 1977. Steward borrowed money to stage a show in Detroit. The show was a success and Hearns knocked out Jerome Hill in round two. Hearns fought 14 of his first 16 fights in Detroit.

When Hearns beat Pipino Cuevas in 1980 at the Joe Louis Arena in Detroit, the Kronk, Steward and the fighter were officially on boxing's map. The success began to attract other fighters to Steward's sweltering basement. There are tales of workmen crowding the gym and watching sparring sessions during lunch breaks. There are other tales of vicious sparring sessions that sorted out the order of celebrity. Steward never denies that working, winning and surviving at the Kronk was hard.

In 1981 Hearns met Sugar Ray Leonard. Before the fight Steward knew there was something wrong. Hearns had messed up with the weight and had ignored his trainer's advice. "He was too light, his face looked slim and I knew he was in trouble but even at that early stage he had started to listen to the people in his entourage," added Steward. The fight ended in defeat for Hearns in round 14.

Hearns and Steward had to wait until 1989 for revenge over Leonard and even then the judges denied Hearns what he so clearly deserved and their WBC super-middleweight fight was officially announced as a draw. Leonard was over twice. "It was a late sweet feeling," admitted Hearns.

Back in 1982 Hearns won the WBC light-middleweight title by outpointing Wilfred Benitez. In 1984 he knocked out Roberto Duran in two rounds to retain the title. Steward is given the credit for devising the plan that left Duran on the canvas. "I knew that Roberto had a habit of knocking punches away with his right glove so I wanted Tommy to hit him in the body and pull the glove down and then throw the right," said Steward. The plan worked. Against Marvin Hagler in 1985 nothing worked. Hearns and Steward parted and all of Steward's champions from the early 1980s left him.

Hearns started to work with fellow Kronk alumnus, Alex Sherer. He pulled off one of his most amazing wins in 1991 when he won the WBA light-heavyweight title by outpointing Virgil Hill, who was unbeaten at the time. Hill was the champion, the clear favorite, but Hearns was paid three million dollars more. "It is an opportunity of a lifetime for me to fight a legend," said Hill.

In 1997 Hearns was still looking for fights. Steward, on the other hand, had a vintage 1997, guiding his new charges, Oscar De La Hoya and Lennox Lewis, through successful world title fights. Steward and Hearns remain friends from a distant time, when the unassuming trainer and the tall skinny kid known as the Hit Man were the most recognizable double act in boxing.

◀ A PREOCCUPIED HEARNS
Tommy Hearns was beaten by Leonard in 1981, and then had to wait years for a rematch. "It has been eight years of living with the pain. I'm fed up with that. It's got to stop," said Hearns before the Leonard rematch in 1989. The day after he added: "I woke up this morning and my mind was clear – Ray wasn't haunting it anymore."

▶ **THE BIG DAY APPROACHES**
Hearns and Duran step up the pre-fight hype. On the day, Hearns knocked Duran out. The stage was set for the Hearns-Hagler bout. "If I get the right clean on Hagler he is going down," promised Hearns.

Pride was at stake in each of the furious meetings in the Nevada heat

▲ **MARVELOUS MARVIN**
"There is a monster that comes out when I'm in the ring. I think it goes back to the days when I had nothing. They're all trying to take something from me that I have worked long and hard for," Hagler once commented.

Marvelous Marvin Hagler lacked the glamor of Sugar Ray Leonard and Tommy Hearns. He knew it, but it didn't seem to bother him when he first won the middleweight title. The resentment increased, however, as the years passed. "Marvin just did what he had to do," said Goody Petronelli, his trainer. No thrills, just raw power and determination.

After seven defenses Hagler was matched with one of his idols, Roberto Duran, in Las Vegas in 1983. It was close and after 13 rounds all three judges had Duran in front. But Hagler was familiar with adversity and reached deep inside, at Petronelli's urging, to find enough in reserve to win the 14th and 15th rounds. His title was safe and he won a split decision.

He had won with old-fashioned skills, not the techniques used by Leonard to beat Duran in 1980. There was talk after Hagler beat Duran that a fight with Leonard would be next. The talk continued until 1987 when they finally met.

In 1984 Hearns knocked out Duran to provide Hagler with an alternative. "When Tommy nailed him, he was jabbing the body, all part of setting Duran up. With Duran concentrating on the body, Tommy dropped over the right and knocked him out," explained Steward. It was perfect, too perfect for Hagler to accept without a response.

Hagler against Hearns for the undisputed middleweight championship, which was known simply as The Fight, was made for Monday, April 15, 1985. Caesars Palace, Las Vegas, was once again the venue.

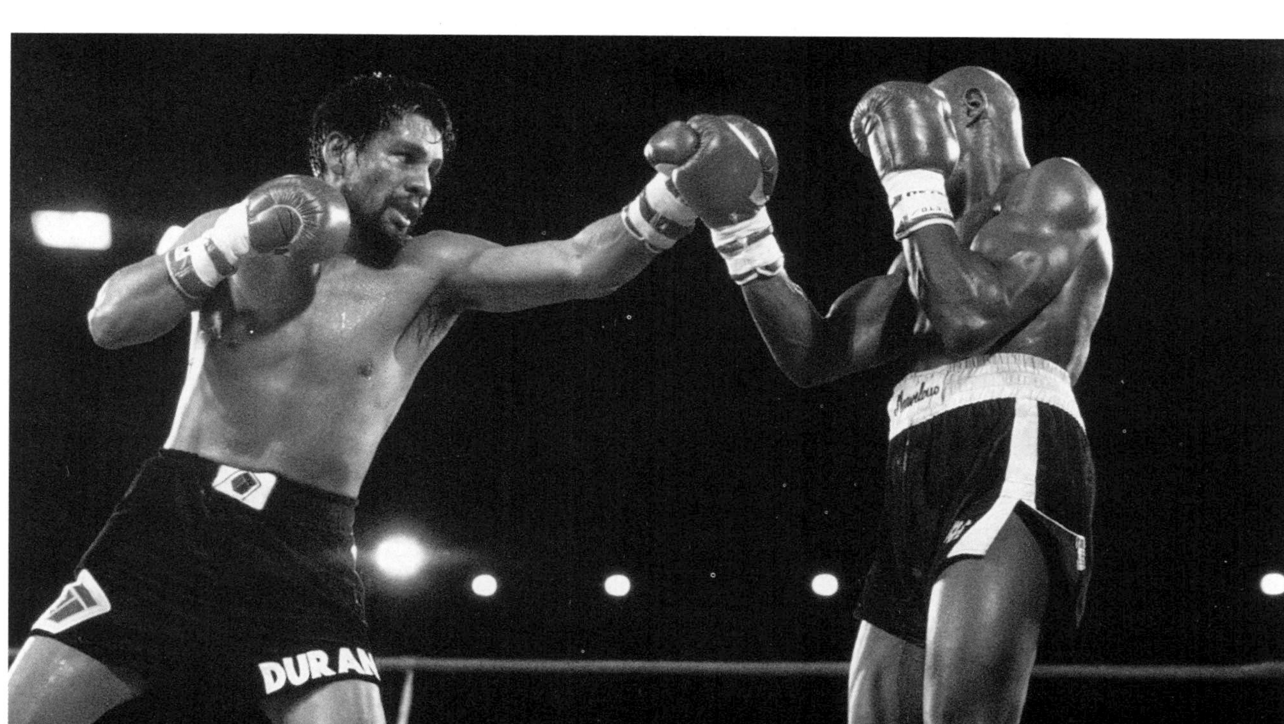

◀ **DURAN V HAGLER**
Duran throws a left at Hagler during their 1983 fight. It went 15 rounds, with Duran losing on points. Duran was Hagler's idol. The fight was close until Hagler's late burst. "If Marvin had put the pressure on in the first 10 rounds it would not have gone 15 rounds," said Goody Petronelli.

MILESTONES OF BOXING

••••••••••••••••••

MONEY, VEGAS AND BOXING

In the early 1980s the city known as Lost Wages was established as boxing's latest resort – a showcase city for the excesses of the sport. The casinos make the fights happen by paying large site fees – the money is returned when the pit drop increases.

Caesars, the Hilton and, in the 1990s, the MGM are the names fight fans know. They have replaced the American ballparks and Madison Square Garden as the venues for famous fights.

Some of boxing's modern classics have taken place in Vegas. Most of the fights between Hagler, Hearns, Duran and Leonard and the complicated series of heavyweight title fights that followed the demise of Ali, for instance, have been staged there.

The dominance of Vegas as a boxing mecca is evident by the fact that there are more current or former boxers living in the city than anywhere else. Some are wealthy, some are struggling and many are on the poverty line. Las Vegas is an easy place for boxing's winners, but there are few of them.

It was a supreme fight and the one that made Hagler truly great

▲ **THE UNFORGETTABLE FIRE**
"Marvin was out to show me that he was more of a man than me. I couldn't have that, so I was slugging with him," said Hearns after his third round knockout loss in April 1985.

The first round of Hagler against Hearns is often reckoned to be one of the most exciting rounds in boxing history. It ended after three minutes of furious punches with Hagler cut high on his forehead between his eyes, but both men had been hurt.

Hagler had planned to go out and mix it with Hearns from the start. He wanted to catch him quick and hurt him before the challenger found his range and started to move and land combinations. Both sets of cornermen watched anxiously as the seconds slowly passed. "Tommy broke his right hand in the first round, but he fought on – he had such a huge heart," said Steward. In the other corner the Petronelli brothers, Pat and Goody, stopped Hagler's cut. "It looked worse than it was," insisted Goody.

The second round was the same. The blood was smeared across Hagler's face and Hearns took some good shots without dropping. Steward remembers the round. "I think if Tommy's legs were okay he would have knocked Hagler out." At the end of the second there was calm but concern in Hagler's corner.

In round three the referee, Richard Steele, insisted Hagler, who was covered in blood from the cut, was looked at by the doctor. They were anxious moments for the champion. Hagler was allowed to continue, however, and he caught Hearns flush on the jaw with a right hook. Hearns was out on his feet and three punches later he was on the canvas. He bravely beat the count, but the referee had no alternative and he waved the fight off.

▶ THE DAMAGE IS DONE

Hagler's cuts are visible as Hearns connects with a right uppercut in the second round. "I felt blood pouring down my face and I knew I had to be the bull. This is what you call a sweet victory. It was war," said Hagler when it was over.

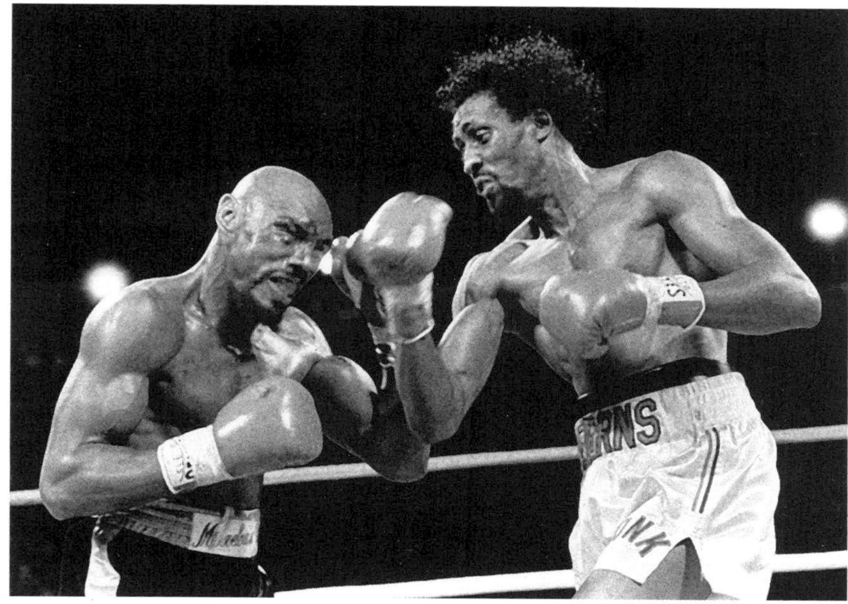

▼ THE SUDDEN END

Hearns is about to fall forward after Hagler's final right severs his senses. Hearns was still for six seconds before he forced himself to get up. The referee gathered Hearns in his arms to end the fight.

THE LOST GENERATION OF HEAVYWEIGHTS

The Noble Art of Self-destruction

▶ **THE SPOON**
Tim Witherspoon celebrates after beating Jorge Gonzalez in 1996. "I could cry all day if I let the past haunt my mind," said Witherspoon, one of the best neglected fighters in heavyweight history.

If there is ever a reunion for the members of the lost generation of boxing's heavyweights it will be a party to remember. John Tate, Mike Weaver, Michael Dokes, Tim Witherspoon, Pinklon Thomas, Greg Page, Tony Tubbs and Tony Tucker: they all belong to a brief period in heavyweight history, a period that was host to the most self-destructive group of fighters to hold titles.

There have been others, and there will be more in different weight divisions who have struggled with addictions, personal troubles and marital chaos, but the lost generation passed the tainted baton to each other during seven years of ignoble combat between 1979 and 1986.

▲ **DODGING POLITICS**
Greg Page won the WBA version of the title in 1984 when he knocked out Gerrie Coetzee in Sun City. David Bey had refused the fight on political grounds and Page later regretted going.

They each fell from grace. Some in awful ring appearances, but most in after-dark encounters in a netherworld of drugs, violence and despair. Their assailants in times of distress were often the people to whom they too willingly surrendered their lifestyles, and often their money. It was a shameful period and the fleecing was obvious. Never have so many talented fighters wasted their lives.

It is too easy to blame Don King, who promoted the shows where world heavyweight titles changed hands at an alarming rate during those chaotic years. King was accused by most of the fighters of taking their money or not paying them enough. His long-running feud with Tim Witherspoon was particularly bitter and was finally resolved when he agreed to pay the boxer one million dollars.

The boxers, however, must share the blame for their individual descents. They came in fat for important fights, they came in high on drugs for other fights and, as the titles were passed back and forth, they just got back in the line and waited.

In 1983 Larry Holmes relinquished the WBC version and accepted the IBF's new championship. With Holmes out of the way, King had two titles to play with and matched Page and Witherspoon, both of whom were managed by King's stepson Carl, in a hitless mazurka for Holmes's old title. Page won, but lost it in a similar fight against Thomas.

In 1986 Witherspoon joined Muhammad Ali and Floyd Patterson as the only boxers to win the world heavyweight title twice. He failed a post-fight drug test and admitted smoking a joint a few weeks earlier at a party. Many of the lost generation of heavyweight champions have spent time in rehab units in their fight against crack and cocaine addiction.

Some of the boxers were brilliant amateurs. Tate, Tubbs, Dokes, Tucker and Page were guaranteed futures before they had their first professional contests and their failure is even more tragic than the frustrated career of Witherspoon, who became a boxer by default. In 1997 Witherspoon was still trying to recapture some glory and recoup some money. Tucker, Page, Tubbs and Dokes were also active in the mid-1990s. Tucker, for instance, lost a vacant WBO heavyweight championship fight to Britain's Herbie Hide in June 1997.

Tyrell Biggs missed membership of the Lost Generation club by just a few years, but his downfall deserves a mention. Biggs was the 1984 Olympic heavyweight champion. A star for the future. However, Biggs skipped the part where you win the world title and then go crazy – he went straight to drug-induced burn-out! He was still fighting in the1990s and was outpointed by Tubbs over three rounds, at a bizarre knockout tournament in December 1993, which lasted one day and featured 16 heavyweights.

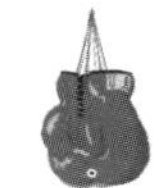

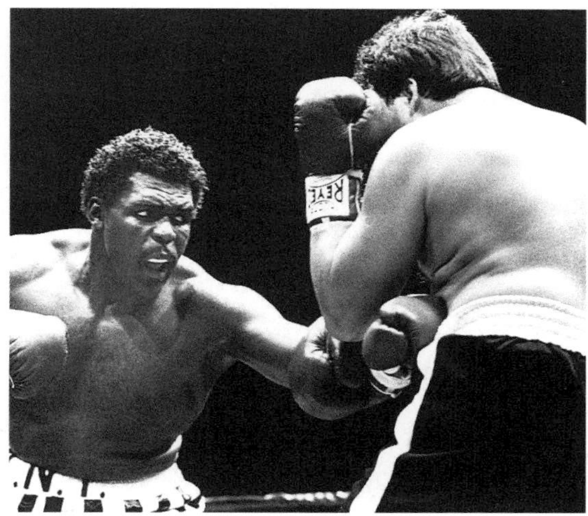

▲ **THEY LOST SO MUCH**

Tony Tucker (top) was one of the sweet boxers. Tony Tubbs (above left) was smooth and cool in the ring. He went with Tucker, Page, Tate and Dokes down a blind alley into a drug-induced decline that sucked their skills and left their futures in turmoil.

The Holmes-Cooney fight was turned into a battle of black against white

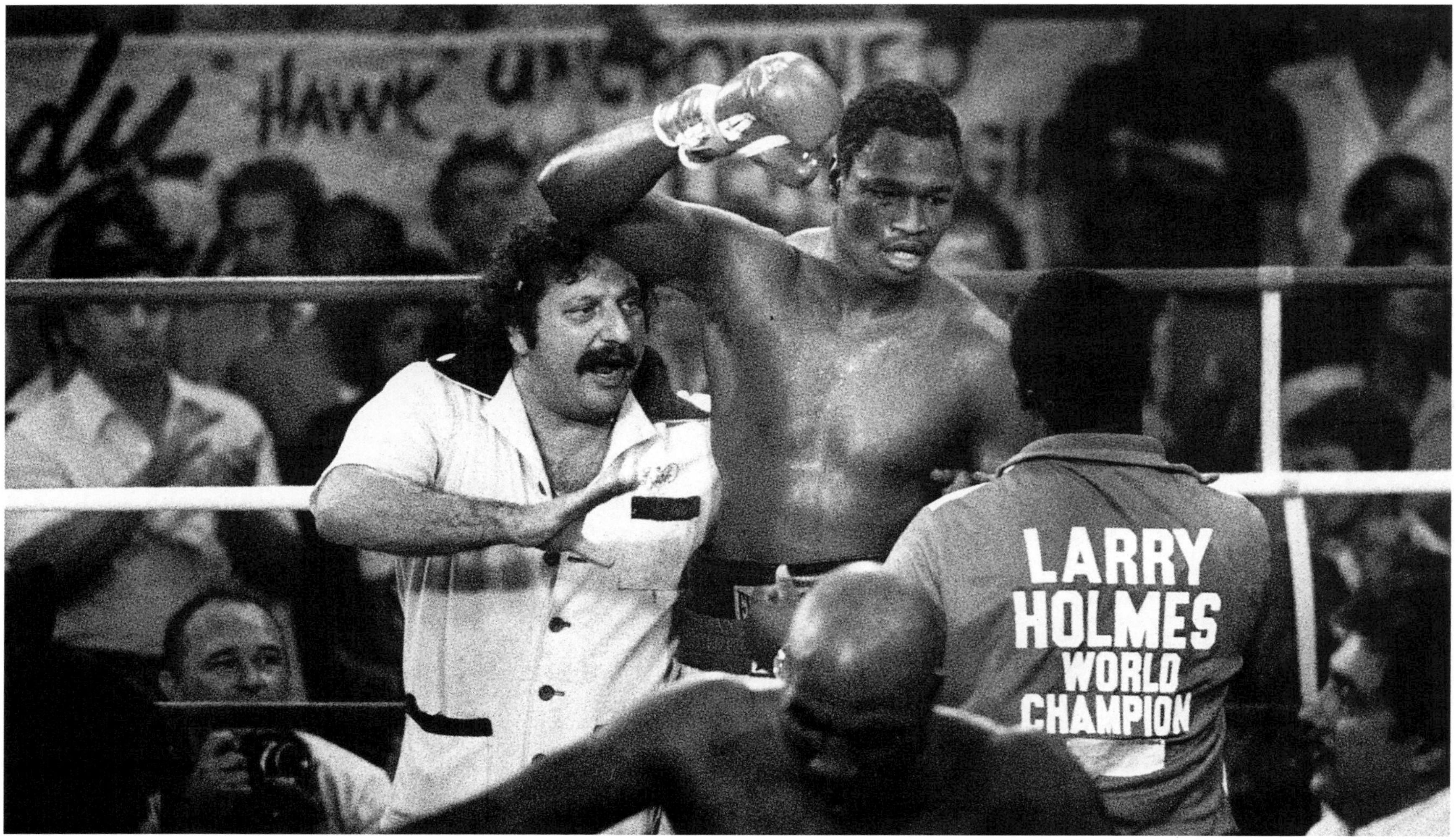

▲ **NO PLACE FOR RESPECT**
Holmes raises his arm in victory as Earnie Shavers is helped to his corner by his trainer in round 11 of their 1979 fight.

Larry Holmes could have ruled the heavyweight division from 1978 until his controversial defeat by Michael Spinks in 1985, if there had been a real effort to unify the titles. Sadly, there was more money to be made from the ongoing carnival of championship fights than there was from a unified series.

Holmes still made news. He beat Ali and then he met Gerry Cooney. The fight against Cooney became a black and white issue. The build-up was ugly but the public enjoyed it. "If I was white for a year, I'd probably make 20 million dollars. Look at all the money Gerry Cooney has made because he is white," said Holmes. In fact their fight was the richest in the sport's history at that time, and they split 20 million dollars.

It was a truly dramatic fight. Cooney started nervously and was dropped in round two. There was a no-foul rule and in the ninth Cooney's left hook landed low and Holmes needed two minutes to recover. The 10th was brutal. It was a real fight and the crowd of 32,000 at Caesars in Las Vegas watched a classic. In round 13 it came to an end when Cooney's friend and trainer, Victor Valle, intervened. "Gerry was finished and there was no point in letting it go further," he said. At the end of round 12 Cooney would have been winning if he had not lost three points for low blows. Cooney never recovered, started to drink and in 1990, during his third comeback, was knocked out by George Foreman.

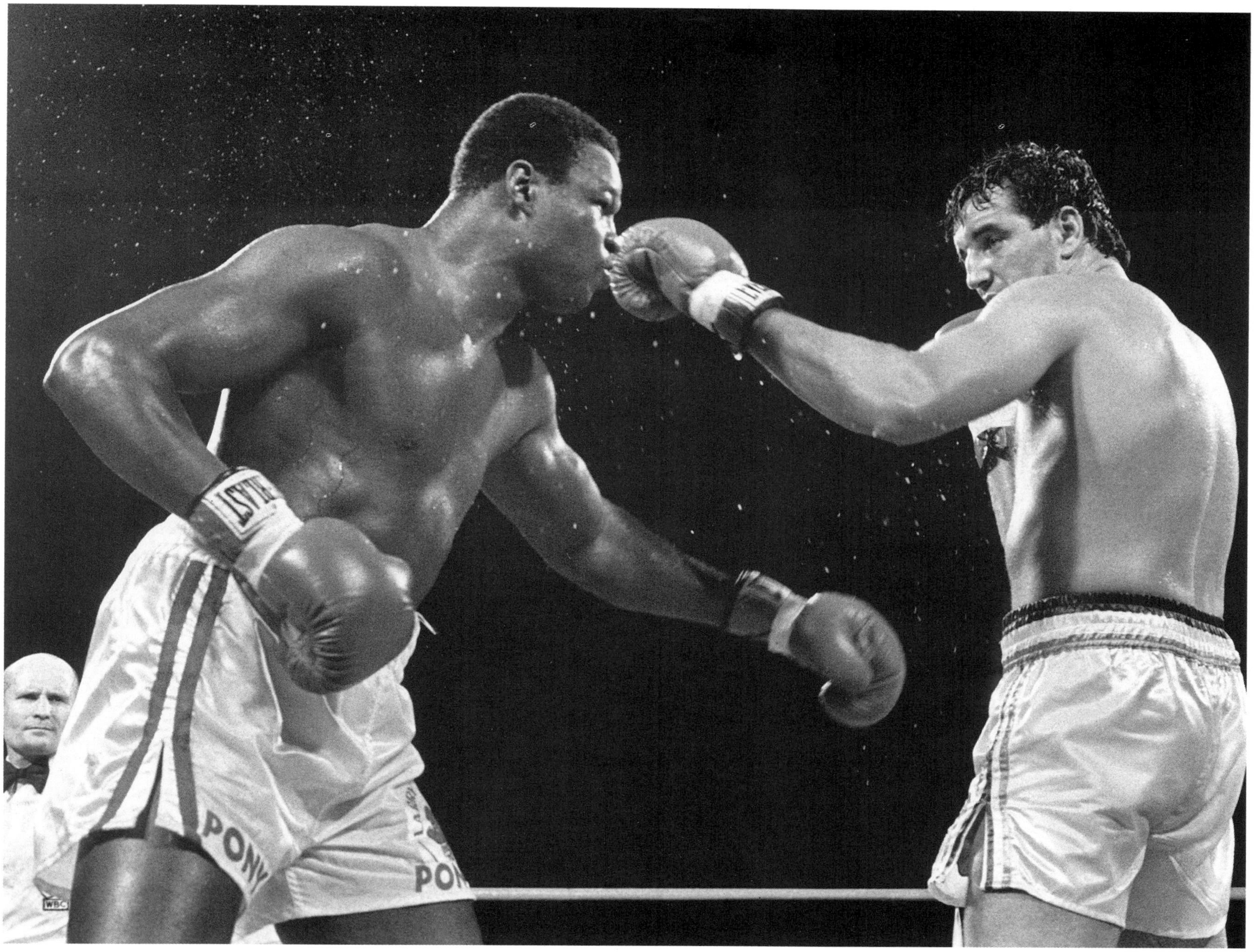

▲ **TOO MUCH PRESSURE**

Gerry Cooney hits Larry Holmes with a left during their 1982 brawl. Cooney dragged the legacy of all white hopes into the ring that year. "I never fought my fight, I was worried about the distance and got things wrong," said Cooney. Holmes won in round 13.

◄ **THE TRUTH IS OUT THERE**

Carl "The Truth" Williams connects with the chin of Holmes in 1985. Holmes won, outpointing Williams in what was the last defense of his heavyweight title.

LARRY HOLMES

Holmes was too Bright to Last

Larry Holmes is famous for his remarks. It took years of fighting to convince the public that he was a great champion and when the recognition finally came he opened his mouth and upset many in boxing's old guard.

After insulting Rocky Marciano, Holmes attacked another institution: Nevada officials. "The referees, judges and promoters can kiss me where the sun don't shine – on my big, black ass," he said after the second controversial points defeat against Michael Spinks in 1986.

He had the same message for officials in Denmark after losing to Brian Nielsen, in 1997. "They tried to poison me in a restaurant and their boy can't fight a lick," Holmes said after the fight, before letting his towel fall to the ground and turning round. "Yep, you know what they can do!"

Holmes was once Muhammad Ali's sparring partner. He was a sparring partner for hire and a good one. "He was just a kid who needed somebody to understand him, somebody to have confidence in him and who cared about him," said Richie Giachetti, the fighter's on-and-off long-suffering trainer.

▲ **PROUD WORDS**

"I know people have never forgiven me for beating Ali. I wanted to be remembered for beating Shavers, Cooney and the rest of the challengers - not just for one fight. Give me the respect," Holmes said.

In 1972 Holmes was disqualified in the Olympic trials against Duane Bobick. In 1973 he turned pro and progress was slow and steady after he had been rejected by top trainers Cus D'Amato, Gil Clancy, Eddie Futch and Angelo Dundee. Holmes went with Giachetti, who at the time had Earnie Shavers. From the start Holmes and Shavers were sparring partners.

In 1978 Holmes beat Shavers to secure a world title fight. Two judges gave him every round. It was a masterful performance. He beat Ken Norton to win the WBC title in his next fight. Holmes then went on to win 19 world heavyweight title fights before the first loss to Spinks in 1985.

"All I ever wanted was nice things for me and my family. There were times when I had nothing, just the money from working with Ali and there were other times when I looked at other fighters making money and it made me angry," said Holmes. He has never denied during his later fights that money is his motivation. "My attitude has been the same: I just want the most money. That is why I liked Gerry Cooney. I had to fight and beat five black fighters to get the money I made from one Cooney fight," claimed Holmes. He has repeatedly used money to justify some of the hard fights in the twilight of his career.

In 1988 he agreed to fight Tyson. He admits he had little chance of winning, but had other reasons for accepting the fight. "I can think of three million dollars why I agreed to meet Mike Tyson," he said. He lost in four rounds but frustrated Tyson on several occasions before going down heavily for the last count. It was a dreadful knockdown.

In 1995 Holmes exposed WBC champion Oliver McCall in Las Vegas. McCall retained his title but Holmes was just two rounds shy of victory. When Holmes was at his best – as he was against Norton or Shavers – it is possible that McCall would have struggled as a sparring partner in his camp.

As the years pass Holmes's status as a modern great increases. He fought on a regular basis and met all of the contenders and pretenders from a period when most of the heavyweights wasted their talents. Holmes is the best heavyweight from the tarnished years between the last of Ali's sweet jabs and the vicious hooks of Tyson. If time had been kinder to Holmes it is possible that he would be held in even higher esteem.

▲ **HOLMES V JONES** *Larry Holmes makes a rotund Leroy Jones suffer during their 1980 fight. Jones went eight rounds before the referee stopped it.*

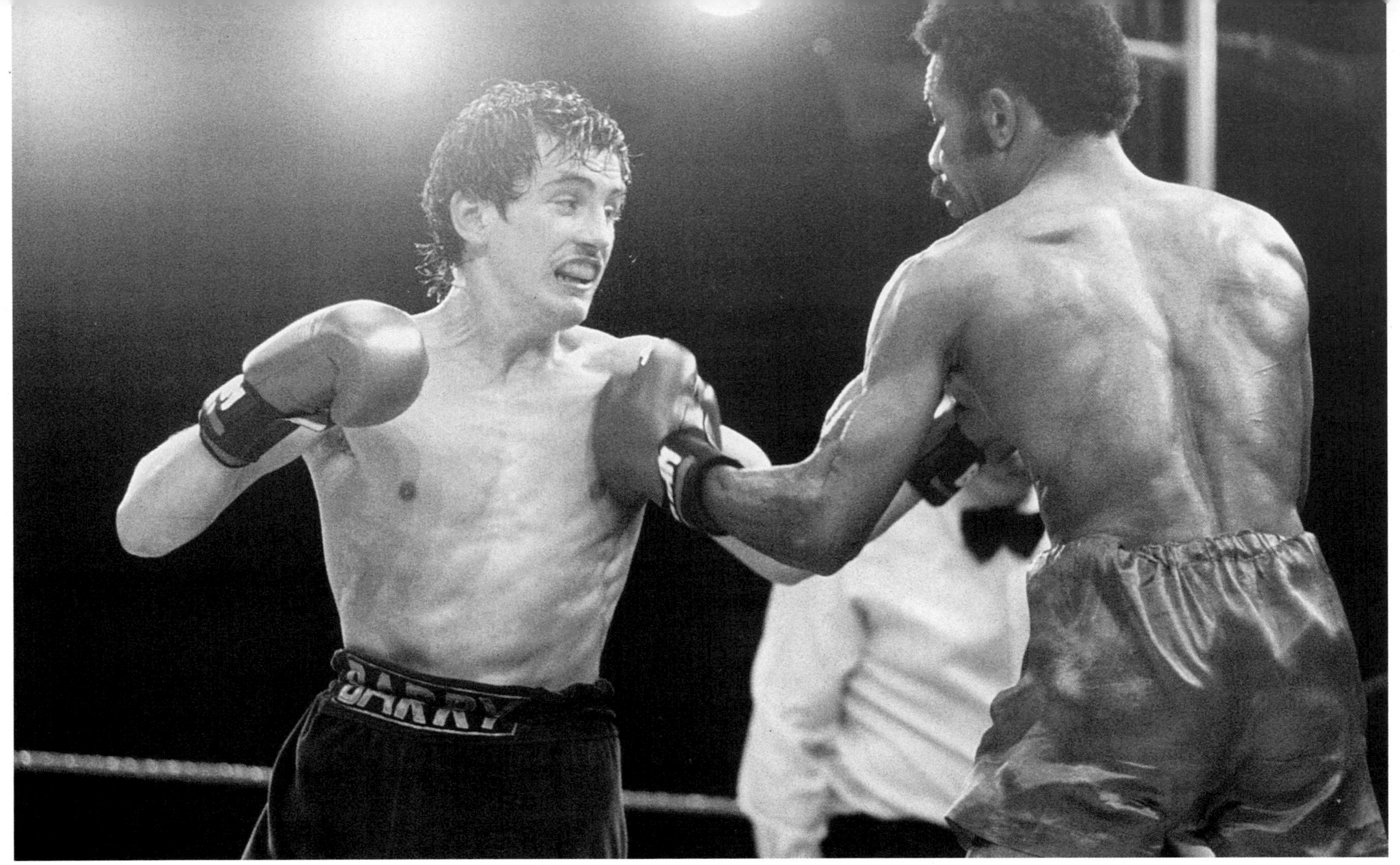

Irish eyes were smiling when Barry McGuigan sought and found glory

▲ **THE OLD MAN FALLS HARD**
Over 26,000 people watched McGuigan challenge fading maestro Pedroza in London in 1985. It was emotional and dramatic and by the end of the evening McGuigan's cult status was confirmed.

Barry McGuigan was a cult fighter in Northern Ireland, his aggressive boxing and personal charm making him the perfect local hero. When he won the WBA featherweight title in 1985 by outpointing Panamanian veteran Eusebio Pedroza in London, his future looked secure. Sadly, it all went horribly wrong.

After two routine, but entertaining defences against average challengers, McGuigan agreed to fight in Las Vegas against Steve Cruz, a substitute from Texas. Cruz had an unexceptional record and McGuigan appeared poised to make a lot of money in America.

Before the move to Las Vegas from the Irishman's training camp in Palm Springs there were rumors about injuries, divided loyalties and imminent splits. The fight was in June, it was too hot and as the sun tortured the two fighters in the ring it was clear that something dreadful was unfolding.

The end of McGuigan's world championship reign was both thrilling and sickening to watch. He was in front on two of the three scorecards going into the 15th and last round and only had to stay on his feet during the final three minutes. However, he could barely stand and Cruz dropped him twice to win a unanimous verdict.

McGuigan was exhausted and was ordered to go to a hospital for a brain scan. An acrimonious fall-out followed between the boxer and his manager Barney Eastwood. The rift has never been healed and when McGuigan returned to the ring in 1988 he was promoted by Frank Warren. He never again reached the emotional highs of the night in 1985 when he won the title.

▶ **BOXING'S NEW HERO**
McGuigan just can't stop smiling. He grew during the fight and when the final bell sounded he was no longer a boy.

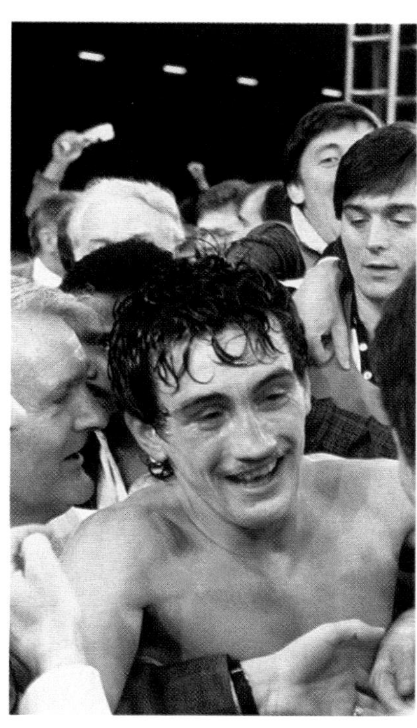

▼ **A JOB WELL DONE**
McGuigan has Pedroza in his sights. The win over Pedroza was a rites of passage, a learning process against a champion who was both too old and dead at the weight. Barney Eastwood had done a marvelous job.

MILESTONES OF BOXING

"NO MAS": DURAN QUITS

It is too easy to overlook the impact of Roberto Duran's two words in his rematch with Sugar Ray Leonard in 1980, but when he turned away and said "No mas" he shocked the boxing world.

In the first fight Duran had laughed at Leonard's attempt to show respect at the end of 15 rounds. He continued to insult Leonard. It was Duran's supreme macho act. The second fight was part of a downfall that no one thought possible. Duran's cornerman, Ray Arcel, tried to lift his fighter. He pleaded for him to get close and stay close but in the ring Leonard was laughing and growing in confidence, while Duran was falling apart.

According to Angelo Dundee, who was in Leonard's corner, the fight was over from the start. "Ray knew what to do and he dominated with his head. Duran had no way out," claimed Dundee. There was a half-hearted story about stomach cramps but nobody was listening. The fight was billed as Stone versus Sugar but on the night it was mind versus heart and Leonard's mind won. When it was over Duran said: "I fight no more." He lied. Despite the damage done to his reputation he continued to box.

Bruno had nothing left after Witherspoon's sustained assault

BRUNO V WITHERSPOON

In 1986 Bruno was given his first title chance against Witherspoon. It ended in dreadful pain for the Brirish challenger. It was obvious that Bruno and the men at his side needed more time at the drawing board.

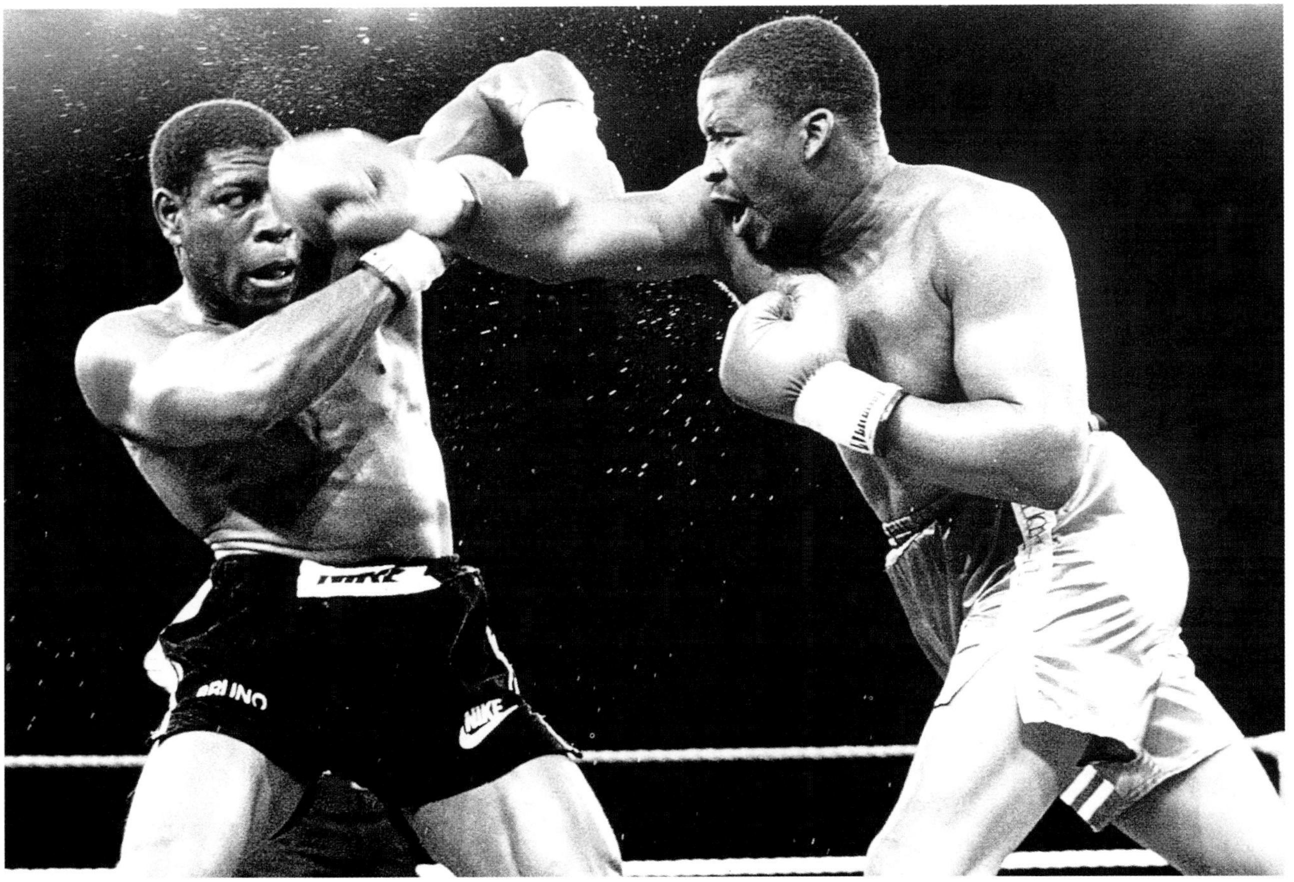

Life continued as normal in the heavyweight division. In January 1986 Tim Witherspoon won the WBA version, his second world title, after 15 dull rounds against Tony Tubbs. In the summer of 1986 the American arrived in London to defend his title against Frank Bruno.

Bruno was a fragile idol, but the British tabloid press created a monster of destruction. Witherspoon had a nice time at his Essex training camp and as the days passed the American's waistline started to grow. A British win was predicted and on the night the foolish turned their hopes into a demand.

In round 11 Bruno was left in a boxing wasteland after the champion had landed enough overhand rights to damage the senses of the brave London fighter. When it was over and Bruno's disfigured face was resting on the shoulder of his manager Terry Lawless, the hooligans went berserk once again. There were 27 arrests.

Bruno fought on. The loss was profitable for him because promoter Mickey Duff and Lawless paid him a fee in excess of his abilities.

However, there was controversy outside the ring. Witherspoon claimed he was not paid what he was promised by his manager Carl King and Carl's step-father Don. It was an ugly story, but nobody really cared too much about Witherspoon, who was later compensated but forever ostracized for his defiance.

In December 1986 Witherspoon was knocked out in one round by James Bonecrusher Smith. "I had no desire or reason to fight," he said. Witherspoon is the greatest of the lost generation because of his sad, bad attitude. "The Spoon", as he was known, was one of boxing's craziest characters.

▲ **ENOUGH IS ENOUGH**

Bruno's bid for the title is over as Witherspoon's punches take their toll. "Against Tim I could tell I was running out of steam but my heart kept me going even when I had no chance," said Bruno. His heart was never under scrutiny.

▼ **BLACK, BRITISH AND FRAGILE**

Bruno looks both relaxed and menacing in a 1982 publicity shot. Despite a gallant showing, Witherspoon proved too strong.

▶ **SHORT CELEBRATIONS**

Witherspoon kept his title but had to sue Don King, his promoter, for money. Witherspoon was eventually paid, but has been on the outside of the ring ever since.

Tyson was the pride of D'Amato and they were boxing's immediate future

The man in the shadows during the mid-1980s was Mike Tyson. He was there in 1985 as the heavyweight title changed hands, and while many fighters were in a state of flux, he was slowly making his way to the top.

In April 1986, Larry Holmes lost a disputed split decision to Michael Spinks. "It's over. This is it. I know I can't win no more. There's no sense in chasing ghosts. It hurts because I worked so hard. I sacrificed so much," said Holmes. But he came back.

Spinks was gracious in victory: "Larry was fighting for his life. He fought to the very end." However, Spinks was looking over his shoulder at Tyson, the man-child from Cus D'Amato's Catskill retreat.

In March 1986 Trevor Berbick, a constant traveler in the heavyweight zone, finally won the title when he beat Pinklon Thomas.

In New York and New Jersey, Tyson kept winning. All of Tyson's opponents were the right men for the job. Many were part of the legion of sparring partners and hired-hands that so many heavyweights belong to. They talked, and a sense of fear developed. There was something disturbing about the kid from Brooklyn and his odd group. Don King worked hard in late 1985 to get as close as possible to Tyson.

In November 1986 Tyson met Berbick for the WBC title. The fight was in Las Vegas, where 17 of the previous 34 world title fights had been staged. The sport was one short fight away from a glorious future. Sadly, Tyson was just a few years away from a hell of his own making, but in the weeks before the Berbick fight the 20-year-old boxer was pure.

◀ **FAIRYTALE BOY**

Tyson devastated his opponents. "Cus taught me. I owe it all to Cus," Tyson insisted. Others blamed D'Amato for Tyson's frailties outside the ring – nobody doubted the influence of the sage from the New York woods on Tyson in the ring.

▶ **THE OTHER BROTHER**
Michael Spinks kept his head, stayed in control and retained his money. "I told Leon that the people around him were trying to turn him against his family. I had different people next to me," Michael said.

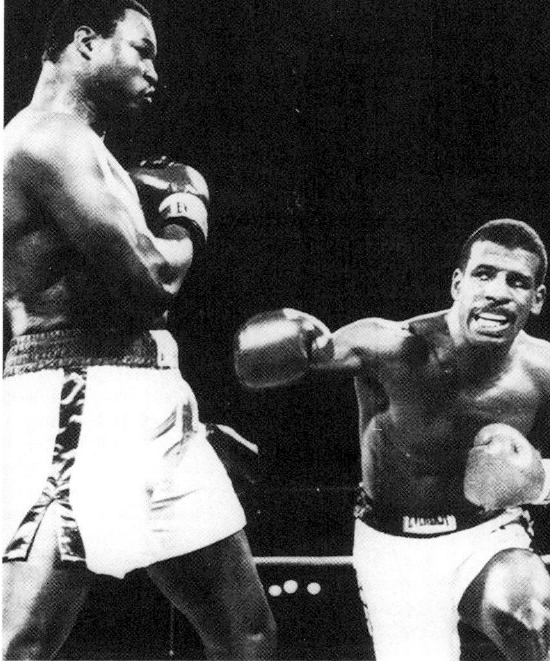

▲ **SPINKS WINS THROUGH**
Larry Holmes backs away from Michael Spinks in the second round of their 1985 title fight in Las Vegas. Spinks defeated Holmes to take the heavyweight title.

◀ **GRUDGE MATCH**
Tyson and Mitch Green go 10 rounds in 1986."Mitch Green was always talking nonsense and saying this and that. I wanted to make his suffer slow," Tyson said. The pair later had a fight outside an all-night tailor's shop in Harlem. Tyson won again.

The NEW *bad boy*

1986-1994

GE MIRA
MIRAGE
USA

▲ **STATEMENT OF INTENT**
"I refuse to lose in the ring," said Tyson after beating Mitch Green in 1986. At the time he looked untouchable, and there were seemingly a string of fighters waiting in line to be sacrificed.

The awesome power of Mike Tyson was first unveiled in 1985. A poor kid from Brooklyn, Tyson lived for boxing and was poised to become the greatest champion in the sport's history.

D'AMATO'S BABE TURNS SOUR

In November 1985 Cus D'Amato died. He left behind his last offering to the sport of boxing, a boxer once so pure and perfect that D'Amato's suggestion that Mike Tyson would be the greatest fighter in history appeared possible.

Tyson was born poor in Brooklyn. He was also born bad and after several scrapes with the law was placed at the age of 13 in the Tryon School for boys in upstate New York. He was nearly 200 pounds, just five foot eight and had an incongruous, high-pitched voice. In Brownsville he was known as Big Head Mike or Little Fairy Boy.

At Tryon Tyson came under the influence of former pro Bobby Stewart. The pair worked together in the gym and in 1980 Stewart made contact with D'Amato. In March 1980, at D'Amato's gym, the trainer watched three rounds of Tyson sparring with Stewart and stated: "That's the heavyweight champion of the world." On June 30, 1980, Tyson was released into D'Amato's custody. He had a legal guardian and a future in the boxing ring.

The troubles did not come to a stop when Tyson left Tryon, however. They never came to a stop. D'Amato concentrated on curbing Tyson's emotions in the ring but ignored his dangerous behavior outside it. The product became too important and indiscretions were overlooked and excused. Unfortunately, Tyson's boxing education failed to include valuable lessons in distinguishing between right and wrong.

In May 1985 Tyson turned professional after 35 amateur contests and a further 19 fights in amateur "smokers." The opponents started to fall. The men from the list of reliable losers made their money in brief and painful encounters with boxing's young star. The news spread as word started to filter through from survivors of undercard beatings. The heavyweight scene was in waiting as Tyson knocked men over and out.

◀ **"RAZOR" IS BLUNTED!**
Previous page: Tyson launches a ferocious right hand at Ruddock during the first of their two fights.

In 1985 Tyson fought 15 times and stopped those 15 opponents in a total of just 22 rounds – 11 went in round one. Some of the beaten men had reputations for losing in style but Tyson ruined them. By the end of 1985 he was being watched and not just by the heavyweights on the championship merry-go-round. There were others with plans.

Tyson's first fight for Don King was in May 1986, against former New York gang leader Mitch "Blood" Green in Madison Square Garden. It went 10 rounds. Two years later Tyson and Green had another fight, again in New York – at four in the morning outside a tailor's shop in Harlem. According to eyewitnesses, Tyson won the rematch.

The last fight in 1986 was against Trevor Berbick for the WBC heavyweight championship. King was the promoter, but Tyson was still managed by Jim Jacobs and his partner Bill Cayton, who at the time did not have a boxing manager's license. Cayton and Jacobs had invited King in. The struggle over Tyson's future guidance was inevitable, and according to Tyson's trainer, and one of D'Amato's loyal boys, Kevin Rooney, the problem was King. "He hung around like a dog," said Rooney.

Before the fight Berbick was not intimidated. "Tyson is just a one-way fighter. He doesn't have a good jab and he is not a smart fighter. I will back him up." He tried but he was overwhelmed. It ended in round two and 20-year-old Tyson was the youngest heavyweight champion of the world.

The heavyweights were now in trouble.

First to go was James "Bonecrusher" Smith, but the fight lasted 12 rounds. Smith was sensible enough to survive but Tyson won the WBA belt. Next, in May 1987, was Pinklon Thomas, the former champion. It went six rounds and Tyson retained both titles. Before the fight Thomas used a line that Evander Holyfield repeated in 1996 and 1997. "He comes from the same mean streets as me. I seen the same things," said Thomas.

"Mike has an image. He thought that by having a certain perception it helped him win fights," said D'Amato protege, Teddy Atlas. The image was simple: Tyson had been told he was savage and ruthless by people close to him and tried to uphold that reputation. In a lot of his fights the image worked, and his opponents' fear helped him.

In August 1987 Tyson unified the titles by beating Tony Tucker for the IBF belt. It went 12 rounds. Tyson was the new unified champion of the world.
In late 1987 he made the first of six defences of the unified world title and stopped Tyrell Biggs, the 1984 Olympic super-heavyweight champion, in seven rounds. Tyson had disliked Biggs since before the Olympics when the two had sparred.

It may have been a great year in the ring for Tyson, but his life away from boxing was starting to come apart. By the start of 1988 Michael Gerard Tyson's life had changed – by the end of the traumatic year the signs of destruction were already clear.

▼ FINAL TITLE SAFE
Tony Tucker went 12 rounds and had the right idea against Tyson in August 1987, but when it was over Tyson had the IBF, WBA and WBC belts. He was midway through his prime first period as champion.

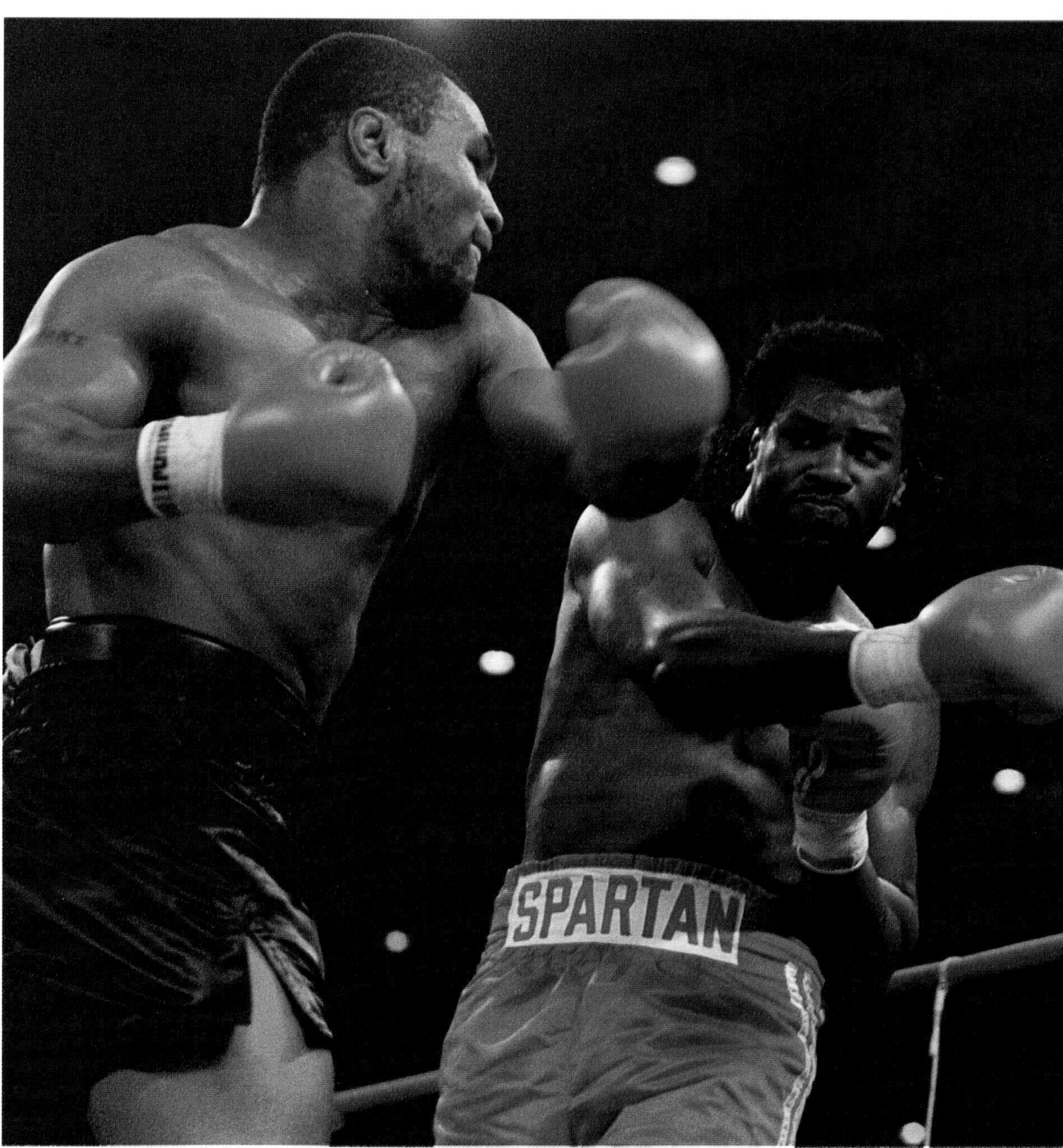

Tyson's destruction of Spinks instilled fear in the division

In March 1988 Tyson lost his mentor Jim Jacobs. It was a shock, nobody had told the fighter that Jacobs was ill! Tyson gained a wife in Robin Givens but their sad marriage was over by October and in November his dispute with Cayton intensified. Rooney was also gone by the end of the year. King was in the background offering promotional agreements. It was a horrible time for the fighter.

In the ring that year Tyson took care of business with three wins, but there were many watching who saw the obvious changes. Tyson was slack.

In January 1988 he had stopped Larry Holmes in round four. Holmes had the right idea but Tyson, after a severe reprimand from Rooney at the end of round two – possibly the last time a cornerman dared criticize Tyson during a fight – returned to his old style and the speed was too much for Holmes. The ending was as savage as any of Tyson's knockout wins.

In March 1988 Tyson took his new bride to Tokyo, where he stopped former champion Tony Tubbs in two rounds. Two days later, after Tyson had returned to New York, he was told that Jacobs was dead. King used the funeral in Los Angeles as an opportunity to move even closer to the fighter.

By the time Tyson knocked out Michael Spinks in June of the same year his relationship with Cayton was in turmoil and his marriage was a sham. Because of the circumstances Spinks had an opportunity. Tyson, however, overcame the pressures to ruin Spinks in just 91 seconds.

◀ **SPINKS'S DELUSION**

Michael Spinks was utterly destroyed in 91 seconds of his fight with Tyson, in June 1988, but after the contest he was in reflective mood. "I thought there was a way to beat him, I still do. On the night it went wrong and he took me out. That is what can happen in boxing."

▼ **THE OLD MAN IS BACK**
"I don't want to hear about age and don't tell me how good Tyson is. I know what I'm doing," said Larry Holmes before his fight with Tyson in January 1988. Holmes was easily beaten in four rounds.

▲ **PRIMED FOR A FALL**
An early studio shot of Tyson in his prime, but there were already signs of trouble. During 1988, several acts of careless behavior dominated his life outside the ropes.

▶ **END FOR THE CITY MAN**
"Each day I would meet with Jim (Jacobs) to discuss what to do with Mike," said Cayton. However, when Jacobs died in March 1988, Cayton was running out of time and Don King was looming large.

▲ **D'AMATO MAN OUSTED**
Kevin Rooney was instructed in the ways of boxing and fear by Cus D'Amato. He was the man Tyson trusted and needed in the corner, but their relationship was soured when Tyson married Robin Givens. "Mike lost control," claimed Rooney.

The British flags stopped waving as Tyson ruined Bruno in five rounds

▶ ANOTHER SAD NIGHT
Bruno throws a left jab at Tyson early in the fight. At one point he managed to hurt the champion with a left hook but in the end there was little for the British fans to cheer about. After the fight, Tyson was in dismissive mood. "How dare they challenge me with their primitive skills. I feel sorry for the guys who want to fight me."

Tyson was out of the ring for eight months before he defended against Frank Bruno in February 1989. The fight had been postponed five times and Tyson had watched as his life changed dramatically in a crazily short period of time. By February 1989 Givens, Rooney and Jacobs were gone forever. King, the "Only in America" man, was in charge.

Tyson left Bruno a wrecked shell on the ropes in round five, but in the first round was caught and clearly hurt by a left hook. The single punch was enough to confirm the worst for the Tyson-watchers. In reality fighting was the easiest part of Tyson's life. It may well have been before, and certainly has been ever since.

In 1989 the ring was still a noble retreat for Tyson, a place of violent sanctuary.

In July he stopped Carl "The Truth" Williams in one round. Williams had a plan and, like Biggs, had sparred with Tyson. It lasted 93 seconds. If Tyson was having trouble in his private life and his reflexes, punches and feet were slowing down, as many claimed, he was still too much for any of his peers.

The lost generation of heavyweights were deep into their declines. George Foreman had just returned after a 10-year absence, Holyfield was not yet big enough and Riddick Bowe and Lennox Lewis were novices. By the end of 1989 the only person Tyson had to lose to was himself.

▲ BRUNO UNDER FIRE

Bruno tries to duck from a barrage of punches in the first round. "I was too stiff, too nervous and just froze when he caught me. We were in Vegas and the pressure was starting to get to me," Bruno offered as explanation. Seven years later Bruno returned to the city of the slaughter and was mauled once again by Tyson.

◄ A MAN IN TROUBLE

Bruno receives a count from the referee after a first-round knockdown. Although Tyson destroyed Bruno, he met with his critics after the fight and furiously denied suggestions that his time was running out. However, after one more quick win he went to Tokyo and lost for the first time in his professional career.

TYSON v DOUGLAS

Fantasy Night in Tokyo for Buster

▼ **DOOM IN NEON CITY**
Tyson's turbulent life outside the ropes finally caught up with him as he groped for his gumshield on the canvas in round 10. Douglas, the underdog, had won. "I just want to get back in the ring. Losing is part of the business," said a resolute Tyson at the fight's end.

The final fight of Mike Tyson's first reign as heavyweight champion ended in diabolical farce, pain and insult.

In February 1990 Tyson was in Tokyo to fight James "Buster" Douglas. It was expected to be easy, with odds set at 40-1 against Douglas winning. In 1987 Douglas had faded and was stopped by Tony Tucker in an IBF title fight. His heart was deemed dubious.

In training Tyson looked awful and was dropped by Greg Page, a former champion. Douglas had beaten Page and there was a suggestion that slow ticket sales inspired the so-called knockdown. Even if it was a set-up, Tyson was not himself.

"I will just hit him and keep hitting him," promised Douglas. Nobody listened, but there were signs that Douglas was a new man. In recent months he had separated from his wife – the mother of his son, Lamar, had been diagnosed with terminal cancer – and in January 1990 his beloved mother died. He was inspired and fearless, whereas Tyson was bored and listless.

The fight was weird from the start. Tyson was not moving his head or his feet. He was easy to hit and Douglas was hitting him. Tyson's cornermen, Aaron Snowell and Jay Bright, were hopeless as the panic increased and the rounds passed. Douglas was resisting. In round five Tyson's left eye started to swell. In his corner the search for an Enswell, the small piece of curved steel that good cornermen sink in ice and use to move swellings, proved fruitless. In its place a condom was packed with ice and rubbed over the eye. It was that type of corner! The strangeness continued until round eight, when Tyson landed a right to send Douglas down. It was all over, many believed. They were wrong. Douglas smashed the canvas in frustration, was lucid, and climbed up as referee, Octavio Meyran, reached nine. The fight started again, but the bell sounded.

Douglas wanted to win and nothing would stop him. In round nine he sought Tyson out in brutal battle, and when the bell sounded it was obvious that boxing would have a new champion. Tyson was stuck in the center of the ring, his mind devoid of desire.

In round 10 Tyson walked out to slaughter and was duly butchered. He went down heavily from a left, after right had landed and frozen him upright, but dazed. On the canvas Tyson worked in slow motion to pick up his gumshield. At ringside King was screaming, and as the seconds of the final count passed, Tyson was on his feet. However, he could not stand alone and it was waved off. Iron Mike was beaten. Seldom in the history of boxing have so many silent witnesses suddenly stepped forward at a fight's conclusion and declared: "I knew that would happen."

Four hours later Jose Sulaiman and Gilberto Mendoza, the respective presidents of the WBC and the WBA suspended recognition of Douglas because in round eight he had been on the floor longer than 10 seconds. King had led the appeal, but it was an action he would regret. "I knocked him out before he knocked me out," claimed Tyson. Within days everybody was backtracking. "Douglas is the true champion," King said in New York. The WBA and WBC quickly agreed.

In October 1990 Douglas collapsed in round three when Evander Holyfield connected cleanly for the first time. "He could have got up," claimed referee Mills Lane. In Tokyo he could have stayed down, but on that wonderful day he had as much heart and desire as any boxer in the sport's history.

▲ **DOUGLAS THE CHAMP** *"This is the dream," said Douglas. "I knew I could do it, I had the determination to succeed and I whupped his ass!"*

Away from Tyson, carnival fighters like Chavez and Whitaker ruled

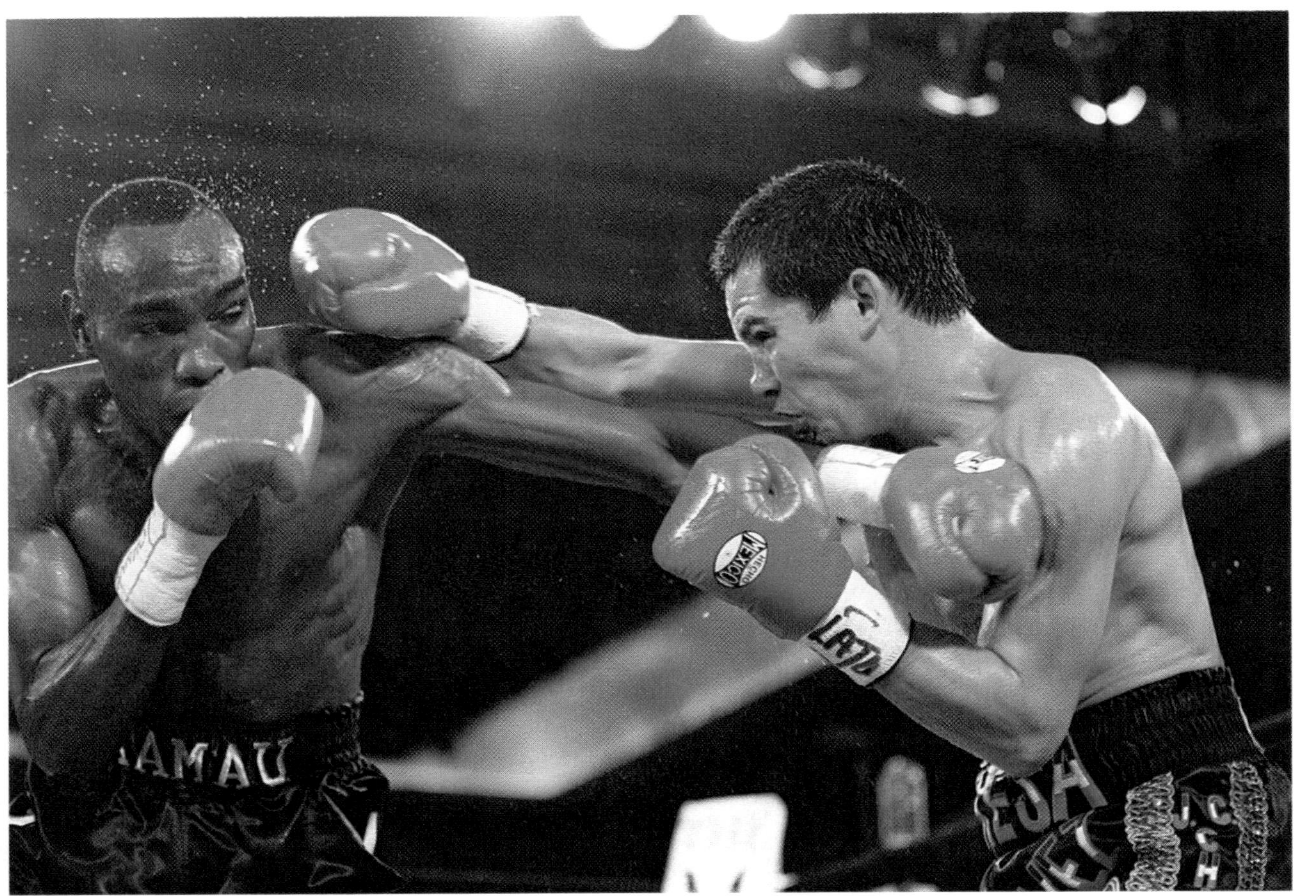

▶ **CHAVEZ V KAMAU**
David Kamau extended Chavez in their WBC light-welterweight title fight in 1995. Chavez won, but his power was starting to diminish after years of training, hard living and weight reduction.

▲ **HAPPY WINNER, BAD LOSER**
"They say Chavez is unbeatable – that suits me. I have heard he is dirty – that suits me. I know he is a bad loser, and that suits me," said Pernell Whitaker before his controversial draw with the Mexican in 1993. "C'mon, I won clearly," he said when it was all over. He did.

Two fighters from the lower divisions dominated the late 1980s and 1990s: Julio Cesar Chavez, who was blessed with a loyal following and a solid chin, and Pernell Whitaker, a gold medalist in 1984 with a tricky and often ugly southpaw style. Both lacked charisma.

Less than one month after Tyson's fall, Chavez stopped Meldrick Taylor with just two seconds left in the last round to add the IBF junior-welterweight title to his WBC super-lightweight belt.

The Mexican idol was losing on two scorecards and was saved when referee, Richard Steele, intervened. Taylor complained later, but had failed to respond to Steele's questions during the dark moments in the ring. It was Chavez's 69th straight win. His first loss was against Frankie Randall in his 91st fight in 1994, although there were many who believed the first loss was actually in 1993 when Chavez drew with Pernell Whitaker in a challenge for the WBC welterweight title.

In 1994 Chavez beat Randall in a rematch and stopped Taylor in round eight but the Mexican had turned from winner to whiner and was losing respect. In 1996 he was cruelly cut and beaten in four rounds by Oscar De La Hoya.

Whitaker won his first title, the IBF lightweight belt, in 1989 and in the same year avenged a controversial defeat by winning the WBC version from Jose Luis Ramirez. In 1990 he beat Azumah Nelson and then added the WBA version after knocking out Juan Nazario in the first. He won the IBF junior-welter in 1992, the WBC welter in 1993 and in 1995 defied the odds to win the WBA light-middleweight championship. In 1997 De La Hoya won a close and disputed points verdict to take Whitaker's WBC welterweight title.

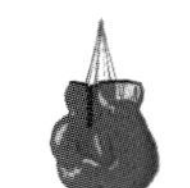

▲ **NO DOUBTERS LEFT**

Whitaker (top) won a title at a fourth weight when he stepped up to light-middleweight to beat WBA champion, Julio Vasquez, in 1995, in another stunning display.

▲ **THE SELF-PROCLAIMED KING**

"When you fight Pernell Whitaker you're not fighting 'Joe Blow' – you're fighting the king," said Whitaker (above) before losing to Oscar De La Hoya in 1997.

MILESTONES OF BOXING

MIKE TYSON BEATS TREVOR BERBICK TO WIN WBC HEAVYWEIGHT TITLE

NOVEMBER 22, 1986. LAS VEGAS.

Mike Tyson became the youngest heavyweight champion of the world at the age of 20 when he stopped Trevor Berbick to win the WBC title in Las Vegas. He knew he would win, knew he would knock out Berbick, and on the night he dominated.

It was classic Tyson. He rolled with each shot and scored from the angles that he had been taught. Berbick was chopped and rocked from the start and his head quickly lost control of the rest of his body. He was willing, but his bravery hurt him in the end.

For Tyson it was the first step. His mentor, Cus D'Amato, had died a year earlier but he left his legacy of fear in the head of the fighter he had spent so many hours creating. "I couldn't have done this without Cus," Tyson would often say.

The world watched two boxing gods on a night of intense emotion

LAS VEGAS CALLING

There were 15,000 spectators at Caesars Palace when Hagler met Leonard in April 1987, and an estimated 300 million watched worldwide on television. Leonard won a split points decision that angered Hagler. "I said I would do it and I did. It was not about beating Marvin Hagler, it was for the title," said Leonard.

Long after their best days, the fighters from the early 1980s were still winning. Sugar Ray Leonard, Tommy Hearns and Roberto Duran refused to leave the arena but in 1987 Marvelous Marvin Hagler retired – and stuck to it – after losing a close decision and his middleweight championship to Leonard.

Before the fight Hagler suggested it would be his last, a perfect win to end his career. "My mind and body are right. I have wanted this for years," he said. Leonard had not fought in three years. Hagler was guaranteed 12 million dollars and Leonard 11. Leonard, who had undergone an operation to repair a detached retina in his left eye, was 30 and Hagler 32.

"I'm going to go for the eye, the nose, the mouth, the neck, the arms, the stomach – anything above the waist. And if he wants to fight dirty, I might go for things below the belt," Hagler replied when asked if he would focus on Leonard's damaged eye.

Leonard was hurt on occasions and was brilliant at other times. Hagler was relentless, his usual aggressive style, but the fight was close and Leonard had the tactics to frustrate. There was a lot of holding but there were also some terrific exchanges. When it was over Hagler was the loser by a split decision.

"He told me at the end. 'You won, man. You beat me'," claimed Hagler. "Leonard fought like a girl. He should have had points deducted for all the holding and grabbing. I fought my heart out." Hagler left Vegas and boxing for good after the fight. Leonard continued to box and was brutally stopped and exposed by Hector "Macho" Camacho, another relic from the 1980s, in 1997.

▲ **A JUBILANT SUGAR RAY**
Leonard celebrates wildly after the announcement of his points victory over Hagler. The defeat signaled the end of the road for the Marvelous one. "I just want to get out of Vegas and get away from boxing." He remained true to his word and never fought again.

◄ **WAITING FOR ACTION**
Hagler and Leonard jockey for position – each looking for an opening – during their long-awaited fight in 1987. Leonard was a master tactician. He constantly moved back and smothered Hagler's attacks during the contest, a move which infuriated the champion.

In Britain a boxing revolution was led by an unlikely fighter

In Las Vegas, in 1990, Nigel Benn dropped Iran Barkley three times and stopped him after two minutes and 57 seconds of round one. He retained his WBO middleweight title, but it was a bad-tempered brawl and Barkley and his handlers were angry at the former British soldier's abuses. "They are crying like babies," said Benn, "I love stuffing it up Americans."

Benn returned to Britain and agreed terms to defend against Chris Eubank. In America nobody paid much attention to the fight, but a crowd of 9,000 packed the NEC, Birmingham, in November, 1990, and watched one of the best-ever British fights. Eubank won in round nine and a golden period in British boxing started. It coincided with the WBO's efforts to establish itself. The WBO had Eubank and he was British boxing.

Eubank retained his WBO middleweight title three times, before winning the vacant WBO super-

▲ **BENN SHARES A JOKE**
Nigel Benn with actor, Pierce Brosnan, in jocular mood in Dublin in 1996.

◀ **THE EGO HAS LANDED**
"My aim is to improve the quality of my life and to achieve my goal. I have selected the noble art as a profession." Eubank was a cult attraction from the start.

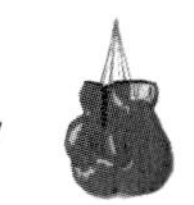

middleweight title and retaining it 14 times. His earnings were far in excess of the amounts American boxers at the same weight made during the time. The eccentric boxer from Brighton created a new audience for the sport in Britain. Purists and old-timers disliked him from the start, but thousands paid and millions watched him on television.

In 1991, Eubank vacated the WBO middleweight title to avoid a mandatory defense against the dangerous young American Gerald McClellan; and agreed terms for a rematch with Michael Watson, a boxer from London, who had knocked out Benn in 1989. In the first fight with Watson the judges decided that Eubank had done enough to retain his middleweight title. The second fight and its tragic outcome are now part of British boxing lore.

▲ **BENN HANGS ON**

Benn avoids a lead right from Eubank during their first fight in 1990. "He (Eubank) is an idiot, a con merchant and I will just take him out as quick as possible," said Benn before the fight, but his words came to nothing in round nine.

◄ **EUBANK EUPHORIC**

A victorious Chris Eubank slowly sinks to his knees in joy, as his beaten foe is consoled by the referee in the background.

Tragic end ruins celebrations of a fight that will never be forgotten

▲ **THE SUPREME SHOWMAN**
Eubank poised to make his trademark ring entrance, before the second fight with Watson in September 1991. "I just want to get Eubank out of my system once and for all," said Watson before the rematch. The pair had met for the middleweight title in June, when Eubank won an unpopular majority decision. The September fight was for the vacant WBO super-middleweight championship.

If the first meeting between Michael Watson and Chris Eubank could be considered a bit of a non-event, the second was undoubtedly a tragedy.

In round 11 Eubank was trailing. Watson connected with a right, followed it with a left and, as an exhausted Eubank started to fall, another right connected. The crowd of 22,00 in the stadium at White Hart Lane in London went wild. Eubank climbed up, however, and nodded at the referee, Roy Francis, that he could continue. Watson leapt forward and was caught with a stunning right uppercut. The punch lifted Watson off his feet and he hit the canvas with a heavy thud, his neck catching the rope. He beat the count, but there was a disturbing look on his face.

At the start of round 12 Watson remained standing in his corner when the bell sounded. For a few seconds nobody in the ring moved and then Francis led Watson out to the center of the ring. The fight finished a few seconds later when, with Watson trapped against the ropes, Francis jumped in. Watson was able to walk back to his corner before he collapsed unconscious. Two hours later he underwent an operation to remove two blood clots from his brain. His recovery has been achingly slow and painful but he can now walk.

In 1993 Eubank and Benn, who had won the WBC title, met in front of 42,000 people at Old Trafford, home of Manchester United. The fight was ferocious and ended in a draw. Benn retired for the third time in 1996. Eubank is still fighting.

MILESTONES OF BOXING

LENNOX LEWIS: FIRST BRITISH-BORN HEAVYWEIGHT CHAMPION OF THE 20TH CENTURY

British heavyweights have been consistent losers in championship fights. Bob Fitzsimmons, who was born in Cornwall but raised in New Zealand, won the heavyweight title in 1897. He never fought in Britain but he was acclaimed as Britain's only heavyweight champion until Lennox Lewis was given the WBC belt in 1993.

Although Lewis, who was born in London but raised in Canada, didn't actually win the WBC title he deserved to when he knocked out Canada's Donovan "Razor" Ruddock in 1992, in an eliminator for the right to challenge the winner of the Riddick Bowe-Evander Holyfield clash. Bowe won the unified title, but threw his WBC belt in a trash can to avoid fighting Lewis and it was given to Lewis on the strength of his win over Ruddock.

Lewis had stopped Bowe in the Olympic final in Seoul, but had to meet American Tony Tucker in his first defence in May 1993 in Las Vegas. Lewis was a clear winner and dropped Tucker twice – something Mike Tyson had failed to do.

◀ **THE FINAL SECONDS**
Roy Francis, the referee, jumps in as Watson is trapped on the ropes in the 12th round.

▲ **ELATION CUT SHORT**
Eubank celebrates his victory as the stricken Watson is helped back to his corner. Watson collapsed seconds later and required emergency brain surgery.

Leonard is humbled as he tries in vain to turn back the clock

Sugar Ray Leonard kept having one last fight. In 1988 he won the WBC light-heavyweight title when he stopped Canada's Danny Lalonde in nine rounds. Lalonde had been persuaded to weigh inside the super-middleweight limit. The fight was also for the inaugural WBC super-middleweight title.

Leonard relinquished the light-heavyweight version and defended the super-middleweight title against Tommy Hearns in 1989. It was called a draw but Leonard had to survive two knockdowns.

In December 1989 Leonard outpointed Roberto Duran in a low-key affair. Duran lost his WBC middleweight title. However, Leonard was stripped of Duran's title in January 1990 and relinquished the super-middleweight version in August 1990. He retired once again.

In February 1991 he was back. "I need to fight at the Garden. I need to fight where the greats have fought," he said. He also believed that WBC light-middleweight champion Terry Norris was beatable. Leonard looked sensational in the gym, dropping sparring partners and sending a speedball flying with a hook. He was 34 and his ego had taken over.

Madison Square Garden looked empty on the night. There were just 7,495 people – a small mob to watch the wake of an extraordinary fighter. Norris was brilliant, Leonard dreadful.

In rounds two and seven Leonard was dropped. It lasted the full 12, but one judge scored a shut-out for Norris and another gave Leonard just one round. "I know now that it is time to go," said Leonard. He went, but he came back yet again.

◄ **TWO OLD HANDS**

Hearns and Leonard were two old men in search of youthful miracles when they fought a controversial draw in 1989, in Las Vegas. The boys from 1981 had become the sunshine men of the prize-ring.

▶ WAITING FOR THE MAN

Norris sits alone in his corner between rounds. "Before the fight I kept hearing about Leonard. He was the favorite and I was the boy who was meant to lose. I let my anger build," said Norris, who retained his WBC light-middleweight title on points.

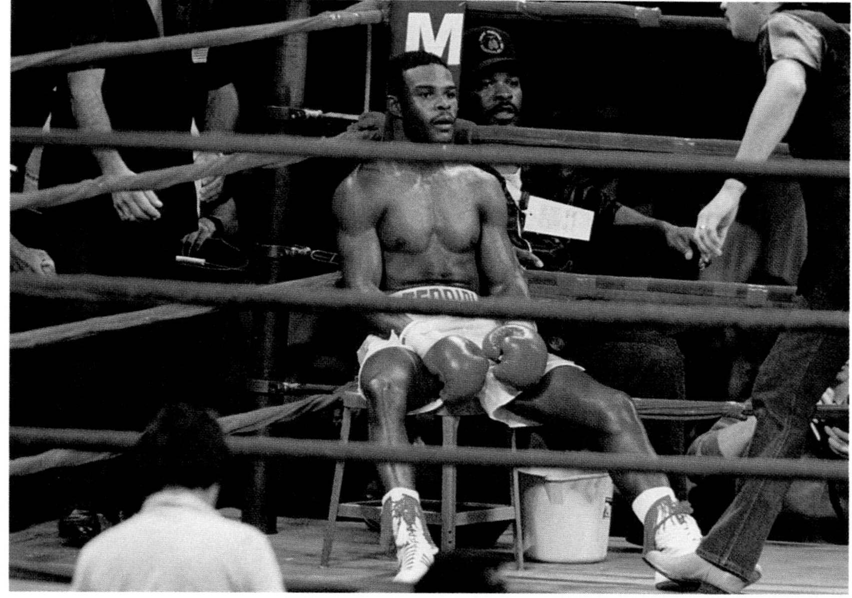

▲ GLORY FOR NORRIS

Norris turns away in victory from a seemingly bewildered Leonard at the end of their contest in February 1991. The gifted, but erratic, Norris had first won the title in 1990 after knocking out John Mugabi. He made 10 defenses, including the win over Leonard before losing to Simon Brown in December 1993.

◀ THE END FOR SUGAR?

"I fight because I like risks – I knew when I got in the ring that it was not there. I'm not a fighter of the nineties, I know that now," admitted a dejected Leonard after the fight. He left the garden of dreams a broken man, but he fought on.

A vintage Hearns revisits past glories by beating Hill in style

▲ **DEFERENCE CAN HURT**
Hill was too cautious, perhaps in awe of the great former champion, while Hearns kept his vulnerable chin in safe places. "It was a masterful performance," concluded a jubilant Hearns. Hill put the defeat down to experience. He later won back the WBA light-heavyweight title, and in 1996 beat Germany's Henry Maske for the IBF version.

In June 1991 it was the turn of Tommy "Hit Man" Hearns, who was 32, to turn back the clock. His task appeared even more daunting than Leonard's had been.

"No sir, that ain't gonna happen to me. There is no way that what happened to Leonard is going to happen to me," said Hearns before his WBA light-heavyweight fight against unbeaten Virgil Hill.

"It's the opportunity of a lifetime to fight a legend like Hearns," said Hill, who was installed as favorite. Norris had been the underdog when he beat Leonard.

The fight was not a classic, but Hearns jabbed and produced a sensible display to win on points. Hill was too cautious and accepted defeat too easily. The win meant Hearns had outlasted his generation. He had succeeded where his bitter rival Leonard had failed by beating a younger champion in a genuine fight. The fight between Hearns and Hill was the final meaningful fight for the Vegas boys from the early and mid-1980s. Leonard would return and Duran would lose to Camacho and Vinny Pazienza, but Hearns left the final mark on this period of boxing history when he beat Hill.

In 1993 Duran fought for the 100th time, stopping Tony Menefee in round eight to improve his record to 91 wins and just nine defeats. Since 1980, however, Duran had won just three of his 10 title fights. His forlorn showing against Leonard in 1989 was an indication of his slow slide. The once praised prizefighter had been gone so long.

Hagler, Hearns, Leonard and Duran belong, like the heavyweights from the 1970s, to a glorious time. Their rivalries will be cherished forever.

▲ THE HEARNS ENTOURAGE
Hearns and his supporters in comical pose after the victory over Hill. However, celebrations were short lived. He lost the title on points in his very first defense, to Iran Barkley. In 1988 Barkley had stopped Hearns in a WBC middleweight title fight, and was one of only three men to have ever halted the Detroit fighter.

▶ ONE MORE FIGHT AGAIN
Hearns proudly parades his WBA light-heavyweight belt, but he did not retire on a high. Both he and Sugar Ray Leonard continue to view retirement as a breathing period between grabs at fame and more wealth. They have each uttered their final words in the ring after several fights, before returning for one more pay day.

▲ A SALUTE TO PAST GLORIES
"Did I look exhausted, did my legs look spent?" said a resilient Hearns when it was over. "I live clean outside the ring and that enables me to continue fighting at this level."

HOLYFIELD v BOWE

Two Men, Three Fights and No Winner

One boxer was too small, and there were doubts about the other's heart. In Las Vegas in November 1992, however, all the pre-conceived limitations of character had to be re-evaluated when Evander Holyfield lost his three world championship titles after 12 pulsating rounds to Riddick Bowe.The fight was one of the very best.

Holyfield had built a heavyweight body on a light-heavyweight frame. The molding of the champion had been a painful inch-by-inch process. He was big enough to knock out Douglas, nimble enough to outpoint Larry Holmes and George Foreman, and human enough to underestimate Bert Cooper before stopping him.

▲ **RIDDICK RULES THE DAY**

Riddick Bowe, his arms aloft, celebrates his dethroning of Evander Holyfield, in November 1992. A year later, however, he lost to the former champion in a return encounter. "I did things right in the first fight and made mistakes in the second. Tonight, I did it right again," said Bowe after his dramatic knockout win in 1995.

Holyfield's cornerman, Lou Duva, had thrown Bowe out of the gym for lacking courage. Bowe's cornerman, Eddie Futch, had a strict plan and had made Bowe lose 40 pounds. Both were confident their fighters would win. The boxers had the same conviction, and it showed as round after round passed and the intensity of the action increased.

Slowly Bowe's extra bulk affected Holyfield. At the end Bowe was the winner and Holyfield was left to contemplate the impossibility of all future tasks against men as tall and heavy as Bowe, who was three inches taller and nearly 30 pounds heavier.

After the fight Bowe insulted Lennox Lewis, the British-born fighter who had boxed for Canada at the 1988 Olympics and stopped Bowe in the super-heavyweight final. "My sister could beat you," Bowe claimed. A month later Bowe dropped the WBC championship belt in a trash can during a publicity stunt in a London hotel.

Bowe, a projects boy from the same part of Brooklyn as Mike Tyson, stopped Michael Dokes and Jesse Ferguson in rapid succession and ignored Lewis. "Beating Dokes and Ferguson is an insult to heavyweight boxing," claimed Lewis, who in January 1993 accepted Bowe's old WBC championship belt.

In November 1993 Bowe was back in Las Vegas face to face with Holyfield. This time the pair had just the IBF and WBA championships to fight for. The rematch was furious, but Bowe was not in great shape. Futch had lost the battle with Bowe's bulge. "I admit I believed I would just take him out," said Bowe. "Riddick thought he would be able to mash Holyfield and not have to go the distance. He trained for a seven or eight-round fight. He didn't train hard. That was a young man's mistake," said Bowe's manager Rock Newman.

The fight was interrupted in round seven by the bizarre arrival of a paraglider in the ring. He landed in the ropes and, as he attempted to disentangle himself, was attacked by members of Bowe's entourage. The fight was delayed for 22 minutes.

"As along as I was moving, Bowe wouldn't swing. The only time Bowe would swing was if I got flat-footed," said Holyfield. He kept moving and regained the title.

Holyfield was never the same after the first fight and Bowe, who at one time had the tools to take control of the heavyweight division, never regained what he lost during the 36 minutes of brutal action on that night in 1992. Their 1993 and 1995 adventures (the last of which Bowe won on an eighth-round stoppage) were brief visits to a former time. Nevertheless, all three of their fights belong in heavyweight history's roll call of great encounters.

▲ **EVANDER STRIKES BACK** *Riddick Bowe throws a left jab at Holyfield during their second fight in November 1993. Holyfield won on points.*

The storm above the ring was the ideal backdrop when Lewis met Bruno

▶ **BRUNO LOOKS GOOD**
Bruno impresses in training before his title fight with Lennox Lewis in October 1993. To British fight fans, Bruno was the beatable hero, but Lewis was a foreign fighter.

▼ **BRUNO WORN DOWN**
In the early rounds it was clear that the damp and cold was having an effect on Lewis – the champion was slow and predictable, while Bruno was superb. But by round six the tide had turned, and in round seven Bruno's challenge was ended.

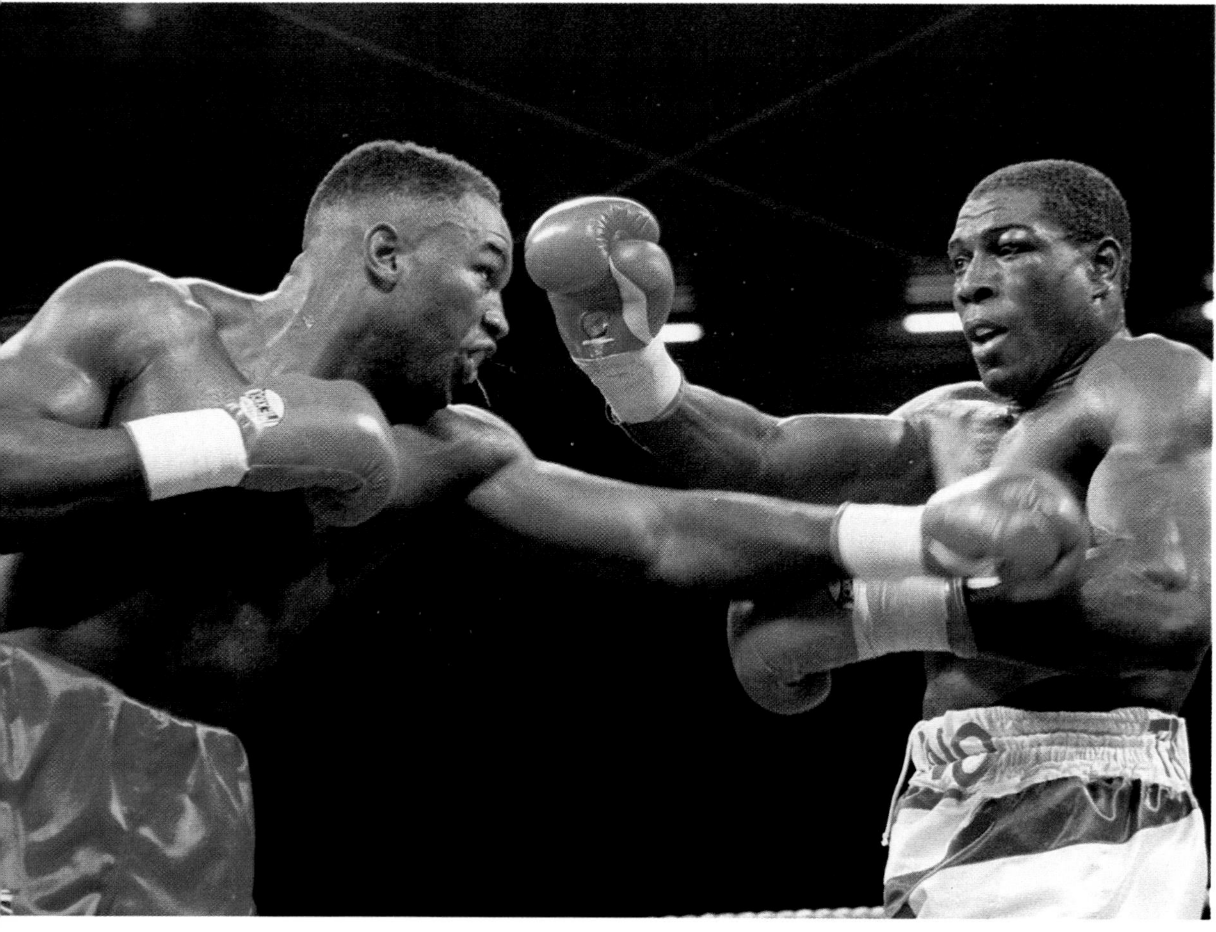

When the drizzle started to soak the ring canvas, the fight between Lennox Lewis, the WBC heavyweight champion, and Frank Bruno, Britain's favorite sporting son, looked in doubt. There had been some raised eyebrows when it was scheduled for an outdoor venue in Wales in October, 1993.

It didn't stop raining, but the fight went ahead anyway. Bruno walked to the ring wearing plastic bags over his boots and old blankets over his solid shoulders. Bruno had no discernible physical defects – he looked good.

Lewis, however, was the massive favorite to retain his title and move closer to the elusive Riddick Bowe. In the run up to the fight the British duo had fallen out. Lewis had been raised in Canada and Bruno insisted that he was using the British flag as a flag of convenience.

When it started, both men were cold and it showed. Lewis was off with his jabs, caught by counters and hurt by a right in the third round. By round six Lewis was behind on points but the numerical deficiency disguised the reality of the action that was taking place in the ring. Bruno's anger had slowed as his body stiffened, and at the end of round six his left cheek and eye were swollen; Lewis was also bruised near the left eye.

It ended in round seven and the British public witnessed their idol Bruno trapped on the ropes for the fourth time in his career. Bruno went stiff and took Lewis's final punches in silence before the referee intervened. Bruno just stood swaying as Lewis celebrated – it was an all-too familiar ending. When it was over the pair did not embrace.

Lewis was ignored by both Bowe and Holyfield, and subsequently by Michael Moorer and George Foreman. A year after beating Bruno, a fighter from the gyms of America, Oliver McCall, knocked out Lewis in two rounds – 12 months later Bruno finally won his world heavyweight title at the fourth attempt when he beat McCall.

▲ **LEWIS GETS THROUGH**
Lewis (top) connects with a left through Bruno's guard as the fight nears a conclusion. "It was a mediocre performance," Lewis later admitted. "I was cold and he caught me too often."

▲ **STILL THE CHAMP**
The champion is besieged by his cornermen, and the Lewis camp erupts in celebration, after the fight is stopped in round seven.

MILESTONES OF BOXING

GEORGE FOREMAN REGAINS HEAVYWEIGHT TITLE

NOVEMBER 5, 1994 MGM, LAS VEGAS.

George Foreman was a sporting icon long before his short right dropped Michael Moorer for the count in round 10. The devastating punch meant that Foreman was the oldest heavyweight champion of the world. He was the new boss, 21 years after first winning the title from Joe Frazier in the Sunshine Showdown in Jamaica, and 20 years after losing it to Muhammad Ali in the Rumble in the Jungle.

Before the fight Moorer's coach, Teddy Atlas, warned his fighter to move. Moorer did for nine rounds and was winning on all scorecards before he was ruined in the 10th. Foreman often looked old as Moorer's southpaw jabs held him at bay, but the finish was stunning. Foreman was back, the linear champion, his redemption complete and his jungle nightmares at an end.

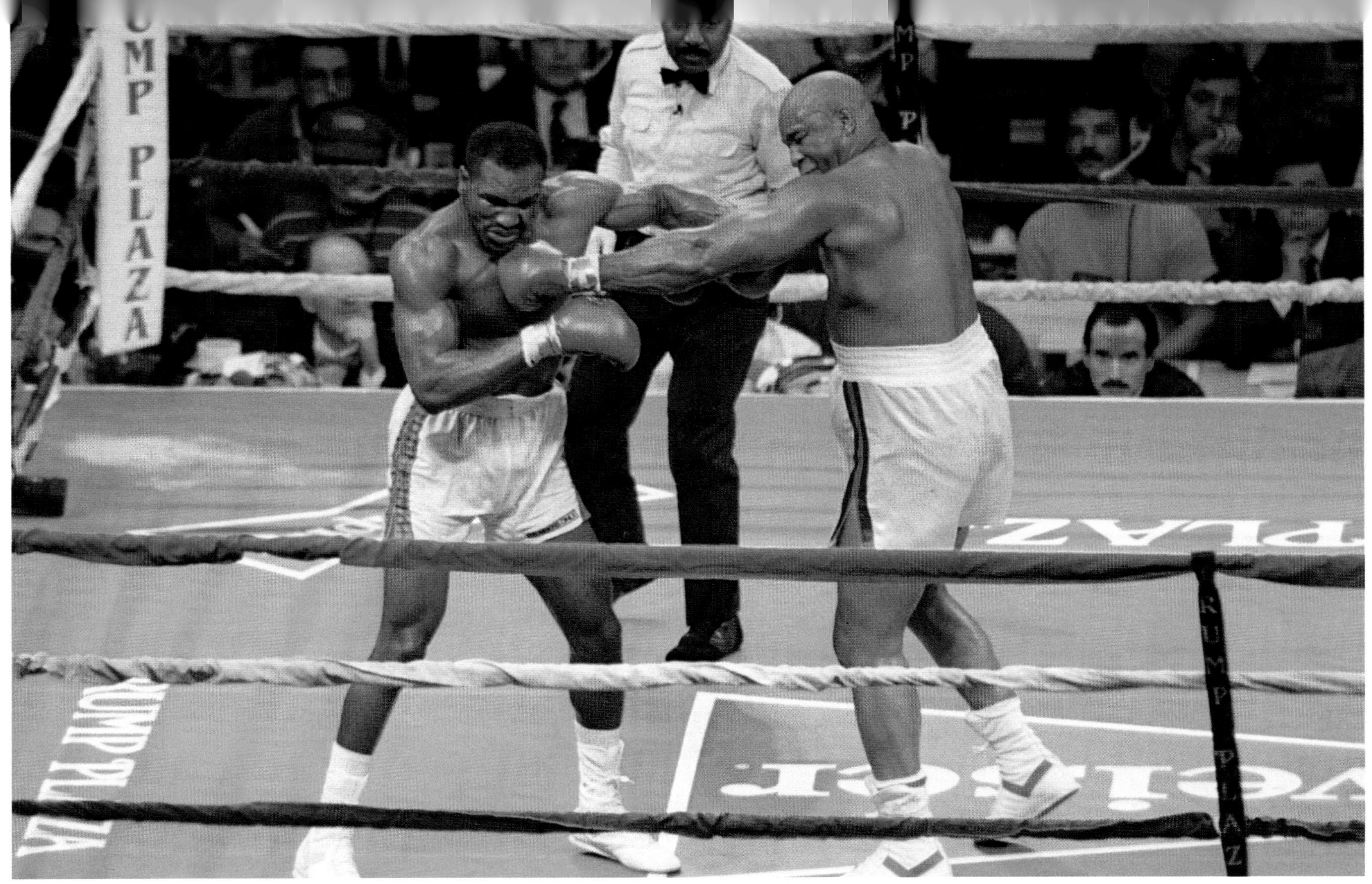

"There is no killer inside anymore" – George Foreman, Tokyo, 1996

▲ **PREACHER STILL HAS IT**
Foreman lost his challenge for Evander Holyfield's unified title in 1991, but his valiant performance convinced the doubters that he was still a force. "Boxing is just a sport. I wish I had this same attitude back then. I would have been heavyweight champion from 1974, to this day," claimed an older and wiser Foreman.

The first part of George Foreman's redemption was when he lost to Evander Holyfield in 1991 for the unified world heavyweight title. It was a hard fight, a moral victory for the hoary warrior. Foreman seemed determined to erase the image of the falling giant crashing dazed to the canvas from Muhammad Ali's punches in 1974. "I never look back. I live in the present. I barely remember the Seventies. If I try and look back it is like an old man looking back at his childhood," claimed Foreman.

He kept fighting, but an odd defeat in 1993 against Tommy Morrison in a vacant WBO fight appeared to end the comeback of the preacher. It was Foreman's 76th fight, his fourth decade of competition and he looked lost. "I need to get the anger back," he said, after returning to his pulpit at the Church of the Lord Jesus Christ, in the Aldine section of northeast Houston.

In the summer of 1994 promoter Bob Arum put together a fight between Michael Moorer and Foreman for the WBA and IBF titles. Moorer was at the time the man who beat the man who beat the man – James "Buster" Douglas knocked out Mike Tyson, Evander Holyfield ko'd Douglas and Moorer beat Holyfield.

The WBA initially refused to sanction the fight but Foreman had his day in court. The WBA walked away with $300,000 in sanctioning fees and Foreman with three million. On November 5, 1994, he had his night in the ring – the passage from George I to George II was complete. Big George was 45 and a grandfather.

▶ **FOREMAN THE SHOWMAN**

Before the fight with Michael Moorer veteran trainer, Angelo Dundee, adjusts the waistband on Foreman's red velvet shorts – the same shorts he wore when he beat Joe Frazier 21 years earlier. Foreman was the lightest he had been in six years. He trained twice each day: once in public, which was a comic performance, and once behind closed doors.

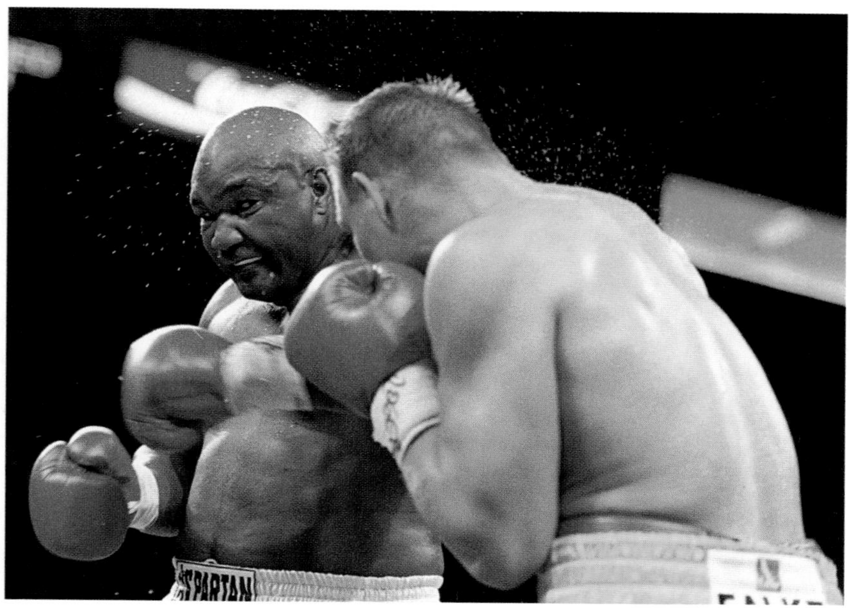

▲ **FOREMAN V SCHULZ**

In their 1995 fight Axel Schulz did enough to win, but the judges went with Foreman. "He was running and hiding," said Foreman after the verdict. "To beat me a man must fight. I will only retire after a true licking, not a boxing lesson."

◀ **LOST ANGER NOT A PROBLEM**

"The other Foreman was more interested in hurting people, the fame and the money. Not in that order – I think I liked the hurting more", said Foreman, who lost on points to Tommy Morrison (seen here landing a chilling right) in 1993.

▶ A NIGHT OF SUFFERING
Chavez lands with a fearsome body shot. "I could hear his pain and that is what I wanted," said Chavez after beating Haugen in a cruel display of evil boxing. Even the hardened men at ringside called for leniency.

145,000 fight fans bay for blood as Chavez cruelly humiliates Haugen

▶ AN AMBITIOUS MAN
Chavez's ambition was to go 100 fights without a loss, and he almost made it: his first defeat, by Frankie Randall, for the WBC light-welterweight title in January 1994, came after 91 fights in 13 years!

Even Don King was speechless when the haunting music accompanied Julio Cesar Chavez's long walk from his changing room to the ring in the middle of the Azteca Stadium, Mexico City. The official attendance figure was nearly 145,000 people.

King called his February 1993 show the Grand Slam of Boxing. Chavez and three other world title fighters – Michael Nunn, Azumah Nelson and Terry Norris – were in defenses, but the crowd were there to watch their man sacrifice the American, Greg Haugen. Chavez didn't let his fans down after they had chanted "Muerte, muerte" (death, death) as Haugen entered the ring.

Chavez penetrated Haugen's limited defense and made him suffer slowly until he slumped motionless in

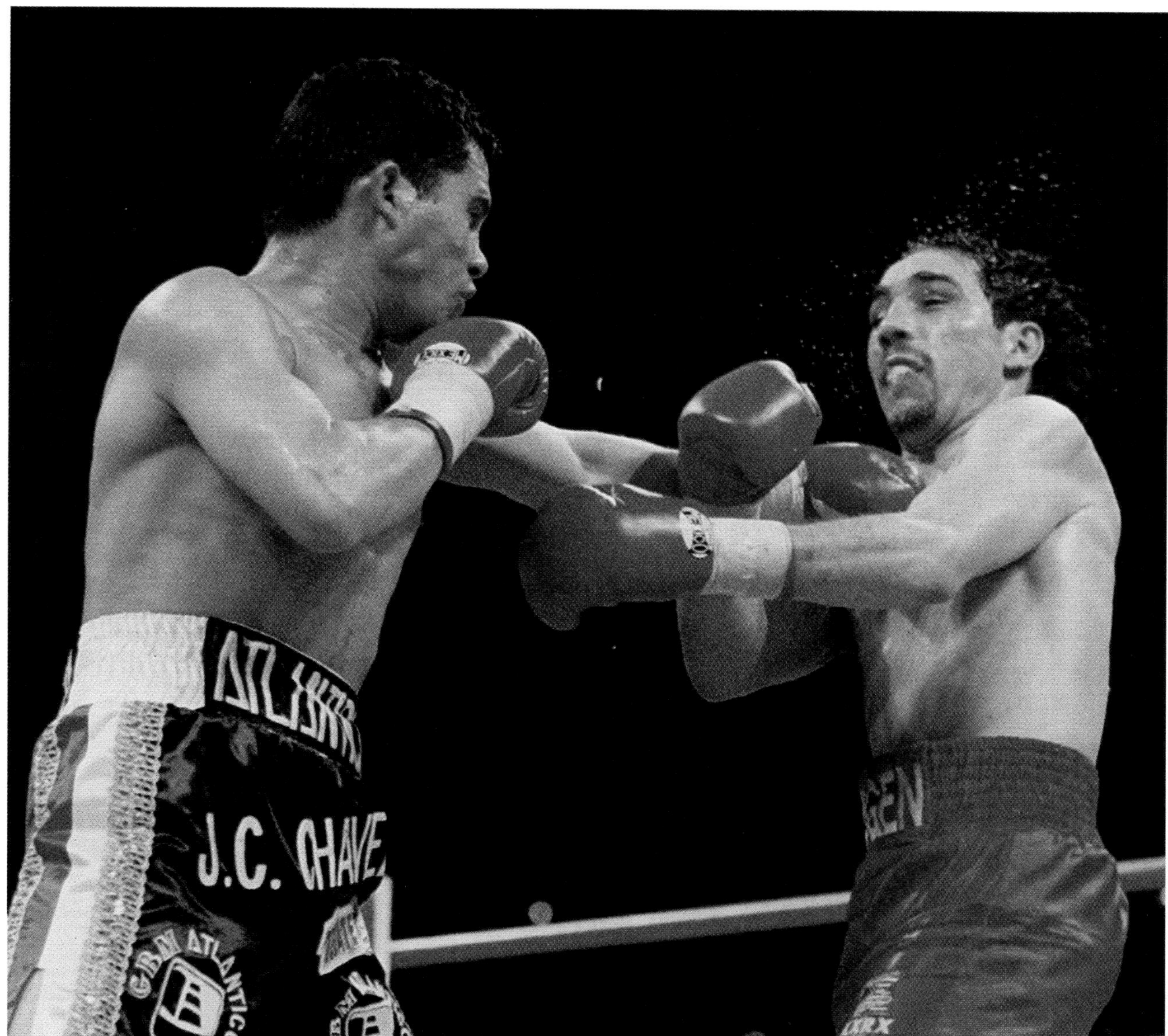

◄ **A LONG NIGHT FOR HAUGEN**
Yet another ferocious punch lands in the face of Haugen during his terrible suffering at the hands of Chavez. The champion had attracted a crowd of around 5,000 when he sparred in the parking lot of the Azteca Stadium before the fight. The atmosphere was unique, the fight savage, and the outcome never in doubt.

▼ **LAST MOMENT OF GLORY**
Chavez receives the adulation from his adoring fans after the Haugen humiliation, but he was a mean loser. His attitude after defeats to Frankie Randall, in 1994, and Oscar De La Hoya, changed the public's perception of the flag-waving warrior.

a corner, the victim of an articulate beating from a master. However, Chavez's win went beyond sporting necessity. As Haugen left the ring he was called a dog. Hysteria had taken over.

At the post-fight conference Chavez continued his assault. "He deserved to suffer. I promised my fans I would punish him and I did." Haugen simply dropped his head at Chavez's cruel words.

The massive spectacle, which was shown on television on a pay-per-view basis, attracted nearly one million viewers, and helped raise the profile of King, who had suffered commercially since Mike Tyson's conviction and imprisonment in 1992.

In Mexico City, however, King was still trying to come to terms with the fate of his most prolific money earner. "Oh boy, Mike would have loved this," he said prior to Chavez beating Haugen.

"I want to punish him and knock him out cleanly" – Mike Tyson, 1991

For Tyson, life after Tokyo was difficult. He was out of control. In 1991 he beat Canada's Donovan "Razor" Ruddock twice, but both were hard, intensive struggles. The first fight ended in round seven and was followed by a brawl in the ring. Ruddock had refused to be intimidated and had caught and hurt Tyson, while his handlers thought that the referee, Richard Steele, was too quick with his stoppage. The rematch went 12.

A fight with Holyfield was planned but on July 19, 1991, Tyson changed his life forever when he raped an 18-year-old beauty contestant at the Canterbury Hotel in Indianapolis. The rape took place at 2 am and Tyson flew back to Cleveland that same morning. When he was arrested he could not even remember Desiree Washington's name.

Tyson was found guilty in February 1992. The trial lasted 17 days and when it was over he dropped his head and simply said "Oh, man." It was the end for him. He protested his innocence and before sentencing promised to change his life. "I have treated women bad, but that is all behind me. I will never return to that way of life," he stated before beginning his three-year sentence.

Tyson was gone and nobody in the business of boxing missed him.

▼ A LOOK OF DISDAIN
Tyson stares at Ruddock as the Canadian tries to clamber up from the canvas in round seven of their first fight in 1991.

▶ NO PEACE FOR TYSON
"Before losing (to "Buster" Douglas) I had a great deal – I mean a big voracious appetite with women and stuff," said Tyson in 1990. "Now I look at womens' eyes and I see the devil." He never found a sanctuary from his urges and in 1991 raped Desiree Washington.

▲ TYSON BEHIND BARS
The American public make their feelings known, as they protest outside the courtroom. The case was a disaster for Tyson. In February 1992 he was found guilty of rape and sentenced to 10 years in prison, although he was given parole in March 1995. He still maintains his innocence.

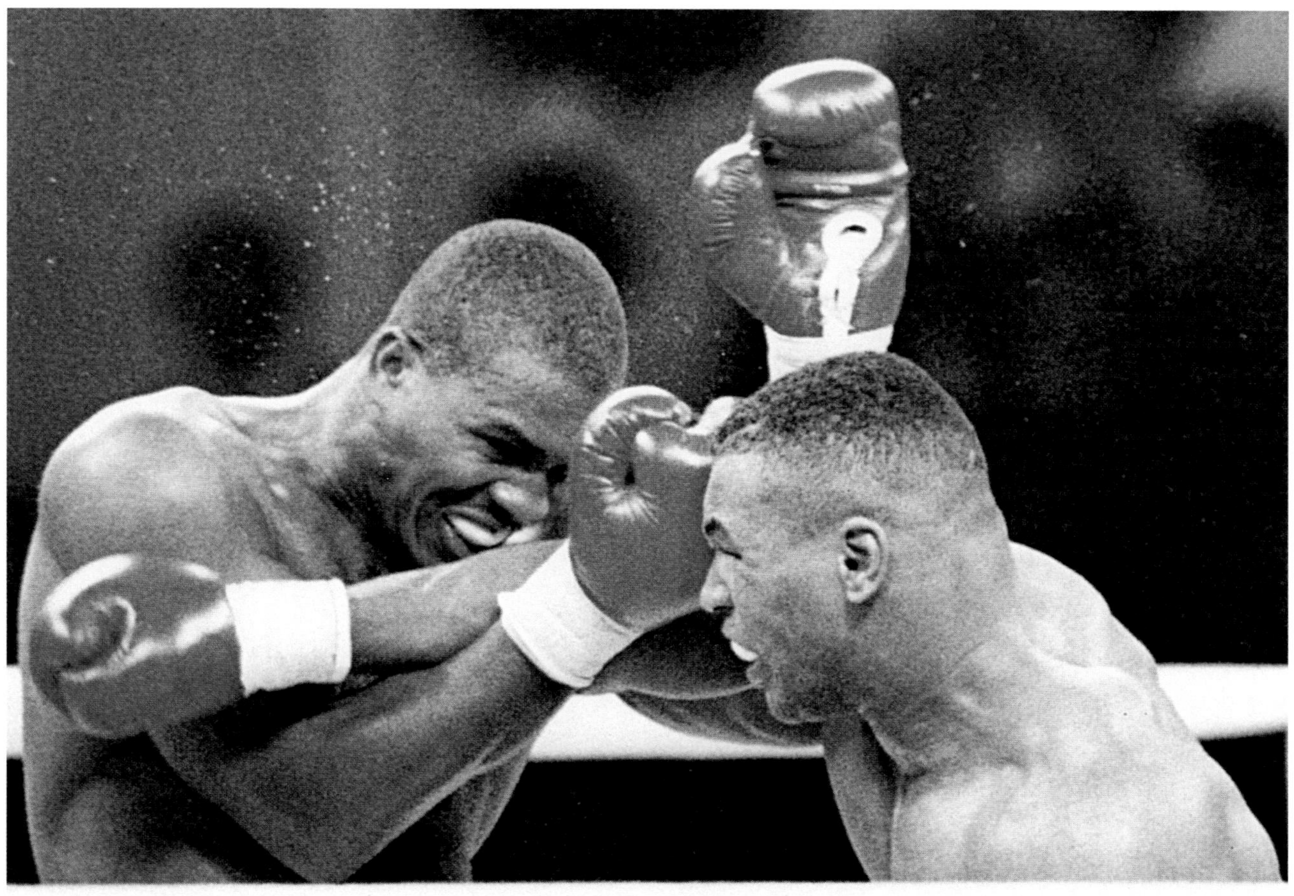

◀ UGLY SCENES RUIN WIN
Tyson on the ascendancy against Donovan "Razor" Ruddock on his way to victory in their first encounter. Regrettably, Tyson's celebrations were marred by an ugly brawl between the fighters' respective cornermen.

WILD DAYS *and* NIGHTS

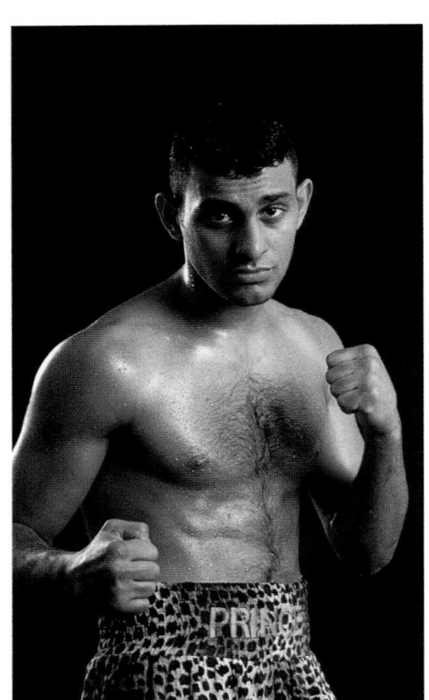

In December 1997, nearly 12,000 people watched Naseem Hamed's debut at Madison Square Garden. Nobody was disappointed by the excitement and in round four Kevin Kelley was counted out. At the same time negotiations for a heavyweight unification fight came to an end and Roy Jones moved up to the division. The future looked good.

TYSON, HAMED AND THE FUTURE

▲ **THE PRINCE OF BOXING**
By 1995 Prince Naseem Hamed was Britain's premier attraction – his confident, often cocky approach, backed up by immense natural talent, has made him an instant hit with the fans.

◀ **A BIG RIGHT HAND**
Previous page: Holyfield launches a big right hand at Ray Mercer during their fight in May 1995.

Mike Tyson walked free from prison in March 1995, but he returned to a sport that, like his shrunken body, had started to fade. Tyson was the salvation that boxing yearned for.

During his absence, the heavyweight division had been in bizarre turmoil. During one stage of the mayhem, Riddick Bowe, having beaten Evander Holyfield in 1992, relinquished his title in dramatic fashion by dumping his WBC belt in a London dustbin, rather than face Lennox Lewis. Lewis thereby became Britain's first world heavyweight champion in 96 years – by default!

Lewis was then knocked out by a former Tyson sparring partner, Oliver McCall; Holyfield beat Bowe for the WBA and IBF titles, but was then outpointed by Michael Moorer, the first ever southpaw heavyweight champion. Then, in late 1994, a further bizarre twist took place when George Foreman knocked out Moorer to regain the world title he had lost to Muhammad Ali 20 years earlier!

However, in August 1995, the Tyson show started in earnest, with Don King again the key player. The first sacrifice was Peter McNeeley, who Tyson duly beat in one round, but the boxing public were unconvinced and the jeers started. Then, in late 1995, Tyson needed three rounds to beat Buster Mathis Jr. There were doubts and doubters, but Tyson appeared capable of beating the other heavyweights.

By the end of 1995 Frank Bruno, Britain's gallant hero, finally tasted glory when he was crowned the new WBC champion; while Holyfield had looked set for retirement after a dreadful knockout defeat in eight rounds against Bowe.

The stage was now set for Tyson, who won the WBC championship in March 1996. Bruno, his old adversary, was hand-picked for his willingness to suffer, his bravery under fire and his limited mobility. Over 5,000 British fans turned the MGM in Las Vegas into a good-natured soccer terrace for a few days. On

the night, the unfortunate Bruno was battered into submission in three one-sided rounds, but the fans and their hero accepted defeat with grace.

After Bruno, Tyson turned his attention to the WBA champion, Bruce Seldon. The fight was a disgrace with Seldon going over in one round. Bruno had taken a ferocious beating but Seldon, the "Atlantic City Express," ducked under a few swings before coming to rest on the canvas at Tyson's feet.

Tyson was then forced to relinquish his WBC belt because an agreement to fight Lewis had not been reached, resulting in a spell of unpleasant litigation between the respective promoters of both fighters.

The awful repercussions of litigation were starting to ruin boxing long before Lewis and Tyson met in court in 1996. It was a good year for the lawyers and a bad year for fighters. And it wasn't just the heavyweights. Throughout the sport there were claims and counter claims, and all of the leading sanctioning bodies faced criticism at one point or another. The situation was rapidly getting out of hand.

The unlikely saviour was Holyfield, who had looked set for retirement only months earlier. In November 1996 Holyfield, the religious warrior, stopped Tyson in 11 rounds in one of boxing's most thrilling shocks. Before the fight, Tyson had made jokes about having to beat two people: God and Holyfield. On the night, there was a third person involved: Tyson. He played a large part in his own downfall and appeared to quit when the going got too tough.

By the end of 1996, Riddick Bowe was out of contention, after two foul-ridden fights with Polish exile, Andrew Golota. Despite having won the contests – albeit on disqualification decisions – Bowe had ended both fights on the floor and was ultimately saved from defeat by Golota's ring lunacy. Bowe was finished and before the Golota rematch his long-term trainer, Eddie Futch, quit his corner in disgust.

However, the early 1990s witnessed the rise of a succession of sweet young stars in the lower weight divisions. Oscar De La Hoya is the darling of the fight business – a boy with a million-dollar smile and a sorry tale of childhood hardship in East LA, he attracts women and the swinging set who adore his clean image. In the ring, the golden boy, who acquired Steward as his coach in 1997, has reduced quality champions to underdogs.

▲ THE KING FACTOR

Don King raises Tyson's arm in victory after his third round defeat of Buster Mathis Jr. in late 1995, but away from the ring the relationship was fraught. "I don't think Tyson wants to fight," said Teddy Atlas, long-time trainer and Tyson's amateur coach. "He's screwed up emotionally and he will be screwed up as long as he has those clowns around him."

Naseem Hamed also makes good fighters cry. Since he was first promoted by Frank Warren in 1994 he has slowly angered the pious who use the sport of boxing as a job. Writers, trainers, promoters, matchmakers and almost everybody else in the business has something negative to say about the boxer known as "The Prince", but his explosive power in the ring is the perfect answer to his critics.

Roy Jones is a third fighter from the 1990s whose talents have not yet gained universal recognition. Perhaps Jones, like De La Hoya and Hamed, is too good for his generation and too bright for his own good. In 1996 Jones won every round to beat the once brilliant Jamaican veteran Mike McCallum. When it was over, McCallum, who had been avoided by middleweights since the mid-1980s, claimed Jones was the greatest fighter for decades. "Hagler, Hearns, Duran, Leonard: forget it man," said McCallum, "Jones would have beaten all of them."

Believe the hype: the Tyson show was back on the road

▲ **MCNEELEY SACRIFICED**

After three years of enforced absence from the ring, Mike Tyson returned to dispose of Peter NcNeeley, in August 1995. Everyone knew it would end quickly and despite his display of confidence (above) McNeeley was duly dumped in round one.

The battle inside Tyson's head had clearly started before his first day of training. His manic stare had intensified during his three-year sabbatical from the ring and Tyson still had to serve his parole – on the outside of the ropes and in the ring.

Meanwhile, his true friends were as thin on the canvas as ever. People made money from Tyson and the more they made the closer they became. After his release, John Horne and Rory Holloway assumed the role of co-managers, but in the shadows lurked King, who secretly controlled every move.

"You never want to go where I have been," Tyson warned in late 1996 before his first fight with Holyfield. Nobody doubted his assertion. He was clearly deeply troubled, and despite surrounding himself with former prison friends, he had no way of escaping the infamy that awaited him. "I don't think anyone can make me happy. Freedom is in the mind, and being on parole makes ... me want to strike out."

Tyson's career can be seen in three distinct parts before he lost to Holyfield. There was the man-child who won the title from Berbick in 1986, the fallen idol who was beaten by Buster Douglas in 1990, and the apparently reformed ex-con. "I'm a better fighter now than I was before prison," he said after his release, "but I wouldn't have beaten that guy." "That guy" was the man Cus D'Amato made and left to boxing. Sadly, "that guy" was also the man who was convicted of raping Desiree Washington and the beast that bit off part of Holyfield's right ear.

◀ **THE TYSON BARRAGE**

Tyson looks impressive in his first comeback fight, as he swiftly ends the challenge of Peter NcNeeley. Later that year, on the eve of the third Bowe-Holyfield fight, Tyson's former trainer, Kevin Rooney, confidently predicted: "Give me three months with Mike ... and he'd beat either of these guys."

▼ **IRON MIKE IS BACK?**

In a disgraceful act of cowardice, Bruce Seldon crumples in a heap on the canvas during the first round of his WBA title fight with Tyson in September 1996. "Mike is back. Iron Mike is back," proclaimed Don King, somewhat inexplicably, after this latest debacle – but few believed him.

Dark clouds loom for McCall as Bruno finally reaches his zenith

▲ **FOURTH TIME LUCKY!**
Bruno reaches out with yet another left jab, the punch which eventually wore down McCall and wrested the WBC belt from him. "The last round was the longest three minutes of my life," said Bruno after the fight. "I knew I just had to stay away and I would win." His finest hour was clouded by rumors of McCall's drug abuse, but nobody made their concerns public before the fight.

When Frank Bruno won the WBC title in 1995 it was the end of an unbelievable odyssey for a man blessed with brawn but cursed by distinct lack of fighting instincts. Bruno's persistent failing was his unfortunate knack of freezing and often dropping his guard, whenever under sustained pressure. It was a weakness that had left him in a perilous state on four occasions, and had sabotaged all his previous title challenges. Against McCall, though, he finally earned his glory.

In a sport where negotiation is crucial, contacts essential, and talent merely preferable, Bruno and dozens of other champions like him have won world championships. In the awful reality of the business of boxing Bruno was as deserving as many and probably more deserving than most.

Elsewhere in the heavyweight world the mass confusion continued. The wild career of George Foreman, the WBU champion, rumbled on. He narrowly defeated Germany's Axel Schulz in early 1995, easily beat Crawford Grimsley in late 1996, and scraped past New Yorker, Lou Savarese, in 1997. He eventually quit the ring in November 1997, after a dubious points defeat to Shannon Briggs.

"I was never fast or nimble, I just knocked people out back then," Foreman said in Tokyo after Grimsley had run for 12 rounds. When asked about meeting Frazier and Ali in one of boxing's halcyon periods he replied: "I can't even remember that far back." Foreman, like fellow ring veteran Larry Holmes, was still fighting and making money in his late 40s.

▶ **A TRUE BRITISH HERO**

Bruno proudly parades his WBC belt in front of the press. A lifetime's ambition is realized for Bruno, after clinging on in the final round to complete a memorable victory.

▼ **GLORY IS SHORT-LIVED**

No one could deny Bruno his glory night in the ring against Oliver McCall, but he came unstuck in his very first defense against an explosive Tyson. "I don't think he (Tyson) has improved since 1989, and I know I have," said Bruno, but the contest was over in three rounds. Bruno had taken the most savage beating of his career and he never fought again.

MILESTONES OF BOXING

GOLDEN BOY BEATS THE OLD WARRIOR

The blood on Julio Cesar Chavez's face could not hide his bitter disappointment at the end of his WBC super-lightweight defense against Oscar De La Hoya, the perfumed Golden Boy from Los Angeles, in June 1996.

Chavez lost his title when the fight was stopped because of a wicked two-inch cut above his left eye in round four. The cut opened in the first minute of round one and Chavez claimed it happened five days before the fight in a late sparring session. At the time of the stoppage De La Hoya's speed and Chavez's disability had turned the long-awaited clash into a one-sided encounter between a brilliant young star and a faded master.

The angry reaction to Chavez's disclosure caused him to alter his story and claim the cut was actually done 25 days before the fight. It was Chavez's 100th fight, and his 34th world title fight, but when it was over the former Mexican idol was in De La Hoya's shadow.

TYSON v HOLYFIELD

Holyfield's Ear was Left Ruined by a Beast

ONE OFFENCE TOO MANY

A visibly distressed Evander Holyfield clutches his right ear in agony after Mike Tyson tore a chunk from it in round three of their rematch in June 1997. The missing piece of Holyfield's ear was later found on the canvas. In the days after the fight Holyfield was in forgiving mood: "The pressure was on him," said Holyfield. "He got hit with some good shots and he reacted. I know he is sorry, but he did it."

Within an hour of Tyson beating Seldon, the debacle was forgotten and the next encounter was already being hyped. At the post-fight press conference Seldon was replaced by Holyfield, who sat down next to King. Tyson was at the other end of the table, his now customary bored expression firmly in place.

As Don King jubilantly announced November 9, 1996, as the date of the fight, Tyson sneered, "I will have fun on the night." Holyfield smiled his smile and left the following morning for the fifth week of his 15-week-long stint at a Houston training camp. Tyson, meanwhile, went to a party. The alarm bells were already ringing.

Holyfield was the rank outsider, the underdog and in Las Vegas there was no indication that Tyson would lose. In the gym his sessions followed a predictable pattern. He hit a procession of static sparring partners and his entourage did the only thing they were required to do – they applauded.

But on the night Holyfield would not be intimidated. He had prayed to be protected from his own bravery and his belief was miraculous. Tyson unwisely made few, if any, concessions to his opponent's ability to find something from some dark place, and paid the price for his complacency.

In round six Tyson was over from a left hook. His body language altered and he started to lose. By round 10 the Holyfield miracle was nearly complete and Tyson, the bully, was saved by the bell. It ended in round 11 and Holyfield was champion for the third time. Tyson was already a blur in the shadows of his enormous entourage before judgement was passed and his diminished status conferred on him. "I lost to the better man," he bravely admitted.

King and his men, Horne and Holloway, were stunned and Tyson entered a muted trance. There was only one thing to do – a rematch. Nobody doubted Holyfield would agree, and a date was set.

The so-called "Bite of the Century" took place on June 28, 1997, and came to be one of the sport's most degrading moments. It ended, in round three, when Tyson tore a chunk from the side of Holyfield's right ear and spat it out. Afterwards, he bit the left ear. It was the final act of shame for the brutal boy, whose money had seldom brought him peace of mind. He was belatedly disqualified by theatrical referee Mills Lane at the end of the round.

The fight's conclusion created hysteria in the crowd of 16,331 and there was later a stampede on the casino floor when people mistakenly believed they had heard gunshots. The MGM later withdrew from its one remaining fight with Don King.

"I don't know what happened that night. It's pretty embarrassing. That was just striking out in total hatred right there. I shouldn't have done that. Just for one moment I forgot that he was a human being," said Tyson three months after the fight. On the night Tyson and his manager Horne disgraced themselves when they made comments about Holyfield.

King and Tyson went missing after the fight – neither met the press. Meanwhile, Holyfield was at the hospital having 15 stitches inserted. Condemnation of Tyson's actions was unanimous and in July 1997 his license to box was revoked by the Nevada State Commission. Although he can apply each year for a new license, he will never get back the respect he once had and there are many who believe he should never be allowed to box again.

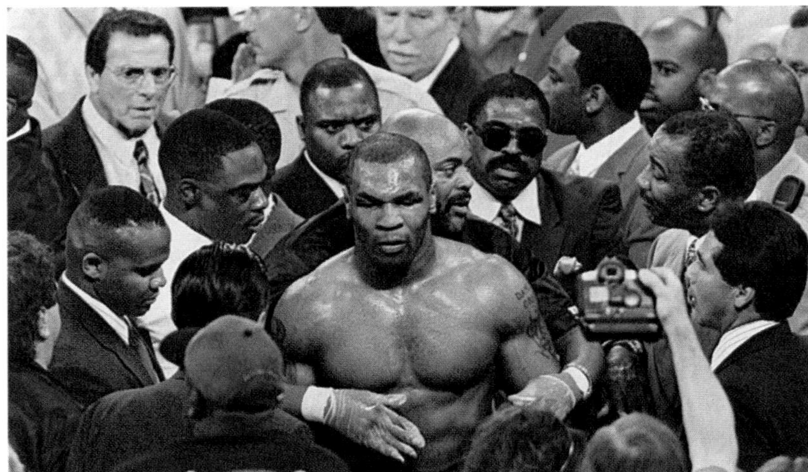

◀ A LONELY WALK BACK *Tyson is led away in disgrace after the shameful ear-biting episode. "I regret what I did. I want to apologize to Evander. He is a great champion and I made a mistake," said Tyson.*

▲ TYSON HUMBLED *Holyfield pressurizes Tyson on his way to beating the champion in November 1996, in one of the shocks of the decade.*

McCall and Akinwande quit, while Golota folds in one round

▶ A BIZARRE CONCLUSION

A clearly troubled Oliver McCall is led away in tears by referee, Mills Lane, as Lewis raises his arms in mock appreciation of a hollow victory. It later emerged that McCall had been battling with a drug problem for some time. "We should pray for his soul," observed Don King after the fight.

In 1997 Lennox Lewis and his promoters were in an awkward position. They had turned down a chance to fight Mike Tyson the previous year, before watching in frustration as Evander Holyfield exposed the bully boy from Brooklyn and took his crown.

Lewis had his chance for redemption in February 1997 when he met Oliver McCall for the vacant WBC title. McCall had dropped and stopped Lewis in 1994, but had since lost his way and found himself back in rehabilitation clinics and under constant supervision.

In the ring McCall broke down, refused to throw punches and was led back to his corner in tears by referee Mills Lane in round five. It was a sad spectacle. Lewis had frozen as McCall's chaos took over.

The next day McCall claimed it was an intentional tactic. "I was waiting for God to let me know when to knock out Lennox," he claimed. Even Don King looked embarrassed!

In July 1997, the unfortunate Lewis was involved in another fiasco, when London-born Henry Akinwande, the former WBO champion, held, held and held and was disqualified in round five. McCall had problems, he was an addict, but Akinwande's performance, or lack of it, was a total disgrace.

"When a fighter gets hurt, that's when you can see if a fighter has guts or not. I don't want to find out," said Akinwande before the fight in Lake Tahoe, Nevada. Sadly, he showed he was a man of his word.

Then, in October 1997, with a dramatic upturn in fortune, Lewis savaged Andrew Golota, in Atlantic City. It ended after a brutal 95 seconds. Suddenly, Lewis was all that he said he was.

▲ GOLOTA POLEAXED

After two rather hollow victories, Lewis savaged Polish emigre, Andrew Golota, in just 95 seconds of a ferocious display in October 1997. "Golota was mine at the press conference. He couldn't look me in the eye and in the ring he was nervous," explained Lewis after his emphatic victory.

◄ MAN IN THE MIDDLE

Referee, Mills Lane, raises the arm of Lennox Lewis to signal his victory over London-born Henry Akinwande in July 1997. Lane was also the official for Lewis's other farcical win, over Oliver McCall in February. Both McCall and Akinwande had their initial suspensions lifted and continue to fight in the heavyweight division.

Super-middleweights steal the show

▶ **BENN V COLLINS II**

Steve Collins (right) launches an assault on Nigel Benn in the second of their two fights in 1996. The fights attracted a total of over 40,000 people – a turn-out which emphasized the allure of the super-middleweight divsion.

▲ **TRAGEDY STRIKES AGAIN**

Gerald McClellan is slumped on the floor in his corner while a doctor examines him. The titantic battle with Britain's Nigel Benn had a tragic outcome for McClellan. Benn was also taken to hospital for observation.

The British super-middleweights have created images in fights that will never be forgotten. Their performances turned a weight class that was at first perceived as an oddity, into arguably the second-most lucrative division in boxing.

In 1995 Nigel Benn defended his WBC version when he survived two knockdowns and a terrible beating to stop former middleweight champion Gerald McClellan, a fighter with a fearsome reputation as a puncher in America. The fight's dramatic end in round 10 was overshadowed by news that McClellan later required emergency surgery to remove a blood clot from his brain. He survived, but he remains blind and deaf.

Also in 1995 over 50,000 people watched Dublin's Steve Collins, who started his career in Boston as an apprentice in the same gym as Marvin Hagler, beat Chris Eubank twice in the Republic of Ireland.

The following year, Collins, the WBO champion, also beat Benn twice. Both fights were in Manchester and were attended by nearly 22,000 on each occasion. Eubank, Benn and Collins are part of British and Irish sporting history.

Also that year, Robin Reid, who won a bronze medal for Britain at the Barcelona Olympics in 1992, won the WBC version in Italy.

In 1997 Collins retired because a fight with Roy Jones could not be made. His vacant WBO title was won by Joe Calzaghe, an unbeaten fighter from Wales, who narrowly outpointed Eubank.

MILESTONES OF BOXING

THE BITE OF THE CENTURY

The unforgivable act of a beast scarred Evander Holyfield and boxing forever on a hot June night in 1997. Mike Tyson chewed off part of Holyfield's ear and admitted his act was senseless.

In July 1997 Tyson was fined three million dollars and his license to fight was revoked by the Nevada State Athletic Commission. Tyson can apply each July for a new license.

"Tyson is not finished as a boxer," said Luther Mack, one of the commissioners after the hearing in Las Vegas which Tyson chose not to attend. Two months later he missed a reconciliation meeting between himself and Holyfield, that Muhammad Ali had organized in Louisville. He claimed that his private jet had broken down on the runway.

"I will not fight the punishment. I will learn from this horrible mistake," said Tyson. In the months after the fight Tyson vanished, there were rumors of wayward behavior and he hinted that there was a chance he would never fight again.

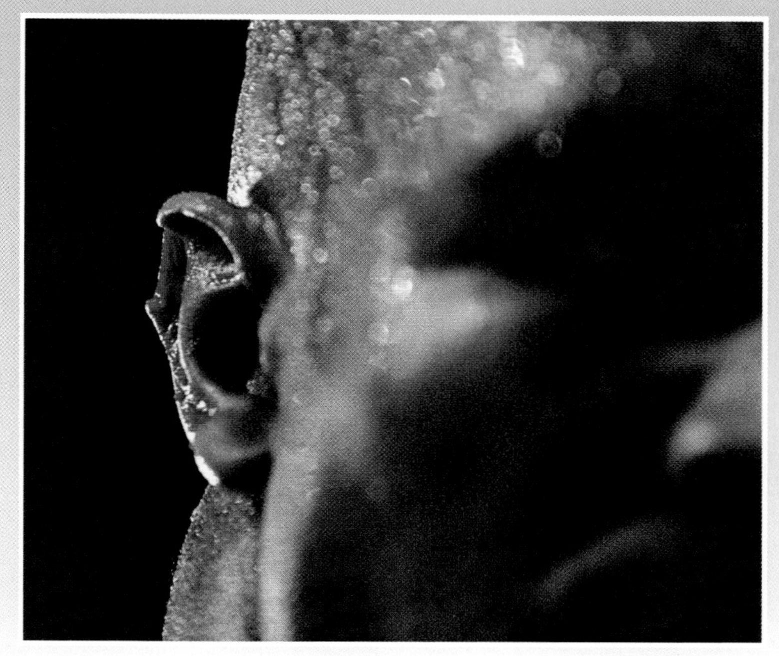

◀ THE CELTIC WARRIOR
Chris Eubank had remained undefeated for 43 fights before he lost his WBO super-middleweight belt to courageous Irishman, Steve Collins, in March 1995. The pair fought again in September the same year, but the outcome was the same. "There is nothing I can do, he is just too strong," Eubank complained to his trainer during the rematch. Collins won every round, prompting Eubank to quit the sport, but he returned in 1996.

Golden Boy fights Macho Man in front of adoring fans in Vegas

▲ **A BRAWL IN VEGAS**
De La Hoya is pushed back against the ropes by the veteran Camacho during their fight in 1997. "As the rounds went by I was ripping to the body and he took some good shots," explained De La Hoya.

Where will it all end? The somewhat farcical senior tour of boxers sunk to new depths in 1997, when Sugar Ray Leonard was stopped in five rounds by the slightly less ancient Hector "Macho" Camacho. Leonard was 40, Camacho 34. In 1996 Camacho had outpointed Roberto Duran.

Camacho's wild spree as boxing's resident lunatic started in the early 1980s when he first won a world title. In 1991, he was arrested for driving with his girlfriend on his lap. "I was doing the vehicular wild thing," he explained.

After beating Leonard, a fight was made between the "Macho Man" and Oscar De La Hoya, who in 1997 hired and then fired, Emanuel Steward. Like many of Camacho's fights it was a dull affair – his fights were seldom equal to his hype. "I came to win and I fought a damn courageous fight," claimed Camacho. In truth, he held and ran, and was at his annoying best.

The fight served two purposes: it gave a clear indication of how good De La Hoya was, while demonstrating just how far back Leonard, Duran, Camacho and the rest of the relics had gone.

De La Hoya had won the WBC welterweight title in early 1997 from Pernell Whitaker in a technical fight that ended with a controversial decision. Whitaker wanted a rematch but Bob Arum, De La Hoya's promoter, refused.

Although wonderfully gifted fighters, Roy Jones and Oscar De La Hoya lacked a certain something, but the third boxer from the time, Naseem Hamed, had the look. He walked the walk and talked the talk. He was a different type of champion – he had a sharp mouth to accompany his fearsome fists.

◀ BAD BOY UNDER THE GLOSS

"He (De La Hoya) has an image. He looks like a choir boy, talks nice and sweet and then in the gym and the ring he changes. He transforms into one of the most cold-blooded killers I've ever seen," said Emanuel Steward shortly before the Camacho fight.

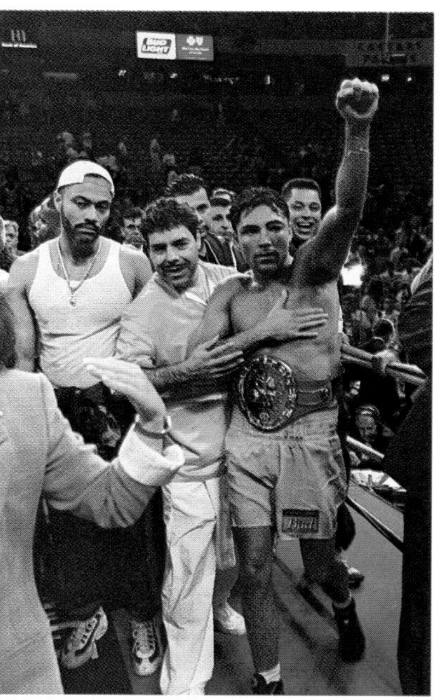

▲ ONE OF THE GREATS

Oscar De La Hoya celebrates his victory over Hector Camacho. "I beat Chavez and Whitaker and they were the best pound-for-pound fighters in the world. It is me now," stated the Golden Boy. However against Camacho and Whitaker there were worrying signs that his power was missing.

▶ STEWARD OUT THE DOOR

De La Hoya is held aloft by members of his entourage after defeating Camacho – however there was tension in the camp. Shortly after the fight De La Hoya split from Emanuel Steward, his trainer of only a few months. There were several rumors, all denied, that Steward was trying to get De La Hoya to leave promoter, Bob Arum, and join Don King.

PRINCE NASEEM HAMED

A Tricky Debut in the Garden for British Fighter

The Naseem Hamed boxing story started when he was only seven years old in a church hall on the outskirts of Sheffield, England. Over the ensuing years he has won amateur titles, dominated the British scene and defended his WBO featherweight title on eight occasions, sometimes in front of crowds in excess of 20,000 people.

Between April 1994 and December 1997, Hamed stopped or knocked out 18, fighters and before he won the WBO world title in September 1995, he met six fighters from the top 10 of either the WBO, IBF, WBA or WBC. He knocked out men who had never been stopped and beat unbeaten fighters. He fought in Britain and the crowds loved his exhilarating style.

In December 1997, he performed his ritual boogie down a ramp to the ring at Madison Square Garden for his American debut. He was 23, the hero of British boxing, and the center of attention for the 12,000 fans in the beloved venue. The decision to take Hamed to America was reached when Frank Warren split with Don King and agreed a deal with Home Box Office (HBO). The publicity before the Kelley fight cost three million dollars and included a 120-foot picture of Hamed's face in Times Square. In the week before the fight, Michael Jackson showed up to watch Hamed train at the Blue Velvet gym in New York City. It was a big fight.

On the night, however, there was panic in the Garden. The fight was savage. Hamed was on the canvas once, and touched down with his gloves four times, before one chilling left dropped Kevin Kelley for the full count in round four. Hamed was close to losing in the second round, but his heart kept him going. It was thrilling stuff. Hamed found extra courage in the most ruthless of boxing's places during the terrible three minutes of round two. He also found enough power to drop Kelley. The fans were going wild, but it was not a perfect American debut by any means. Hamed was exposed at times by Kelley in a brutal and breathless fight.

"We all know what went wrong – I just hope people recognize what went right," said Hamed's promoter Frank Warren. "Naz was an unknown from Sheffield, he came to New York, to Kelley's backyard, he attracted 12,000 people, climbed up from knockdowns to take out the local hero. That is what happened and that's a bloody good British success story." After the fight Hamed admitted his mistakes. "I tried too hard to entertain at the start and then I was caught," he said.

Kelley had trouble walking from the ring when it was all over, but was still critical of his opponent. "Hamed is not as good as he thinks he is," he said, but his face and legs belied his opinion. However, many of the press on both sides of the Atlantic agreed with Kelley. True, Hamed deserved some of the criticism but the general tone of the condemnation was ridiculous.

In round four Hamed cast a shadow over Kelley's defeated body before the last count reached 10. The relief on the faces of his trainers, Brendan and John Ingle, when the fight was called off said all that had to be said. "It will be different next time," promised Hamed. Everybody involved agreed – it has to be different next time.

▼ WHISPERING FISTIC GURU
Brendan Ingle (left) has worked with Hamed since the boxer was a boy of seven, but their relationship has not always been easy. "Naz has taken a bit of this, a bit of that and sometimes he forgets who showed him," said Ingle.

▲ **PRINCE HAS THE LAST LAUGH** *A blistering left from Hamed dumps his opponent on the canvas for the full count in round four. "Do you think I will ever fight that way again?" said Hamed after the fight. "The truth is simple: I took his best shots and got up, he couldn't take mine."*

Butterbean and Martin prove surprise attractions in the 1990s

Butterbean is just one of modern boxing's eccentric acts. Christy Martin, the coal miner's daughter, is another. Both have made more money than ordinary boxers at their weight.

In the early 1990s Butterbean, or Eric Esch, was a construction worker in Alabama, but by the mid-1990s he was the undisputed king of flab and the IBA, one of 12 sanctioning bodies, gave him their super-heavyweight four-round championship title. It is the world's least significant belt and has to be a full 60 inches long to go round Butterbean's gut.

"I have the urge to win just like I have the urge to eat ice cream," claims Butterbean. The fans love the freak show and because he has so few skills he is seldom in a dull fight.

Christy Martin is the best known of the female boxers to emerge in the 1990s. She is a natural fighter, not a natural boxer, and has gained her fame on the undercard of Don King's shows. Critics claim that she has ignored other women, many of whom were former kick boxers from Europe, who fought for women's world titles.

Both Martin and Butterbean provide new boxing fans with some quality entertainment, but whereas Butterbean's talents are crude and limited, Martin and her fellow fighters are being afforded greater credibility. Women's boxing has existed since the 1920s, but Martin has brought it to the forefront. As women continue to expand and develop their skills the fan base will undoubtedly grow

▲ MARTIN TAUNTS ROBINSON
Christy Martin easily defeats Melinder Robinson (above) in four rounds in July 1996. "I fight for Christy Martin," she explains, "I'm not at the front of any revolution."

▶ A HUG FOR THE BEAN
"I'm the best four-round fighter in the world," says Butterbean, who is pictured here after beating George Clarke in one round. At 322 pounds he is undeniably a high-profile attraction.

▲ NOT RUNNING SCARED
"If they run I can still catch them," explains Butterbean. At the super-heavyweight end of the business credibility is a distant notion with no real meaning.

MILESTONES OF BOXING

THE END OF THE ANCIENT DAYS

Big George Foreman quit the ring in 1977 after losing to Jimmy Young and in November 1997 he quit again after a dubious points loss to New York's Shannon Briggs.

Foreman was six weeks shy of his 49th birthday and taking part in his 81st fight. He was the missing link in boxing's journey from the past to its future.

His fight with Briggs was for the "linear" championship - it was the title Foreman kept after the WBA and IBF stripped him, and after he decided to relinquish the WBU version.

"I have not lost since knocking out Michael Moorer in 1994," he said before losing to Briggs. After his victory, Briggs became the unlikely recipient of the linear championship, while Foreman was left to reflect: "I'm done. I'm going home, it has been a great ride," he said.

New stars are poised to take boxing into the next Millennium

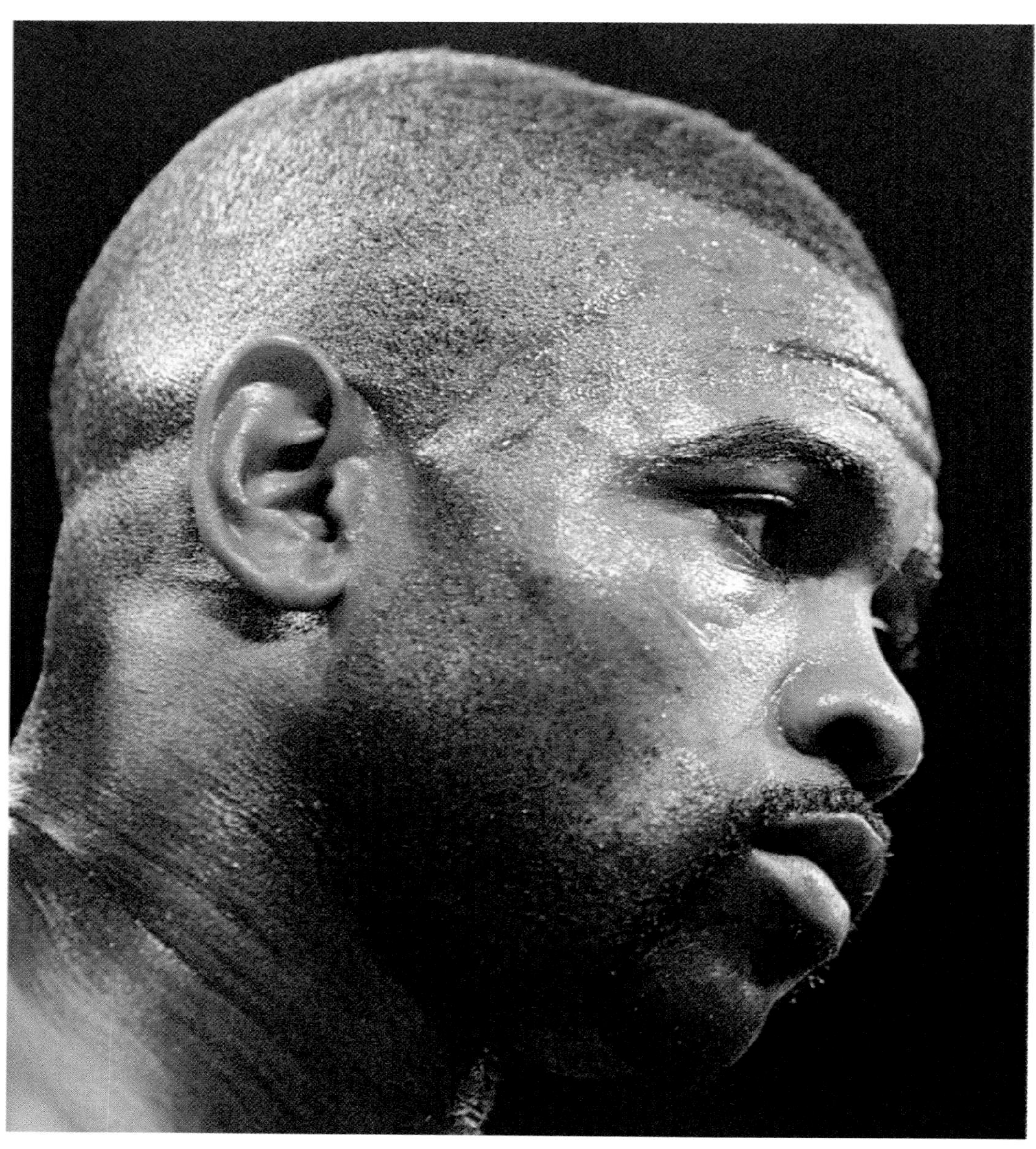

▲ **A NEW HEAVYWEIGHT**
In late 1997 Roy Jones decided to step up to join the ranks of the heavyweights, but refused fights with both WBO champion, Herbie Hide, and James "Buster" Douglas, leading to speculation over his future intents.

The news that Roy Jones may join the heavyweights put a bizarre seal on 1997. It was a year that started with the tears of Oliver McCall, and also included the maiming of Evander Holyfield's ear. There seemed no end in sight to the amazing scenes at the top of the sport's mad realm, and there was also little hope of a heavyweight unification fight when negotiations broke down between Holyfield and Lewis.

Elsewhere some great potential fights vanished. The loss suffered by Terry Norris in a supposedly routine WBC light-middleweight title defense, against Keith Mullings, ruined a planned showdown with Oscar De La Hoya. However, WBC welterweight champion De La Hoya only has to look across at WBA champion, Ike "Bazooka" Quartey, or the IBF's Felix Trinidad for a potential unification fight.

There is a chance for one of these fighters to attain greatness in the welterweight division, but he will have to be willing to prove himself against the other champions. De La Hoya has the opportunity. At featherweight, Hamed has fewer options but a move through the weight divisions could produce some of the fights of the decade.

Jones had relinquished the middle, super-middle and light-heavyweight titles in his pursuit of excellence. He could have met Dublin's Steve Collins in late 1997 but both parties wanted too much money. Collins opted to vacate his WBO super-middleweight title when he refused to fight Joe Calzaghe, who beat Chris Eubank for the belt. Calzaghe is just one fighter for the Millennium. There are dozens of others.

Ricardo Lopez ended 1997 as WBC strawweight champion and boasted an unbeaten record of 46 fights. He is a brilliant operator at the bottom of a pile of fighters in a sport dominated by excessive personalities. It has been the same since fists and gloves were first used. If Lopez, and not Jones, could move to heavyweight there would certainly be some fun. A fairy tale, once upon a distant fight: Lopez v Tyson for New Year's Eve 1999!

◀ HOLYFIELD MUST WAIT
After two stunning wins against Mike Tyson the only man left in the heavyweight division for Holyfield to fight was Lennox Lewis. However, initial negotiations broke down and the fight now looks unlikely to take place until at least the end of 1998.

▼ JONES LANDS A LEFT
Roy Jones (left) easily beat James Toney when they met in Las Vegas in 1994. The victory helped establish Jones as one of the finest fighters in the world.

▲ A MEXICAN IDOL
Ricardo Lopez is the forgotten man of boxing, but at the start of 1998 he was undefeated in 46 fights and held both the WBO and WBC strawweight titles. Many consider him to be the best pound-for-pound fighter in the world.

Picture Credits

Allsport Picture Library:
3-5, 7, 127 (top), 129 (right), 148, 149 (right), 152-153, 157 (bottom), 158 (top left), 160, 161 (right), 171 (top and right), 177 (bottom), 180-181, 183, 187 (left), 192, 193 (top and bottom), 195 (top right and bottom right), 196, 197 (top and bottom), 198-200, 202-251

Allsport/Hulton Collection:
10-11, 14, 15 (bottom), 16, 18, 20-26, 27 (top), 29, 31 (top right and bottom), 33, 35-36, 37 (right), 38-40, 41 (top), 45 (right), 49, 52-54, 57 (bottom), 61 (top), 63 (bottom), 65-66, 68, 69 (bottom and right), 72, 73 (right), 74-76, 78, 83, 86, 88-89, 91 (top and right), 93, 96, 97 (top left), 100, 101 (top and bottom), 102 (top), 104-105, 107-110, 111 (bottom), 112-115, 117, 121 (top and bottom), 122, 123 (bottom right), 125, 127 (right), 129 (bottom left), 130 (bottom), 131, 133 (left), 136-137, 139 (right), 142, 143 (bottom), 144, 149 (top and bottom), 151 (top), 156, 157 (top left and top right), 163, 165, 167, 170, 171 (bottom), 182 (left), 194, 195 (left)

Alpha Sport:
106, 128

Corbis:
19, 27 (bottom), 28, 30, 31 (top left), 32, 37 (top and middle), 41 (bottom), 42-44, 45 (bottom), 46-48, 50-51, 55 (top and right), 56, 57 (top), 59-60, 61 (bottom), 62, 63 (top), 64, 67, 69 (top), 71, 73 (top and bottom), 77, 79, 81-82, 84-85, 87, 90, 91 (bottom), 94-95, 97 (top right and bottom), 98-99, 101 (right), 102 (bottom), 103, 118-120, 121 (right), 123 (bottom left), 124, 126, 127 (bottom), 129 (top left), 130 (top), 132, 133 (right), 134-135, 138, 139 (left), 140-141, 143 (top), 146-147, 150, 151 (bottom), 154-155, 158 (bottom), 159, 161 (left), 162, 164, 166, 168-169, 172, 174-175, 178-179, 182, 184-185, 187 (right), 188-191, 193 (right), 201

International Boxing Hall of Fame:*
4-7, 45 (top), 58, 61 (right), 70, 80, 92, 145, 176, 186, 187 (top right), 256

Mary Evans Picture Library:
8, 9, 12-13, 15 (top), 17

Mirror Group:
34, 55 (bottom), 111 (top), 116, 123 (top), 177 (top left and right), 197 (right)

***** The Publisher and the International Boxing Hall of Fame wish to stress that every effort has been made to contact the copyright holders in cases where ownership is unclear.

The Publishers would like to extend their very special thanks to Lee Martin and Mark Goldsmith at Allsport Picture Library for their unstinting efforts in researching and compiling the photographs used in this book.

Allsport Picture Library
3 Greenlea Park
Prince George's Road
London
England
SW19 2JD

Tel: 0181 685 1010

Index

G

H

I

J

K

L

M

N

O

P

Q

R

S

T

U

V

W

Y

Z

POLICE GAZETTE
FRANCISCO CHRONICLE
ART OF BOXING
ROBERT FITZSIMMONS
IS THE CHAMPION